D1582022

Construction project management

Construction project management

John Bennett

Professor, Department of Construction Management
University of Reading

Butterworths
London Boston Durban Singapore Sydney Toronto Wellington

First published 1985

© John Bennett 1985

British Library Cataloguing in Publication Data

Bennett, John
    Construction project management.
    1. Construction industry—Management
    2. Industrial project management
    I. Title
    624′.0684   TH438

    ISBN 0-408-01544-6

Library of Congress Cataloging in Publication Data

Bennett, John, P. A.
    Construction project management.

    Includes bibliographies and index.
    1. Construction industry—Management.
    2. Industrial project management.   I. Title.
    TH438.B434   1985   624′.068   85-7807

    ISBN 0-408-01544-6

Photoset by Butterworths Litho Preparation Department
Printed in Great Britain at the University Press, Cambridge

Preface

I wrote this book, first because I wanted to set down what I have learnt from thirty years in the construction industry, the last nine working in academia with time to read and think about the way construction projects are managed. In writing I have learnt much of how my practical experience and my more recent research into current practice fits into established management theories. I wrote secondly to give others an opportunity to know of my ideas and to comment on and criticize them. I hope, of course, that at least some of my readers will find something of value in the book. Those in practice I hope will find ideas which will help them to make their part of the construction industry more effective and more efficient. Those in academia I hope will find a coherent body of theory which will help their own research.

I came to the University of Reading from practice where, following a traditional education and training as a quantity surveyor, I had, for eleven years, first in Nottinghamshire and subsequently in Hampshire, been encouraged by colleagues to try new ways of managing construction. In this respect Henry Swain, Henry Morris and Colin Stansfield-Smith made major contributions to my thinking. I arrived at the University with a head full of questions provoked by this experience but sharpened by a brief period of work in the USA. I wanted to know why construction projects are managed in different ways; why some approaches work with certain projects but not with others; how we should choose the appropriate methods for each project; how far should clients be involved with their projects; why very large projects so often go wrong; and other questions about roles and relationships and also the likely consequences of computer developments on construction industry practice. In a sense this book records the first tentative answers to these questions. In doing so it provides the basis for a deeper understanding of the issues involved in managing construction projects and so lays the foundations for the next stages of my research.

The book is the end product of nine years' reading of management literature. In particular it is greatly influenced by the published work of Jay

Galbraith, Henry Mintzberg and Alfred Kuhn. Their ideas have provided me with a pattern which makes sense of my direct experience of construction management, or quantity surveying, as it tends to be called in the UK. The pattern consists of the concepts defined in the glossary at the end of the book and the relationships between them which are described in the main body of the book. This set of ideas begins with fundamental assumptions about teams which I see as the basic component of construction project management and builds on them logically by deduction so that the whole is internally consistent.

Together with colleagues in the Department of Construction Management I have had the opportunity particularly over the past six years of undertaking research which has allowed me to test the validity and usefulness of the pattern. This includes work funded by the Science and Engineering Research Council and work funded by professional institutions and major clients of the construction industry. The support I have received from the Royal Institution of Chartered Surveyors has been especially valuable in providing access to a wide range of contemporary practice.

I am particularly grateful to Leonard Fletcher, Geoffrey Townsend, Brian Drake and Norman Harris for helping me to understand issues raised by this research. I have also gained much from my work as Chairman of the Standard Method of Measurement Development Unit. Dr Martin Barnes has made a huge contribution to the thinking of the Unit and Geoffrey Beard has ensured that we kept our feet on the ground. More recently, work with the Coordinating Committee for Project Information, so ably chaired by Alex Gordon, has thrown much light on the way the orthodox professional approach works in the UK.

The largest contribution to my thinking has been made by colleagues in the Department of Construction Management. They have all at various times provided ideas which have found their way on to these pages but Professor Bill Biggs, Professor John Paterson, Dr Roger Flanagan, Peter Goodacre, Colin Gray, Norman Fisher and Laurence Holt deserve special thanks. Brian Fine has worked on a part-time basis in the Department and his brilliant and original approach to construction management has sown the seeds of many of the ideas in the book. I have also been helped by a number of outstanding research assistants in particular Dr Neill Morrison, Dr Susan Stevens and Richard Ormerod. During the last three years the Department Advisory Board chaired with total competence and unfailing good humour by Sir Peter Trench has provided cogent practical criticism of the Department's teaching and research. This too has produced new ideas and put old ones into much sharper focus.

I must also acknowledge the contribution made by all the interesting people in the construction industry who unwittingly have provided the basis for the characters I have used in the book to illustrate the principles of construction project management.

The book draws on ideas from all these various sources and from others which I have omitted to mention, but the end product is my own responsibility, particularly the areas of remaining obscurity and error.

I must also thank Jean Wild for typing the manuscript from my scribbled, altered and amended drafts. Finally, I must above all, thank my wife Sue and my children Stephen and Kate for providing the encouragement and support needed to write this book.

John Bennett
University of Reading
1985

Acknowledgements

Permission to include material from the following sources was generously given by the publishers.

The Logic of Organization, by Alfred Kuhn and Robert D. Beam; Jossey-Bass Ltd (1982)

Architectural Practice and Management, RIBA Publications (1973)

Cost Planning and Computers, by Department of Construction Management, University of Reading; Property Services Agency (1981)

Coordinating Working Drawings, CP60/76 by D.T. Crawshaw; Building Research Establishment (1976)

Contents

List of tables

Chapter 1

Basic components of projects

Pete James deftly applied the mortar from his trowel to the end of a brick and slid it along the mortar bed into position as he had done with hundreds of thousands of bricks before. Then he picked up another brick and trowelfull of mortar from where his labourer Tony Bronoski had placed them and repeated the actions. As he did so he felt rain begin to fall on his face and hands. He looked across the scaffolding to where his mates Doug Henderson and Mike Williams were standing. They had already stopped work and were looking at the deep black clouds gathering overhead. Pete tipped the unused mortar away, wiped his trowel clean, gathered his tools together into their bag and began the descent to the site hut.

Pete, Tony, Doug and Mike had worked together as a bricklaying team for just over two years. They had worked on 13 different construction projects and the present one was by far the worst. The bricks they were using chipped easily and so they had to watch each one for defects. This slowed their work, particularly as they were not entirely clear whether or not the architect would accept slightly chipped bricks in the less prominent parts of the building. Also they had run out of bricks on two occasions and had to wait while the site agent arranged for an emergency delivery from the brick manufacturer. They had further problems because the design details were complicated which meant that they frequently had to wait for one of the site manager's team to set out the next stage of the work.

In addition to this, many of the details were very difficult to build but the architect had refused to consider changing them. As Doug had said, it was hard to see why, since he had changed practically everything else. However, their main difficulty was having to wait for the steel fixers to position their joists at each floor level and, even worse, having to wait for the plumbers to fix metal cavity gutters and damp-proof membranes at every few courses. Doug had suggested a way of leaving gaps for the other trades which would have allowed the brickwork to continue uninterrupted. The architect had said it would affect the stability of the work but Pete suspected he did not know what he was talking about. Be that as it may, the overall result was that their work progressed slowly and uncertainly. Pete saw these problems in terms of two important consequences. First, the team's earnings were low because they earned very little bonus. Perhaps even worse, they did not

enjoy their work and so niggled about small problems, took sick leave when
they could easily have managed to work and, if Pete was honest, the work
they produced was not to their normal quality standards.

   As Pete reached the ground it was raining hard. When he reached the hut
the rest of his team had decided to pack up for the day. This meant their pay
would fall to the basic wet-time rate. Pete wondered how his wife would face
yet another week short of money.

As Pete, Tony, Doug and Mike trudged home through the wet, cold streets
it is unlikely that they gave much thought to all the other construction
teams around the world. Yet the four men have much in common with the
millions of other teams who provide the basic components of the project
organizations, brought together to construct each of the buildings and civil
and heavy engineering projects which shape so much of the human
environment. Indeed, they have a good deal in common with all the teams
who, throughout history, have laid bricks wherever and whenever society
has needed construction.

   Some things, however, have changed. Today construction is faster, more
complex and more efficient than in earlier times. According to the visitors'
guide, Salisbury Cathedral is the only English cathedral, apart from St
Paul's, built to the design of one man and completed without a break. The
building interior is 135 m long, the nave and aisles 23 m wide and the nave
24 m high. Building work started in 1220 and by 1265 all was finished.
Finished that is, except for the cloisters 1263–1270, the Chapter House
1263–1284 and the spire 1334–1365. The building consists almost entirely
of one undivided and virtually unserviced space. A very large proportion of
the work is masonry and it is unlikely that more than half-a-dozen trades
were involved in the whole building. The result is unquestionably
beautiful, but by the standards of today's great cultural symbols, it is an
essentially simple building which was built slowly and used massive
amounts of labour.

   Sydney Opera House is a notorious modern example of a great cultural
symbol. It is considerably larger than Salisbury, seating in excess of 5000
people in its two auditoria and its small theatre. Building work started in
1959 and was complete in 1973. It is an extremely complicated building
which required many specialist designers. These include architects,
structural engineers, acoustics designers, electrical engineers, mechanical
engineers, heating and ventilating engineers, air-conditioning specialists
and lighting designers. The work of all these specialists was interdependent
so that none could be given a complete and clear definition of design
requirements. The brief for each designer had to be developed through a
process of trial and error. The design solutions proposed had not only to
meet demanding technical criteria but also high aesthetic standards. The
amount of design work was enormous with the structural engineering firm
of Ove Arup alone spending 370 000 man-hours on the project between
1957 and 1965.

Construction was equally complicated and dominated by major errors. A large part of the foundations built in 1961 had to be demolished in 1963. Major changes were made to the function of the main spaces. The big auditorium originally designed for opera was changed into a concert hall. The space for opera was moved to the small auditorium, making it the smallest opera house in the world except for specialist ones like Glyndebourne. It is too small to house the stage sets required for full-scale grand opera and so cannot fulfil its original purpose. Its final cost was $A 102 m compared with the estimated cost provided for the committee selecting the architect and the design of just over $A 7 m.

Sydney Opera House is, without doubt, one of the world's great buildings. It is vastly more complex than Salisbury Cathedral. Although it is also considerably bigger it was built in about half the time taken for Salisbury. Even so this performance is so much worse than normal modern construction standards that it is included in the book of great planning disasters[1] which has been freely drawn on for this description.

Today's demands for speed, complexity and efficiency in construction have given rise to the need for management. This is a recent development in practice and even more so in education. Indeed the first university courses in construction management were established during the past 20 years.

The recognition of the new need for educated management in construction had led to a deeper understanding of construction project organizations. This has emerged by trial and error in practice and by thought and research in academia. Both provide important insights to guide future practice and research. This book describes the fundamental principles so far identified in the new subject of construction project management. In doing so it is intended to help practitioners to plan and control their projects by providing them with a structured way of thinking about their work. At the same time it is intended to help researchers in construction management by defining the basic concepts which make up their subject. These twin-related aims begin with Pete, Tony, Doug and Mike, or at least with the teams of which they are one representative example. Construction teams are taken as the basic elements from which construction project organizations are assembled.

Construction teams

Since it plays such a central part in the book, it is important to establish the idea of teams straight away. We have already met Pete and his bricklaying team. Their work related to that of the steelfixing team and the plumbing team. The work was directed by the site manager's team and designed by the architect's team. On any construction project, apart from the smallest and simplest, there will be many other teams each bringing a useful combination of knowledge and skills to the work. Teams are formal groups consisting of few enough persons that each can take explicit cognizance of each of the others. It is usually considered that between two and twelve or perhaps slightly more persons are the practical limits on the size of effective teams.

Obviously all teams are different. They comprise different people. They have different capabilities and capacities. They are motivated by different rewards and threats. Their experience is different. They have different attitudes to site safety, to aesthetic quality and to moral issues. It would be easy to continue listing general or indeed even specific differences between all the teams which make up the construction industry.

It is, however, more useful to concentrate on similarities. By identifying important characteristics which teams have in common we may be able to establish some general principles which will help in thinking about particular teams on particular construction projects.

It is sufficient, for this purpose, to concentrate on three general characteristics of teams[2].

The first important characteristic of teams is that they are able to gather information and retain it as knowledge. We are centrally interested in knowledge about construction or that which has some influence on construction. Thus, the first important characteristic which all construction teams have in common is that they have some knowledge of construction.

It is, of course, possible to imagine a construction project which, for whatever reason, worked with teams who started with no knowledge of construction and had to be trained. Although even in that extreme case it is difficult to imagine people with no knowledge whatsoever of the construction industry or its products. It is, therefore, safe to ignore that obviously hypothetical possibility and assert that all construction teams possess the ability to gather and retain relevant knowledge.

The second important characteristic is that teams are able to make choices based on their own values. That is, they prefer some things to others. Generally, teams are likely to prefer more money rather than less if everything else remains the same. They may prefer more money to more leisure time. They may prefer safer working conditions to more money, and both to more leisure time. The values which any particular team put on these things and all the others which may influence their view of construction are likely to vary. What is common and consistent is that all teams make choices based on their own values.

The third important characteristic is that all teams can take actions. That is quite simply that they can do things. Pete, Tony, Doug and Mike can work together to lay bricks. The architect's team can work together to design buildings and to inspect the quality of the resulting building work. Generally, teams are practised in the things they can do which are relevant to construction. Thus, Pete has laid hundreds of thousands of bricks and so he can, with pride and justification, call himself a skilled bricklayer. This ability is the third characteristic which is common to all the teams which make up the construction industry. This is self-evident because a team which was unable to take some relevant actions would be of no interest or value to any construction project. It may well be thought at this stage that each of these three characteristics is too obvious to be worthy of comment. It will, however, be shown that each is important and that these three characteristics are sufficient to help understand some important facts about construction projects and the way they are managed.

There is one combination of the basic characteristics which is so important that it must be given a separate name and identified in this initial description. This is the combination of a team taking some action and then having knowledge of the results of their action. It is called 'feedback'.

Feedback can be immediate and direct. Thus, when Pete lays a brick he receives information about the state of the mortar bed he is working on from the reaction he gets through the brick as he slides it into position. Generally this confirms that the mortar is fit for its purpose, but if it has begun to harden so that it will fail to form a proper joint in the brickwork Pete will sense this and, if he is well motivated, will change the mortar immediately. On the other hand, feedback may take months or even years. Thus, the architect's action of producing the first sketches for a building design may have to wait a very long time before it is joined in a feedback loop by knowledge of the appearance of the actual building.

In managing construction we are generally interested in short-term feedback. That is feedback which is available in time to influence the actions of the team while they are still involved with the project.

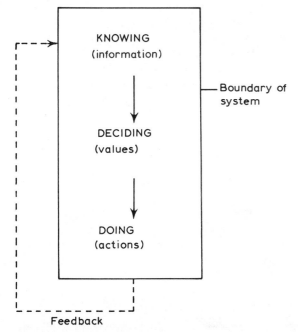

Figure 1.1 Basic characteristics of teams

Longer-term feedback is valuable in that it helps build knowledge which may help future projects. It is, however, of less interest than short-term feedback in managing any specific construction project.

The basic characteristics of teams are shown in *Figure 1.1*. They are sufficient to allow us to regard teams as controlled systems.

Controlled systems

The concept of system is an important one in much contemporary thought. At its simplest it means any group of things which relate to each other in a sufficiently regular way to justify our attention. On this basis construction teams clearly qualify as systems. There are many aspects of the behaviour of teams which justify our attention. Some have already been described and more will be described as the book develops.

However, construction teams can be more precisely classified in systems terms. They are controlled systems. This means that the components of the system maintain at least one aspect of their behaviour within some specified range or return it to that range if the particular variable goes beyond it. A controlled system maintains the variable within its specified range despite changes in forces which influence that variable. For Pete and his team the quality of their brickwork must meet specific standards irrespective of the weather. The team adjusts its work according to changes in temperature, humidity and wind speed in order to maintain a quality of work which they know to be acceptable. They do this with very little explicit thought to the matter. Experience has taught them the kind of adjustments to make to keep the variable of quality within the range defined by what they know the project architect will accept. Typically construction teams seek to control a number of variables. For example Pete and his team are concerned about safe working conditions, their total earnings and their leisure time in addition to the quality of the work. They try to maintain each of these variables within a range which all members of the team accept implicitly.

Control may be exercised, in part at least, by almost subconscious processes and be directed towards a range of values which is never explicitly identified; nevertheless, the basic components of teams shown in *Figure 1.1* are all necessary and all have a part to play in maintaining control.

We can consider control as forming a cycle beginning with an action. The system taking the action gathers information about its effects and compares them with the range of acceptable values. Then, if the information gathered, that is the feedback, falls within the acceptable range the system repeats the action. If, however, the feedback falls outside the acceptable range the system will change its action. It will continue to change until the resulting feedback is within the range of acceptable values.

Two conclusions of some importance to managers flow from the essential nature of control. First, teams generally will seek to expand the range of acceptable values. They do this to avoid constraints on their behaviour so that they have greater freedom of action. Secondly, teams, as with all systems, seek to control not their actions, but their feedback. The corollary of these two facts is that managers, in seeking to control construction teams, must establish the range of acceptable values and ensure that feedback closely relates to the actions they want from the team.

On each new project Pete, Tony, Doug and Mike need to learn the standard of quality required by the architect. It is very difficult to define quality in construction work with precision. As far as brickwork is concerned it is fairly common to build a sample panel of brickwork and agree with the architect that it represents the quality he or she wants. It often requires several panels before the architect will accept that Pete and his team have got the quality right. There is an obvious process of negotiation as Pete seeks to find the minimum acceptable standard, that is to expand the range of acceptable values. While, at the same time, the architect seeks to get the best possible brickwork for his building, that is to reduce the range of acceptable values. Once a panel is agreed Pete's aim now is not directly to build to the agreed standard but rather to get the architect to accept the team's work. One obvious way for Pete to control his feedback is to build good brickwork. In the main this is what he and his team do. However, he has been bricklaying long enough to know that it helps to be friendly and polite in all his dealings with the architect. It helps to admire his design or to compliment him on the choice of bricks. In these and other ways Pete and his team and indeed all teams seek to control their feedback.

Team interactions

Construction projects require the work of a number of teams. On large projects this may amount to hundreds of teams spread over many years but even the smallest is likely to need more than one kind of work and so need more than one team. Do-it-yourself projects seem to provide the only obvious exception but by definition they are outside the construction industry.

Given that teams normally have to work with other teams it is necessary to understand how they interact. Just as there is a great variety of different kinds of team so there are many ways in which they may interact. We have already seen how Pete and his team's work is interrupted by the steelfixers and plumbers; how they must wait for the site manager to set out their work; and their complex relationship with the architect.

As with teams we need to identify the things which interactions between teams have in common rather than attempting to list all the differences. We are looking for a set of ideas about interactions which will help us to understand how teams work together. It will clearly be helpful if these ideas are related to the idea of teams as controlled systems which we have already described. Thus, we are interested in interactions concerned with knowledge, with values and with actions. We have already seen that most interactions involve all three components. Thus, an interaction between Pete and the architect about the quality of a particular piece of brickwork may well involve knowledge about the working characteristics of the bricks, the purpose of the brickwork, the weather and a number of other pieces of information. It may require reference to the quality standard established by a sample panel and is likely to cause the architect to make choices based on the values he places on the building, his reputation, his time and on good relationships with the craftsmen. Similarly, Pete will take account of his own values including pride in his work, the bonus he will lose if the work has to be pulled down, and relationships with the architect on this and perhaps future projects. Both will be taking a number of actions, talking, pointing, picking-up bricks, looking at the current work and other similar work nearby and, in extreme cases, making veiled threats. Most interactions between teams involve a similarly rich content.

It is, however, useful in thinking about and seeking to understand interactions between teams to separate them into three categories which match the basic characteristics of teams.

We can therefore first recognize a class of interactions which are primarily concerned with communication of information. This envisages knowledge originating in one team which it wishes to impart to a second team. First the knowledge must be turned into words, numbers, or symbols which the other team are likely to understand. Then these words, numbers or symbols must be transferred on to some communication medium. This may be spoken words or drawings, or a written document, or electrical impulses in a telephone line. Then the medium must be transferred to the second team. They in turn must identify the words, numbers or symbols and then interpret them. All five of the steps of source, coding, medium, detection and decoding are essential for communication to take place.

The second class of interactions between teams are those primarily concerned with transactions of values. Essentially a transaction involves one team agreeing to provide something of value to another team in return for something else of value. Thus, Pete and his team agree to provide bricklaying knowledge and skills to the site manager's team in return for money. The amount of money depends on a number of factors including the amount of brickwork the team produces and the time they are prevented from working due to various causes, etc. Some of these factors are the subject of a formal agreement entered into after preliminary negotiations between Pete and one of the site manager's team. Others are the subject of day-to-day negotiations as the work is carried out and as problems arise.

In construction, the initial or major bargain is often expressed in a formal contract. In Pete's case this consists of a letter from the site agent describing the work they are to do, roughly when it will be required, the agreed rates of pay and the working rule agreements which govern their other terms and conditions of employment. However, the major bargain provides only a general framework of agreement. There are inevitably many further matters which have to be settled as the work progresses. The exact date on which Pete and his team were to start work was in fact agreed in the saloon bar of the *Three Compasses* public house. The part of the building they are to work on next is agreed as they progress and the positions at which bricks are to be unloaded is agreed by Tony Bronoski, the labourer, as lorry-loads arrive. Each of these decisions involve choices based on values.

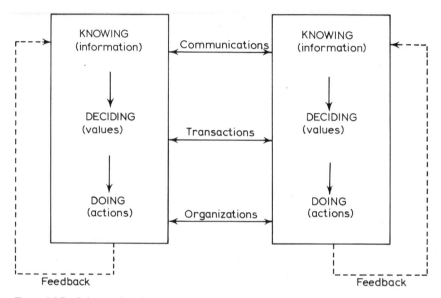

Figure 1.2 Basic interactions between teams

The third class of interactions between teams is that primarily concerned with organization to take coordinated action. Clearly teams do organize their work so that it fits together. The work of Pete and his team is organized to relate in a predetermined way with that of the steelfixers and the plumbers. However, this is achieved by means of communications and transactions and the concept of organization does not add anything to this analysis. Therefore, organization is merely a useful term to describe the coordinated actions of separate teams. The three classes of interaction between teams are shown in *Figure 1.2*.

Types of team

The basic analysis of teams and the interactions between them helps us to draw a distinction between two kinds of team. The first kind is that whose work essentially consists of producing and communicating information. We have already seen that in order for it to be communicated, information must be encoded on some medium which comprises matter and/or energy (henceforth expressed as matter–energy). However, the architect produces drawings essentially for the information they convey rather than primarily seeking to produce a drawing which is a work of art. Clearly the end purpose of the architect's drawing is a building, but its actual production is the work of other teams. The essential purpose of the drawing and indeed of all the architect's normal range of work is to produce and communicate information. Teams which are essentially concerned with information form part of the control sub-systems of projects.

The second kind of team is that whose work consists essentially of modifying matter–energy. In the construction industry this consists largely of transporting and assembling materials and components. The work of Pete and his team has been described to illustrate various characteristics of this kind of team. Such teams form part of the operating sub-systems of projects.

It is the operating sub-system which directly produces the end product. Construction projects typically bring together many different kinds of work involving different technologies. Thus bricklaying involves quite different technological principles from structural steelwork, heating and ventilating systems, painting, television surveillance systems, sewage treatment plants and the many other kinds of work which make up the construction industry. It is not practical for any one organization to have detailed knowledge and practical skills in all of these kinds of work. As a consequence, the industry tends to be fragmented into small specialized firms. Individual construction projects bring together an appropriate mix of these teams.

It is the task of the control sub-system to coordinate the work of the specialized teams which make up the operating sub-system. The control sub-system in construction projects is likely also to consist of specialized teams. This is because the coordination of construction work requires a wide range of knowledge and skills. There is a tendency for this to be concentrated in small specialized firms of architects, engineers, surveyors, builders, managers and other professionals. There are also multi-discipline firms which bring together various mixes of professions. However, even in such firms there is a tendency towards grouping by professional discipline rather than by project. So in general the control sub-system comprises a number of teams.

The distinction between the control and operating sub-systems has, thus far, been expressed in terms of the essential nature of the direct end product of their work. The distinction can usefully be re-expressed in terms of the basic interactions between teams. The control sub-system essentially communicates information and the operating sub-system essentially organizes to undertake actions on matter–energy to produce construction work. Both engage in transactions of values. These include transactions with other teams inside their particular sub-system and transactions which cross the boundary between sub-systems. Thus, we can say that the control sub-system is responsible for providing information and making decisions based on values. The operating sub-system is responsible for making decisions and taking direct construction actions.

The operating sub-system consists of teams all of whom produce direct construction work. There are, however, three distinct kinds of work within the control sub-systems of construction projects. They can each conveniently be regarded as an area of responsibility for providing information and making decisions.

First there is a client responsibility. The client is the person or organization whose motives concerning a project constitute its objectives. The client owns the project and so is responsible for financing it. However, their vital role in considering construction project management is to define the objectives of the project. These may well include explicit statements about the amount and timing of finance available. If not explicitly stated, clients normally impose limits on their financial commitment in one way or another. However, there are many other matters of equal or even greater importance about which clients may have views. These typically include the function, size and location of the end product and a date by which it is required. Objectives can and often do include a much wider range of matters. In the public sector these may include creating extra jobs to reduce unemployment. In the private sector these may include creating a favourable image with potential employees or customers. Whatever they may be, the client's essential responsibility is to establish the project objectives and to ensure that the project organization is directed towards achieving them.

The second distinct area of responsibility within the control sub-system of construction projects is design. That is to select all the parts of the end product and their relationship to each other and to the site on which the project is situated. Typically design moves through broad stages, with the client's objectives as its starting point, it progresses through general descriptions of the appearance, layout, functions and processes of the whole building or engineering product, to detailed drawings and specifications of every part. However, this is usually a far from smooth sequence of work. Design typically proceeds by proposing tentative design solutions, evaluating them against selected objectives and modifying the design in the light of this evaluation. The modifications often mean back-tracking through several previous stages of design development. *Figure 1.3* illustrates the general nature of design development[3].

It is usual for there to be a number of design teams each responsible for different aspects of the end product. Their work has to be coordinated so that all the elements which they design fit together and in total meet the clients objectives in respect of such matters as function, size, performance and quality. The design teams' work also has to be coordinated with the rest of the control sub-system and with the operating sub-system. In addition, the work of the teams within the operating sub-system has to be coordinated. It is the complexity of the coordination needs of construction projects which give rise to the third area of responsibility within the control sub-system. This is management.

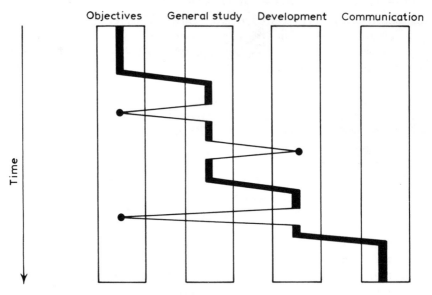

Figure 1.3 General nature of design development

Management is responsible for the project organization. That is, with how things are done, with the behaviour of the teams within a project, and in particular with interactions between them. It has therefore particular responsibility for meeting objectives concerned with costs, time and resource use. These responsibilities involve decisions about teams, the role they will play and the relationships between them, including formal contractual relationships. Management may, particularly on large and complex projects, involve several specialist teams each responsible for one aspect of organization.

We have now identified four major areas of responsibility which together make up construction projects. They are illustrated in *Figure 1.4*. Each area may involve the work of a number of teams. It is necessary for the work within each area of responsibility to be coordinated so that it produces a coherent whole. That is, it is necessary for the objectives to be consistent one with another. Similarly, all the parts of the design must function together to produce the desired performance. Also the separate aspects of management must relate to each other so that the project is carried out efficiently. Obviously the work produced by the construction teams must fit together so that the end product functions as one coherent whole.

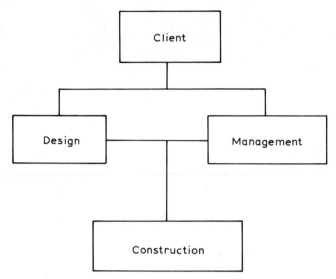

Figure 1.4 Major responsibilities in construction projects

It is also necessary for the four major areas of responsibility to be coordinated. That is, designs and organizations must relate to clients' objectives and to each other. Equally, construction work must take account of the frameworks provided by designs and organizations.

Major responsibility boundary principle

Coordination within the major areas of responsibility and between them both warrant separate consideration. This does not necessarily mean that the major responsibilities must be allocated to separate teams. However, where individual team responsibilities cross the major area boundaries there is likely to be an increased requirement for coordination. This can be seen by considering *Figure 1.5*. Both diagrams represent eight teams responsible for two major areas of responsibility A and B. It is assumed that the work of all teams within each major area needs to be coordinated but that coordination between areas is achieved at a higher level and so is restricted to a single link. *Figure 1.5(a)* shows the situation when the responsibilities of individual teams do not cross the major area boundaries. This produces 13 pairs of teams which need to be coordinated as shown by the lines between teams. *Figure 1.5(b)* shows the situation where two of the teams have responsibilities which cross major area boundaries. The same rules for coordination have been applied as in the first case but now there are 20 pairs of teams which need to be coordinated. The increase would probably result in practice in far more problems to be resolved and therefore in greater costs. This conclusion is clearly of some importance in construction project management and we will consider some practical

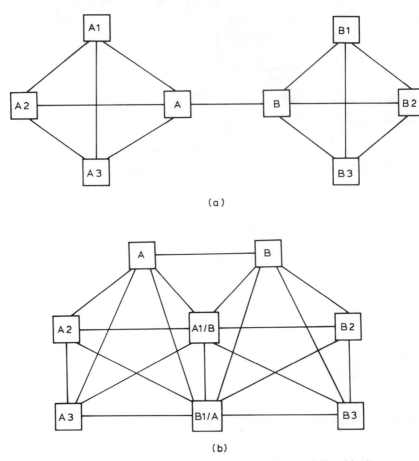

Figure 1.5 Coordination needs of eight teams in two areas of responsibility. (a) All teams within one area of responsibility; (b) two teams cross responsibility boundaries

implications before leaving it to later chapters for more detailed consideration.

The orthodox approach to building projects used in the UK breaks the major responsibility boundary principle. The architect's orthodox role combines design responsibility with part of the management responsibility; the general contractor's role combines construction responsibility with a second part of the management responsibility; and the quantity surveyor's orthodox role has emerged as yet a further management responsibility whose primary purpose is to coordinate the other two management responsibilities. It is little wonder that the UK orthodox approach to building projects is widely regarded as inefficient; nor is it surprising that attempts to improve matters tend to concentrate on establishing a clear management responsibility[4].

On the other hand, many experienced commentators on the UK building industry criticize it for separating design from construction. This appears, on the face of, to conflict with the principle that team responsibilities should not cross the boundaries of the major areas. Yet, for example, the British Property Federation's recent proposals for the design and construction of building[4] place considerable importance on giving the builder responsibility for parts of the design. This idea does not necessarily conflict with the principle of not crossing the boundaries of the major areas of responsibility. It does, however, highlight the need for a tighter definition of design and of construction.

We have observed that Pete James and his team have knowledge about bricklaying. This includes knowing the various situations and circumstances in which particular bricks can be used; the type of mortar required with various combinations of bricks, imposed loads and exposure conditions; several different brick bonds and how to apply them to awkward details; how window and door frames should be built into brickwork; the proper arrangement of damp-proof courses around openings, at ground floor level and in parapet walls; and how to make basement brickwork watertight. They have knowledge about many other matters concerning brickwork which, therefore, could either be made the subject of a design decision or could be left to Pete and his team to decide.

Taking the choice of mortar as an example, designers can either select and specify the mortar in detail or they can leave the choice to competent craftsmen. The end result may well be the same or it may be either better or worse in each case. What is clear is that less work is required if the designer leaves the decision to the specialist construction team. When the designer selects the mortar he must produce a complete specification, indicate clearly on the drawings exactly where that particular mortar is to be used and ensure that the bricklayers have the information when they need it. The bricklayers in turn must find the appropriate information, read it, understand it and put the resulting understanding into effect. It may well be that they decide that the designers choice of mortar is inappropriate or even occasionally that it is wrong. They may decide that they should question the designer or that they should put his decision right but not tell him so as to avoid offending him. In all events it will be somewhat more difficult for them to undertake the work confidently and well if they are working with mortar which they believe is not right for the particular work. Beyond this there is likely to be a tendency for the bricklayers to blame the mortar for any deficiencies in the resulting brickwork.

It is these kinds of consequences which lead to the suggestions that constructors should be given responsibility for detail design. Historically in the UK and still today in many parts of the world, the craft and specialized construction knowledge possessed by construction teams, is regarded as part of construction not as part of design. That view is taken in defining the two terms in this book.

Accepting these practical definitions in no way interferes with designers' ability to retain control of the complete design. They are free to decide, to rely on craft and specialist knowledge where it is appropriate or to adopt design solutions which fall outside the competence of that body of knowledge. In the second case they must communicate what they require to the constructor and make sure that it is understood and put into practice properly. However, where established construction knowledge is appropriate it is most efficient to use it. Thus, we see that the boundary between design and construction varies according to circumstances but on any one particular project in respect of each element the boundary is in one place.

In much the same way the boundaries between the other major areas of responsibility vary from time to rime and from place to place. Their exact position depends on the knowledge and skills which are commonly found together in a single team. This normal practice of the local construction industry and, as we shall see in later chapters, the nature of projects should be used to guide the division of responsibilities into client, design, management and construction areas. The important point is that coordination must be provided both between the teams inside these areas and also between the areas; and these two coordination tasks require careful consideration by clients and their construction project organizations. The main practical consequence of this principle is that it is important to define the boundaries between roles clearly and carefully. A further practical consideration is that it is an advantage if the roles so defined match the pattern of skills and knowledge available in the local construction industry.

Information systems

Thus far we have considered construction projects as comprising the coordinated actions of teams. In this view projects are acting systems. In describing projects in these terms it has been necessary to refer to another type of system which needs to be understood. This is information systems.

Information systems are abstract systems. That is they consist of words, numbers and symbols which represent particular concepts. These concepts usually, and in the context of construction projects, practically always relate to physical objects. That is, they stand for some particular matter–energy. Or rather they represent some interesting characteristic of the real world object. Thus, it may be helpful to think of the need for a team of bricklayers and to make judgements about the capabilities of bricklayers in general without having a particular team of bricklayers available. Knowing Pete and his team can be a rich and rewarding experience but they bring with them a complex combination of attributes which may be confusing to have in mind at certain stages of projects. Thus, we abstract concepts which are useful and give them names or signs which stand for the objects or their characteristics. Information systems use these words, numbers and symbols to help us undertake construction projects.

It is important to recognize that information systems and the acting systems they represent are related but are not the same thing. Thus, in an information system we can define roles, that is the instructions to a team specifying the actions which it is required to take including interactions with other teams both inside and outside the project. Roles are not part of the acting system. It is the role occupants, the teams, who form the acting system. Roles form an important part of project information systems. Clearly there is a close link between role and role occupant but they are not identical.

In general the information system consideration of any particular matter precedes that matter being given expression in a project's acting system. Thus, projects begin in the information system.

They begin with the project objectives. The more clearly and completely they are stated the more likely it is that the client will get what he wants. Thus, to state an extreme case, a developer who had built six identical factory units on an industrial site and who now wants the seventh built by the organization which built the first six, is very likely to get what he wants. On the other hand, if he commissions an architect to design and organize the construction of a new head office which he hopes will enhance his company's image, and then goes on holiday overseas for a year while the work is carried out, without providing any further information, he may be disappointed with the results. Most project objectives fall somewhere between these extremes. Typically clients are certain about some aspects of the construction they need but have given little or no thought to other perhaps equally important matters. Thus, an important and early part of many project organization's task is to determine which matters the client has objectives about and, of course, to establish exactly what they are. Experienced clients are likely to produce a full statement of objectives without outside help but clients unfamiliar with the construction industry, or with the particular type of building or engineering product, are likely to need expert help. Whichever situation exists the client's best interests are most likely to be served if he defines clearly all his objectives and makes sure that all the teams which make up the project organization are aware of these objectives and are working towards them.

In practice the client's statement of objectives normally comprises a formal document called the brief. Experienced clients tend to devote considerable attention to maintaining and refining very detailed descriptions of their requirements. One of the most successful UK development companies maintains on a wordprocessor a description of the materials and components to be used in every part of the office buildings which they finance. In addition the function and performance of each type of space commonly occurring in these buildings are fully specified. This complete description is included in the contracts which the company enters into with design and management teams. The teams are required to use the standard brief unless they can propose an improvement. To be accepted a proposed improvement must be shown to produce demonstrable net benefits in costs, time or performance. Once accepted the improvement becomes a part of the standard brief and is incorporated in the wordprocessor record. Typically two or three improvements are found on each new project. So the brief gradually develops with the client fully in control of his statement of objectives and by including it specifically in contracts with all designers and managers he ensures that his requirements are fully taken into account as each new building is produced. This approach to briefing is discussed in more detail in Chapter 8.

The next major component of the information system is a description of the end product. This is normally produced in the form of two-dimensional drawings and written specifications. These descriptions are the result of what is usually a long process of modelling the project's end product in gradually increasing degrees of detail. The formal drawings and specifications are needed to form part of the contracts for construction and to communicate the designers' intentions to the constructors. The earlier models of the end product which lead up to the formal documents may include three-dimensional drawings, physical models which are often very elaborate and full-size prototypes of new elements used in the design of particularly complicated details. There is a growing tendency for the description to make use of computer graphics systems. This is almost certain to emerge as the normal method of working in the future. Systems currently in use in practice produce two- and three-dimensional drawings and very realistic three-dimensional images using full colour on visual display units. These systems make it possible to create the illusion of moving around or through a finished building or engineering product. It is technically possible for the computer automatically to call up the appropriate specification clauses as materials and components are incorporated in the design model. These developments are likely to increase the speed of the design processes very considerably but in no way alter the need for a description of the project's end product.

As the description of the end product is produced, so a parallel description or model of the project organization must be developed. As described earlier, this is expressed in terms of the roles which must be played for the project to be completed successfully. The roles may be expressed in costs, times or descriptions of the work to be done. Common examples of the resulting documents include budgets, schedules, cost plans, bar charts, bills of quantities, method statements and networks. They usually model the direct construction work. However, as the management responsibility becomes more clearly developed in practice, so the value of modelling the complete project organization is being more fully recognized. Techniques are emerging which enable the design and the organization to be planned in parallel each reinforcing and constraining the other so that all the client's objectives can be given their proper weight.

Figure 1.6 shows a combined budget and bar chart produced during the early stages of a project. It provides a framework for the subsequent development both of the design and the organization. It is computer

Work package		BUDGET £,000s		1981				1982				1983				1984			
		Design & management	Construction	1	2	3	4	1	2	3	4	1	2	3	4	1	2	3	4
1	Strategy	200	-																
2	Substructure	45	427																
3	Superstructure	52	418																
4	External envelope	35	729																
5	Internal sub-division	10	429																
6	Concealed fittings	54	732																
7	Surface finishes	37	219																
8	Exposed fittings	103	1521																
9	External works 1	32	217																
10	External works 2	17	184																
11	Set up site	25	53																
12	Site organization	180	312																
	Totals	790	5241																

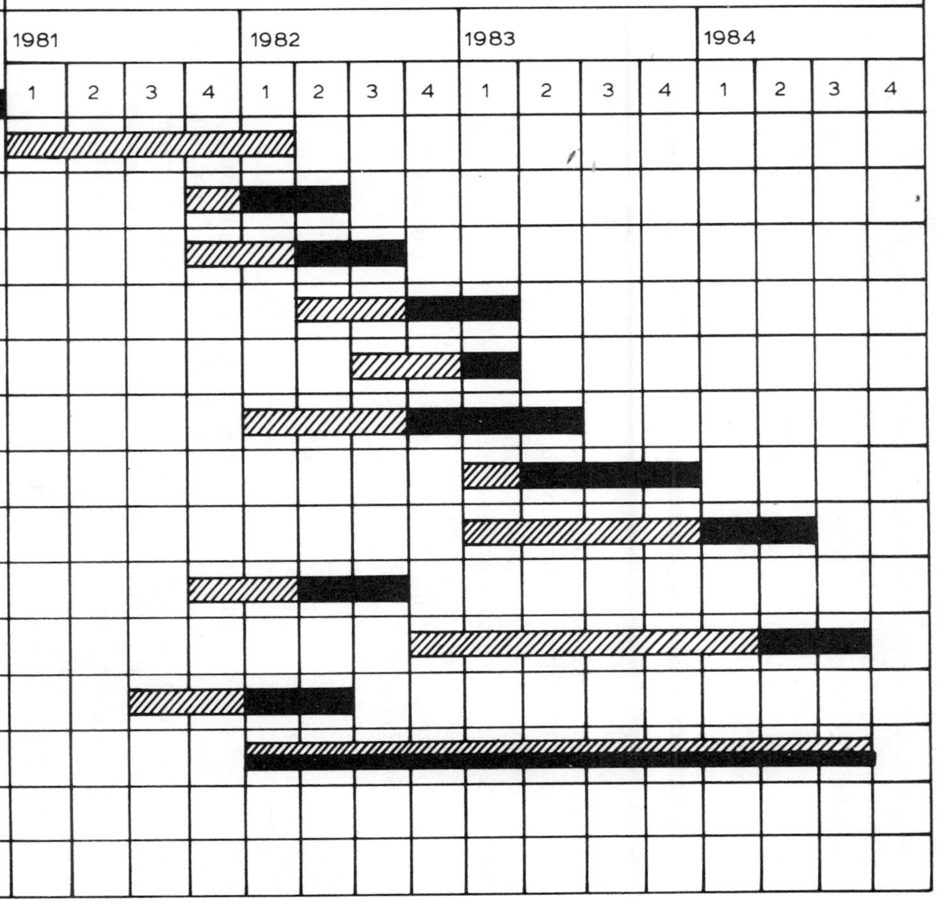

Figure 1.6 Budget and schedule at an early stage of a construction project

produced and this is now very common. Future developments promise to provide computer systems which integrate the management information with the designer's information. This will in no way reduce the need for a model of the organization. It will, as with design, simply increase the speed of the essential processes. It seems likely that computers will also enable more useful models of the organization to be developed.

The simple bars in *Figure 1.6* do not provide a very clear image of the direct construction work they are intended to represent. It should be possible to produce instead three-dimensional pictures perhaps simulating the construction work on a visual display unit in the foreseeable future. Certainly the possibilities arising from using computer graphics for construction management are very exciting[5].

In considering the project information system we have identified three major components. These are, objectives, a model of the end product and a model of the organization. These three components are not developed in isolation, neither are they developed as a simple sequence of objectives, design and organization. They need to be developed together in a fully interactive manner.

Project phases

The initial development of objectives, design and organization forms a separate phase of construction projects. This is a strategic phase which has different characteristics from a subsequent tactical phase. The purpose of the strategic phase of projects is to establish the nature of the end product and of the organization required to produce it in sufficient detail to be able to define fully the project roles. Once clearly-defined roles have been established the project moves into a tactical phase.

The distinction between strategic and tactical phases is important because the nature of the work involved and of the interactions between role occupants is essentially different in each. *Figure 1.7* shows the main components of the information system at the level of detail so far described. It clearly indicates the distinction between the interactive strategic phase and the more regimented execution of clearly defined roles.

During the strategic phase projects are essentially problem-solving organizations[6]. That is they work in a relatively unstructured or organic style through teams comprising different kinds of skills and knowledge. They are seeking original answers to the key questions about their project which cannot be provided by existing established answers.

The decision-making process moves through distinct stages and there is merit in deliberately following these. The first step is to identify and clearly define the questions to be answered. This means separating the questions which may require an original answer from those clearly settled by the client's brief. The questions so identified should be defined as precisely as possible.

The next stage is to develop a number of answers. This may draw on a very wide range of skills and knowledge and a number of different methods of working. It may involve brain-storming sessions, several teams working on rival answers in competition, or original research and development work. The aim is to develop a choice of answers.

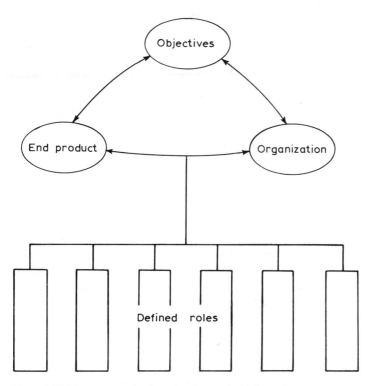

Figure 1.7 Main components of construction project information systems

The third stage is to consider the consequences of each of the answers. This evaluation may be made by those proposing the answer or by separate independent teams. Their job is to relate the answers to the client's stated objectives. So the evaluation may involve a simple ranking of the options identified or may involve careful measurement of performance, costs, times or other aspects. As well as being complete it is important that the evaluation is as objective as possible.

The final stage is to choose one of the answers, or some combination of the features provided by the answers presented, or to decide to seek further information. The further information may take the form of re-defining the original question, seeking further possible answers or a more searching evaluation of one or more of the answers under consideration. Thus, the outcome may require the client to review his objectives or it may lead to a clearer definition of the end product or of the organization. On the other hand it may lead to a widening of the decision-making process in a search for a better answer.

Problem-solving can be and indeed often is, an expensive process. It is also likely to lead to difficulties during construction because original designs tend to generate unexpected or unusual combinations of circumstances which have to be sorted out on site as they arise. It can also produce better answers than any which existed previously. This of course is the main reason why designers and managers are attracted to a problem-solving method of working. However, on any one construction project, original answers inevitably increase the risk of poor performance. The more original answers on any one project, the greater will be the risks. Therefore, the initial strategic decisions which determine how far established answers are to be used and how far original answers are to be sought are obviously of crucial importance. It is vital that the client takes full responsibility for these decisions and that he ensures that he has sufficient information to understand their implications on the benefits he will receive and on the costs and risks that he will face.

Essentially the strategic phase seeks to bring into balance the client's objectives, a model of the end product and a model of the project organization. It may take many years and many people to achieve this balance on a large, complex, innovative project. This is especially true when the project is of major political interest. Sydney Opera House has already been mentioned and it suffered from deliberately political decisions aimed at ensuring a start on site before the 1959 State elections. As we shall see in later chapters politicians and others often interfere with construction projects and cause them to take an extraordinarily long time. On the other hand, all the strategic questions may be settled very quickly and involve little expense. It is, as we shall see, the nature of the client's objectives combined with his power to pursue them, which very largely, determines the schedule for the strategic phase of construction projects.

The product of the strategic phase of construction projects is the definition of a number of roles. Each role represents work which is required for the completion of the project in accordance with the agreed strategy. Once defined roles have been identified the project organization becomes more concerned with tactical issues and so the style of working changes. Now the primary need is to select competent teams for each of the roles and to motivate them so that the project is completed efficiently.

Teams need to understand their work. That is, they need to know what they are to do and then once their work is underway they need to know how they are doing. Arbitrary changes, failure to provide the necessary materials or tools, interruptions which prevent a steady flow of work or work which is difficult for no obvious reason, all serve to alienate workers. Avoiding such bad effects requires, first of all, that the teams are competent to carry out their roles. Generally this means selecting teams who have carried out similar work successfully in the recent past. Where this is not possible it may be sensible to review the role definition to consider whether it can be changed to a task which is within the competence of the teams available. Alternatively, the project may have to be expanded to provide training. In all events it is essential for efficient work that the team accept that the work is within their competence and that the targets specified in the role definition and the rewards are reasonable.

Once a team is appointed, efficiency requires that they have clear instructions on the work they are to do; are provided with everything they need to do it; and are then allowed to get on with their work without interruption. It helps if they are reminded of the purpose of their work frequently by an enthusiastic manager. The team should regularly be briefed on progress, any changes planned for the near future which affect team members and any actions needed to make the team more effective. Managers should be seen to be concerned to improve working conditions and safety. They should deal with grievances promptly. Above all, the managers should regularly walk round each team's place of work. This should be at least once a day. While walking the job, managers should observe the work, listen to anything the workers wish to say to them and be prepared to give praise and encouragement. At the same time managers must be clear about the rules and procedures which apply. They should seek to gain the support of the teams for those rules and criticize or otherwise discipline anyone who breaks them. These basic principles of motivating teams are well understood[7]. They depend on a clear definition of the team's role, competent execution of any work by others which interacts with that of the team and on not changing the role definition once the team is appointed. These principles and conditions for success are of central concern during the tactical phase of projects.

All projects completed successfully move through strategic and tactical phases. However, there is not a clear break between the two in respect of whole projects. Partly this is because roles are not defined and allocated to teams all at the same moment. This takes time and so both strategic and tactical work may take place simultaneously although this should not be on the same element of the project. Mixing strategic and tactical work relating to any one element tends to lead to inefficiency and increased costs. Another factor of some importance which prevents there being a clear break between the two phases is the need to arrange construction project organizations in hierarchies.

Project hierarchies

Large and complex construction projects are necessarily arranged in hierarchies because of practical limits on the size and capacity of teams. There is much evidence which is consistent that teams of between 2 and 15 people are the most effective[7]. Also there is much evidence that effective teams, or rather their managers, tend to plan their work in terms of a relatively small number of sub-tasks[8]. Large and complex construction projects will require the work of many hundreds of teams if each is to be relatively small. Since such numbers are beyond the capacity of effective managers there is no choice but to see projects as hierarchies, which means that the strategy for a total project will divide it into a fairly small number of sub-projects. As far as the top level of responsibility in the project is concerned, the sub-projects become its tactical level. However, each sub-project becomes a complete project in itself as far as the teams responsible for it are concerned. Their project moves through a strategic phase which results in the definition of sub-sub-projects or of defined roles depending on the size and complexity of the total project. The process of sub-dividing continues through as many levels of a hierarchy as are needed to arrive at defined roles small enough to be carried out by teams of between two and 15 people.

Figure 1.8 shows the essential features of a project hierarchy in terms of the information system. It also illustrates an important principle. This is that each of the major components of the project information system needs to be connected to the equivalent components in the sub-projects and similarly it needs to be connected to those in their sub-sub-projects. This is to ensure that, first of all, the lower level teams are fully informed of what they are to do and secondly, that the higher level teams are provided with feedback.

The coordination links needed in the acting system on large, complex, innovative projects are more numerous than those indicated in *Figure 1.8*. The richer pattern of links is described in Chapter 4. The links shown in *Figure 1.8* are those which are essential in the information system of projects.

Thus, we see that in large and complex projects the tactical phase for a higher level team becomes the total project for a lower level team. That project has both a strategic and a tactical phase. This is true right down to the work of individual teams. For example, when Pete James and his team won the contract for the brickwork on their 13th project they had to decide exactly what work was to be done, how it was to be done, how it was to be allocated between the team members and a number of other strategic issues. Once these matters were settled they could get on with the direct construction work.

The essential differences between work at the top of the hierarchy and at the bottom, lie in the discretion exercised in the strategic phase. Pete is employed in the project to lay bricks rather than to do any other kind of work. An architect employed on the same project may do a number of very different things and, to a large extent, it may well be for the architect to decide whether he or she makes a model, produces a drawing, builds a computer system, writes a specification or does something else.

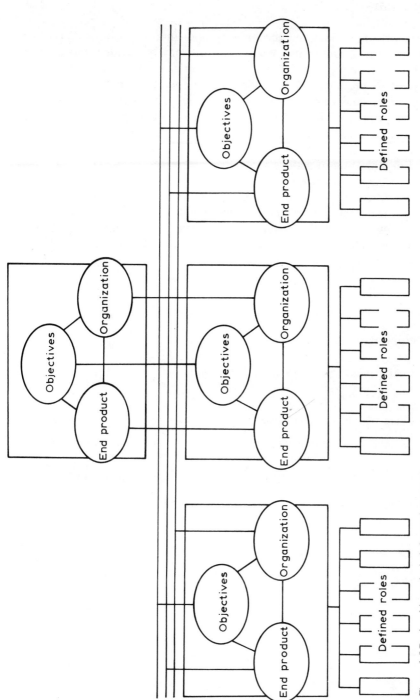

Figure 1.8 Project hierarchy in information system

Summary

We have now identified the basic components of projects. There is an acting system comprising teams, and this may be divided into a control sub-system undertaking client design and management responsibilities and essentially producing information; and an operating sub-system undertaking direct construction work and essentially modifying matter–energy. Teams can usefully be regarded as controlled systems which have knowledge, values and the ability to take actions. They rely on feedback. Teams interact by communication of information, transactions of values and organization of actions.

Projects also include an information system. It is divided into a strategic phase concerned with objectives, models of the end product and models of the project organization; and a tactical phase concerned with defined roles.

Finally we saw that large and complex projects inevitably adopt a hierarchical form. These concepts provide the basic raw material which we shall use in subsequent chapters as we consider construction project management.

References

1. HALL, P., *Great Planning Disasters*, Weidenfeld & Nicolson (1980)
2. For a justification for the choice of just three characteristics and for much of what follows from this selection see: KUHN, A. and BEAM, R. D., *The Logic of Organization*, Jossey–Bass (1982)
3. Figure 1.3 is based on a diagram in *Architectural Practice and Management Handbook*, RIBA, London (1973)
4. See for example: *Manual of the BPF System: The British Property Federation System for Building Design and Construction*, The British Property Federation (1983)
5. The range of systems which link computer graphics and data handling is well described in: KROUSE, JOHN K., *Computer-Aided Design and Computer-Aided Manufacturing*, Marcel Dekker (1982)
6. For an excellent description of how organizations should approach problem-solving see: HEIRS, B. and PEHRSON, G., *The Mind of the Organization*, Harper & Row (1977)
7. For much sound advice on managing work see: REVANS, R. W., *Action Learning*, Chartwell–Bratt (1982)
8. This aspect of construction managers work is well documented in: BENNETT, J. and ORMEROD, R., *Construction Project Simulator, Final Report of SERC Research Grant*, Department of Construction Management, University of Reading, Occasional Paper No.12 (1984)

Chapter 2

Project types

It was a bright clear morning as Pete James, later than usual, turned in through the site gate knowing that today he would finish his work on the project. There were about 250 bricks still to be laid and he and Tony could finish before lunchtime. Doug and Mike were spending the morning looking at two other projects where they had been offered work. Pete was already looking forward to lunch in the Three Compasses *public house when the team would decide which project to work on next.*

Pete put his coat in the site hut and collected his bag of tools. As he came out of the hut he stopped to look at the building he was helping to construct. The sunlight slanted across the rows of arches highlighting the intricate patterns around each one and the dark shadows emphasized the ornamental bands which marked each floor level. The brickwork looked good to Pete. Then he saw that Tony was already on the scaffolding mixing the mortar for the last few bricks.

As Pete climbed to the top of the building he noticed that the floor decking was in place on the first three floors. Inside the building the plumbers were fixing pipes, the electricians were fixing conduits and the heating fitters were fixing large silver ducts to the underside of the floor slabs. As he reached the top the scaffolding seemed to be full of people. The foreman of the window team was arguing furiously with the architect about the position of the fixing pads in the openings. The rest of the window team were stood around them listening and grinning. Overhead the tower crane was swinging a large curved roof panel into place under directions from the roofing foreman armed with a two-way radio. The plumbers were still fixing their damp-proof courses at the head of the brickwork and would soon be held up unless Pete finished his work quickly.

Pete did not like projects as crowded as this one had now become. Everyone was in each others way and repeatedly falling over each others materials and equipment. He had heard that the site manager was under pressure to finish quickly, which presumably was why he was flooding the work with labour. Despite the congestion the work went very well that morning and Pete and Tony had finished by eleven o'clock. They said goodbye to the site manager, collected their outstanding money and set off for the Three Compasses.

The two projects on which the team had been offered work were very different from the one they had just left. The first was a new factory on the industrial site down by the railway and the second was in the centre of town where three large houses were being refurbished and turned into offices. Pete knew that the refurbishment work would suit them best. There would be problems to be solved as they worked and the brickwork would have to be good quality. The factory just needed fast bricklaying and would probably pay higher wages. The team might benefit from well-paid, straightforward work as a change from all the difficulties of the project they had just finished. But Pete knew they would soon get bored with laying somewhere between 700 and 1200 bricks each, day after day in endless straight lines. They might as well be machines.

Doug had seen Pete and Tony coming across the town square and had two pints waiting on the table in the corner by the dartboard as they entered the saloon bar. The four men weighed up the advantages and disadvantages of the two projects. The money was better on the factory but Red McGregor was the site manager and would push everyone very hard to get a fast completion, the office project was nearer their homes and nearer the Three Compasses *and they would certainly need an extra labourer on the factory project but would be working outside. Refurbishment work was always very dirty and dusty and got very hot in the Summer. Mike and Doug said they felt the office project was the happier one. The men working there seemed to be enjoying the work and had said that the site manager and architect were reasonable people. So it was agreed that Pete would go to the office project that afternoon and make all the arrangements for them to start next morning.*

As he sank his third pint Pete began to wonder if they had made the right choice. The two projects were very different and both different from the one they had just finished.

He was thinking of the differences from the point of view of the brickwork and its interactions with all the other kinds of work. However, construction projects vary from each other in many different ways. Each is unique at least in being in a different physical location from every other building or civil and heavy engineering product. This is likely to result in a particular combination of ground conditions, weather and access constraints not exactly matched by any other project. Also the end products vary from each other in many major and minor matters. Even identical houses are made from materials which vary slightly in their constituents, performance, size and shape. The major elements will be slightly different in size and relative position. The defects and errors will vary. The processes which produce them will be different. Almost certainly the teams which design, manage and construct them will be somewhat different.

So we may safely accept that all construction projects are different from each other. However, we need to find some similarities between projects in order that we can learn how to design, manage and construct them. Unless we find some basis for thinking about projects in a consistent manner we will not know which parts of our experience and knowledge are relevant to particular new projects.

Generally when construction projects are classified they are grouped together on the basis of their main function. CI/SfB[1] is a well-developed classification scheme and in providing for the end results of the construction process it includes categories based on primary function under the following main headings: utilities, civil engineering facilities; industrial facilities; administrative, commercial, protective service facilities; health, welfare facilities; recreational facilities; religious facilities; educational, scientific, information facilities; and residential facilities. These are useful in bringing together information about the functional design of buildings or civil and heavy engineering products. However, there is no necessary reason why buildings which serve the same function should produce similar construction management tasks. Indeed it is possible from a construction management point of view for a school building to be more like an office block, a factory or a hospital than other school buildings.

Construction project management is essentially concerned with identifying the roles needed to undertake particular projects, with appointing teams to undertake those roles and with coordinating their actions so that all work towards agreed objectives. We need, therefore, a means of classifying projects in terms of the number of roles and teams involved and the relationships between them.

In order that we can concentrate on whole projects rather than the details of individual roles and teams described in Chapter 1, we will use, initially at least, the concept of an idealized construction role and team. The role is a standard size and requires the work of a standard team which produces a standard quantity of output at a standard cost in a standard time.

This provides a way of looking at construction projects which is not wholly unrealistic. As we saw in Chapter 1, construction teams tend to be roughly the same size. Also in practice, there tends to be a natural tempo of work on any one project. This may be planned or it may emerge quite naturally as teams undertaking various kinds of work in sequence follow each other from workplace to workplace. The size of the teams or the number of teams, and the timing of their work in practice are adjusted so that there is a reasonably regular tempo of work[2]. So, although the primary reason for thinking initially in terms of standard roles and teams is to allow us to concentrate on important characteristics of whole projects, this provides a view which is not wholly divorced from practice. In any case, once we have identified all the important characteristics which the idealized model reveals, we shall relax the assumptions on which it is based in order to consider the behaviour of real projects.

Project characteristics

We will first consider a project comprising several roles, each of which requires a team undertaking a different kind of work. Such a project is shown in *Figure 2.1*. It comprises six standard roles undertaken by six standard teams whose work is carried out in a simple sequence. Each team's work may begin when the preceding team has finished. Thus, the minimum time for the project shown in *Figure 2.1* is six standard time units. It is also clear that the cost of the project in *Figure 2.1* is six standard units of cost.

Figure 2.1 Project comprising six teams in sequence

Standard roles allow us to measure the size of projects. Thus, a project comprising seven or more roles is bigger than the one shown in *Figure 2.1* and, equally obviously, one comprising five or fewer roles is smaller. Size is the first important characteristic of construction projects. As we have already noted it has a direct effect on total time and costs.

We can model a bigger project by adding more roles to the sequence. Thus, we could think of a project comprising 30 roles in a simple sequence. Alternatively, we could imagine a 30-role project comprising five repetitions of the work of six teams. This is shown in *Figure 2.2*. In this new project when team 1 has finished its work, two things can happen. Team 1 may repeat its work in a new location and team 2 may carry out its work in the first location. In practice, the separate locations could be individual bays in a large, single-storey building, separate floors in a multi-storey building, separate buildings in, for example, a housing project or indeed any other sub-divisions of projects.

Within our definition of standard roles the project in *Figure 2.2* is the same size as a project comprising 30 roles in a simple sequence. Also, within this definition, the cost of the two projects is identical. However, the time is very different. While the simple sequence will take a minimum of 30 standard time units the project in *Figure 2.2* has a minimum time of only 10 standard time units. This is a sufficiently dramatic difference to justify distinguishing between projects with these different characteristics. We shall regard the number of roles requiring different kinds of work as a measure of complexity and the number of times this work is repeated as a measure of repetition. Thus the 30-role sequential project is more complex than the one in *Figure 2.2*. Conversely it is less repetitive. Complexity and repetition are the second and third important characteristics of construction projects.

We can see something of the effect of these two characteristics from *Table 2.1* which lists the minimum time in standard time units for various 30-team projects. Clearly, within our idealized model of construction projects, repetition results in greatly reduced completion times.

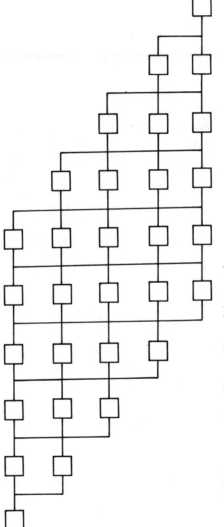

Figure 2.2 Project comprising five repetitions of six teams in sequence

TABLE 2.1. Various 30-team projects

Complexity	Repetition	Minimum time
30	1	30
15	2	16
10	3	12
6	5	10

We can now look at the effects of interactions between teams. First we can observe that any delay between the completion of work by one team and the start of work by any following team will, in the projects considered so far, increase the total time. Such delays are common in practice. They may arise from chance interactions between teams or they may be planned. The effect of introducing one standard time unit buffer between the work of each team is shown in *Table 2.2*. This suggests that the effect on time of delays or planned buffers between the work of separate teams is likely to be both absolutely and relatively greater in complex projects than in repetitive ones. Thus, the benefits of earlier completion in repetitive projects are enhanced by the effects of interactions between teams.

TABLE 2.2. Various 30-team projects with one time unit buffers

Complexity	Repetition	Minimum time with buffer	Increase over minimum time
30	1	59	29
15	2	30	14
10	3	21	9
6	5	15	5

The idealized model of construction projects enables us to consider the effect of using several teams each undertaking the same kind of work. Thus, the project shown in *Figure 2.2* could use five teams of each of the types required working in parallel. This might represent five houses or five bays being built simultaneously. During the finishings and fitting out stages of multi-storey buildings it could represent work on five separate floors. The minimum time now reduces to six standard time units or, if we can assume one time unit buffer, it reduces to eleven units. So not surprisingly the use of more teams leads to a significant reduction in the total time.

The decision to introduce planned time buffers or to use several teams of the same type directly affects the speed with which a given project is likely to be completed. It is, of course, also possible to use buffers and several teams of the same type in combination. This would produce a total time somewhere between those resulting from using the alternative strategies separately. Clearly these types of decision have significant effects. Therefore, speed is the fourth important characteristic of projects.

Within the idealized model of projects, a consistent measure of speed is provided by calculating the number of roles completed in each unit of time. *Table 2.3* lists the resulting speeds for the projects considered earlier. They vary from 0.5 to 5.0 roles per time unit. It can be seen from the right-hand column of *Table 2.3* that slow construction generally results from complexity, the use of buffers and using only one of each kind of team, while fast construction generally results from repetition, using extra teams and having each one start as soon as the preceding team has finished its work. These principles are reasonably self-evident. The benefits we derive from constructing the model are first, that it helps to reveal how the individual characteristics behave in combination and secondly, we have a means of measuring the effects. The third benefit is that by adding one more important characteristic the model will begin to provide insights which are far from self-evident. Before moving on to the next important characteristic which is more subtle than the first four, we need to establish a more precise terminology. This should help to ensure that the insights provided by the very simple model are not lost as we add more features.

TABLE 2.3. Speed of various 30-team projects

Complexity	Repetition	Buffer	Teams	Minimum time	Speed
30	1	0	30	30	1.0
30	1	1	30	59	0.5
15	2	0	15	16	1.9
15	2	1	15	30	1.0
15	2	0	30	15	2.0
15	2	1	30	29	1.0
10	3	0	10	12	2.5
10	3	1	10	21	1.4
10	3	0	30	10	3.0
10	3	1	30	19	1.6
6	5	0	6	10	3.0
6	5	1	6	15	2.0
6	5	0	30	6	5.0
6	5	1	30	11	2.7

The four characteristics of size, complexity, repetition and speed are all the important ones that we can derive from the concepts of standard roles and teams without relaxing any of the assumptions on which they are based. We will use the following notation for the concepts and the relationships between them which we have identified to this point.

A = number of roles requiring different kinds of work = complexity,
R = number of repetitions of roles requiring similar work = repetition,
S = size of projects = number of roles,
T = number of teams,
ω = standard unit of time,
p = standard unit of costs,

M　= minimum time for projects in which $T = A$,
N　= minimum time for projects in which $T = S$,
B_n　= buffer of n standard time units,
V　= speed of projects,
C　= costs of projects.

The following relationships exist

$$S = AR \qquad (2.1)$$
$$M = \omega(A + R - 1 + B_n (A - 1)) \qquad (2.2)$$
$$N = \omega(A + B_n (A - 1)) \qquad (2.3)$$
$$V = \frac{S}{M} \text{ or } \frac{S}{N} \qquad (2.4)$$
$$C = pAR \qquad (2.5)$$

Variability in productivity

The assumption in the idealized model which we must relax in order to move closer to real projects is that each team produces a standard quantity of output in any given period of time. It is part of the human condition that work takes either more or less time than we expect. Sometimes we are pleasantly surprised when a task is completed quickly, but perhaps more often, we have to cope with delay. Variability in human productivity is commonplace. A direct illustration of this at the level of individuals is provided by popular participation in marathon running. Typically, those who finish events like the London or New York marathons have times which range between a little over 2 hours and 6 hours. There is, in addition, always a number, usually a surprisingly small number, who fail to finish. So there is a wide range of performance amongst marathon runners which can be described as 4 hours ± 50%. It is, of course, the case that any individual runner can make a reasonably accurate prediction of his own time. However, before we use individual predictability in athletic performance to guide us in construction projects, we must take into account two factors. First, we must recognize that running a marathon is a very tightly defined and essentially simple task in which most of the competitors have directly relevant experience. These circumstances are difficult to achieve in construction projects. Secondly, during the strategic stages which is when major project decisions have to be taken, we cannot be certain whether the teams who will carry out the direct construction work at some time in the future will be the equivalent of Olympic medal winners or fun runners. Neither can we be sure how many workers there will be in each team. We can expect between two and 15 in most of the teams but then we cannot be sure what tools and equipment they will use. We cannot be sure how strong, how fit, how well-motivated nor how skilful they will be. Therefore, any single estimate of the time to complete the work comprising any construction role is unlikely to be accurate except within wide margins.

This is confirmed in practice since variability in productivity is commonplace in all construction work. Bennett and Ormerod[3] in reviewing the available evidence have attempted to find measures which describe the range of man–hours expended per unit of work. This suggests that the range recorded in practice is of the order of ±50 to 60%. This relates to the effort expended in completing the task at the workplace and does not take account of time lost due to bad weather, lack of materials or information or other factors external to the team. The figures quoted represent the variability in productivity of one team for a given task, in a given situation. It is probable that the recorded figures understate the actual variability. It was found by Bennett and Ormerod[3] that with work study data the observed times are adjusted to allow for the effort expended by the workers and the working conditions. Time judged to be used inefficiently in eating, talking or idleness is not recorded. Extreme values are eliminated and other steps are taken in order to produce a narrow and consistent range of results. This is done because current methods of predicting the times and costs of construction projects rely on single values for each item of work. Therefore, all attention is concentrated on the average values and the size of the range of results is largely ignored. This narrow view is reinforced by published research data which are often adjusted to eliminate extreme values largely in order to preserve a degree of credibility with practitioners who are used to using doctored data. However, as will soon become apparent, the variability of productivity has important effects on models of projects.

We shall initially take a range of ±50% as a measure of construction variability in productivity in developing our model of construction projects. This is as good a figure as can be obtained from the available data, if anything it probably understates the variability experienced in practice and is sufficiently large for our purpose of identifying the important characteristics of construction projects. At least it is sufficiently large provided that we regard all levels of productivity within the range as equally likely to occur.

It is often assumed when we get a series of results which form a regular pattern, that provided we take a large number of results, the average will tend to be consistent and therefore we can ignore the variability. It is the case that the average will tend to be consistent but in construction projects, variability affects the interactions between teams and so simple average is misleading. It is perhaps easiest to see why if we look at a simple case. *Figure 2.3* shows a 16-role project with equal complexity and repetition. The productivity achieved is shown in the boxes representing each role. They have an average of 1.00 and a range of ±50%. The planned start for each team is given and it is assumed that teams do not start before that time. Actual schedules based on the data given in *Figure 2.3* are listed in *Table 2.4*.

TABLE 2.4. Progress on the project in *Figure 2.3*

Team	Repetition	Time	Start	Finish	Comment
1	1	0.50	0.00	0.50	
1	2	1.25	0.50	1.75	
1	3	0.50	1.75	2.25	
1	4	1.25	2.25	3.50	
2	1	1.50	1.00	2.50	Planned start
2	2	0.75	2.50	3.25	
2	3	1.25	3.25	4.50	
2	4	0.50	4.50	5.00	
3	1	1.00	2.50	3.50	Start delayed by team 2
3	2	1.25	3.50	4.75	
3	3	1.50	4.75	6.25	
3	4	0.50	6.25	6.75	
4	1	0.75	3.50	4.25	Start delayed by team 3
4	2	1.00	4.75	5.75	Delayed by team 3
4	3	1.00	6.25	7.25	Delayed by team 3
4	4	1.50	7.25	8.75	

The planned time for the project is seven standard time units. Variability in performance has caused delays which extend the time to 8.75 time units. This is an increase of 25%. We can also examine the effect of this time over-run on costs. *Table 2.5* lists the costs under the alternative assumptions (a) that each team starts in accordance with its planned start and (b) that each team starts when its first workplace is available.

TABLE 2.5. Costs on the project in *Figure 2.3*

Team	Planned start	Finish	Costs
1	0.00	3.50	3.50
2	1.00	5.00	4.00
3	2.00	6.75	4.75
4	3.00	8.75	5.75
		Total (a)	18.00

Team	Actual start	Finish	Costs
1	0.00	3.50	3.50
2	1.00	5.00	4.00
3	2.50	6.75	4.25
4	3.50	8.75	5.25
		Total (b)	17.00

The planned cost for the project is 16 standard cost units. Assuming that each team arrives at the planned time and incurs costs until its work is complete increases the total cost to 18 units. Alternatively, assuming that each team arrives when its first workplace is available and incurs costs until its work is complete produces a total cost of 17 units. These are increases of 12.5% and 6.25%, respectively. Under both assumptions the costs of individual teams increase as the project progresses further which suggests that we are unlikely to remove the effects of variability by adding yet more teams to provide, as it were, a larger sample. To see why this is so we need to look more closely at the interactions between teams in total projects.

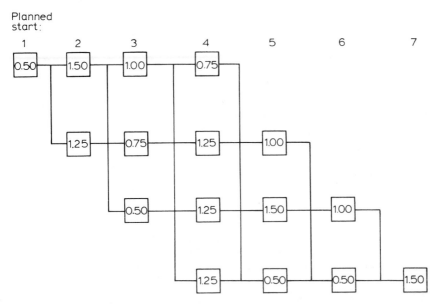

Figure 2.3 Project with variability in productivity

Legard[4] has analysed the consequences of including variability in models of construction projects. His analysis suggests that two factors work in combination to produce the increases in time and costs compared with results which assume fixed and consistent productivity. The first is the length of the routes from the start to the finish of the whole project comprising a sequence of interdependent roles. Thus, in *Figure 2.3* the sequences of teams and repetitions of 1.1, 2.1, 2.2, 3.2, 3.3, 4.3, 4.4 or 1.1, 1.2, 1.3, 2.3, 2.4, 3.4, 4.4 provide alternative routes. Both are seven standard units long. There are many other routes and all pass through seven roles. Given variability of performance, the actual time to complete each route will be different. Clearly the minimum with a range of ±50% is 50% of the standard route length but because of interactions between teams which cause delays, the maximum can be very large. The longer the route and, therefore, the greater the risk that delays will occur, the higher the maximum is likely to be compared with the standard route length.

The second factor which is important when we include variability in models of construction projects is the number of routes. This has an influence because the more routes through a project the greater the chance that one of them will become very long. It is, of course, the longest route which determines the overall time of projects just as it is the weakest link which determines the strength of a chain.

We can calculate the number of routes through a project from the equation:

$$H = \frac{(A + R - 2)!}{(A - 1)! \times (R - 1)!} \tag{2.6}$$

where H = the number of routes.

It can be seen that the number of routes increases rapidly as projects get bigger. This is illustrated in *Table 2.6* which lists the number of routes through projects of different sizes. Clearly with so many alternative routes through large projects, the chances are very high that one route, and indeed, that many routes, will be very long. So we see that when we include variability in models, large projects inevitably take relatively longer than small ones. This principle will help us in subsequent chapters to understand why large projects frequently over-run their estimated times.

TABLE 2.6. **Number of routes through various projects**

Complexity	Repetition	Routes	Routes per role
5	5	70	2.8
10	10	48 620	486.2
25	25	25 trillion[1]	40 billion[2]

1. approximately; trillion = million, million
2. approximately; billion = thousand, million

Within the idealized model costs are equal to the sum of the times for which each team is involved in the project. *Table 2.5* shows the costs in a small project under alternative assumptions about the start time for each team. Both sets of data show that the costs of individual teams increase as more teams are working simultaneously. This is because the chances increase that earlier teams will do their work slowly and so delay later teams. As projects get larger the number of routes which can potentially delay each team increases rapidly as shown in *Table 2.6* and so the costs of each team and therefore of the project also rise. So it is inevitable that when we include variability in models, large projects will have higher unit costs than small ones. And we shall see in later chapters this principle helps to explain why large projects frequently over-run their estimated costs.

We shall also see that variability influences the times and costs associated with complexity, repetition and speed. Therefore, variability in productivity is included as the fifth important characteristic of projects.

Causes of variability

Variability has many causes and it would be impossible to list them all. It is, however, helpful in understanding how construction projects are managed to consider some of the factors which influence the likely range of variability. This will also serve to illustrate the nature of variability and the kind of influence it may have on the times and costs of construction projects. We will consider four factors and call them innovation quality standards, intricacy and learning curves.

Innovation refers to work which falls outside the normal range of work of local construction teams. It may, therefore, arise from extending the scope of an established form of construction or from using a form of construction new to the local industry. It may arise from original design details or a novel overall configuration of the end product. Alternatively, it may arise from designs established elsewhere but used for the first time in the local industry. Most innovative projects involve a mixture of these cases. Variability of performance tends to increase as more of the factors apply to more parts of the end product. Very little live data exist to provide a direct measure of the effects of innovation. However, realistic results are produced by using variability in the range ±50% for work within the normal competence of the local industry increasing to −50% to +300% for projects comprising a large proportion of original design deatils in an original overall configuration. Projects which fall between normal work and totally innovative work are likely to experience levels of variability in productivity between these two sets of figures.

TABLE 2.7. Output per employed worker–year in construction in 1973 ($ thousand) 'Labour productivity in 1980: an international comparison', by A. D. Roy in *National Institute Economic Review* No. 101 (August 1982))

Country	1973	1980
West Germany	14.5	17.3
France	11.2	13.2
USA	11.6	11.0
UK	10.7	9.5
Japan	7.6	7.1

The second factor to consider is quality standards. Conventional wisdom tells us that higher quality costs more and takes longer to produce than lower quality. This view, however, conflicts with the widely reported coincidence of high quality and high productivity in Japanese manufacturing industry. It is therefore necessary to consider more carefully the effect of quality on productivity. *Table 2.7* lists the productivity in various national construction industries. This shows West German productivity in construction as significantly better than in other countries. Buildings in West Germany are particularly impressive because of their high technical quality. This suggests that high productivity and high quality can co-exist in construction. Certainly the converse is possible as both manufacturing and construction in Britain have, in the past, all too often been criticized for combining low productivity with low quality.

On the other hand, within any given national industry, increases in quality are reflected in higher prices. In part this is caused by marketing strategies which exploit the natural human expectation that quality costs money but is also due to real differences in costs. This suggests that there are two different factors at work. The first is strategic and relates to the general overall quality of the end product. This tends to increase the general level of costs and times as better materials and higher levels of skill tend to be more expensive. However, once the strategic quality standard is established, attempts to achieve high quality in the work of individual teams seems, if anything, to reduce times and costs. It is rather as though good management results in good performance in quality, times and costs and conversely poor management produces poor results across the board. In terms of the model of construction projects the two factors can be incorporated by linking an increase in quality with an increase in the level of standard units of time and costs but with a reduction in variability of productivity.

This is a speculative analysis but it does make sense of the available data drawn from a wide range of sources. No direct measure of this effect exists but it is plausible to envisage a clear management commitment which demands high-quality work from the construction teams having the effect of halving the range of variability experienced on projects where quality is largely ignored.

The third factor which is likely to influence the general level of variability in productivity is the intricacy of the work. The more complex the details of construction work the greater the chance that parts will take a very long time to complete. By way of example the volume of reinforcement in the concrete foundations of the National Westminster Bank tower in the City of London in parts exceeds 25%. The placing of the final bars in such situations required extensive computer calculation and unusual construction methods. Essentially the computer identified clear pathways through the forest of vertical reinforcement for each horizontal bar which was then placed at the entrance to its predetermined path and driven home by sledge-hammer. The time and costs of such intricate work is inevitably variable as previously completed work obstructs access to the current work. It is likely that intricacy has the same order of magnitude of influence on variability as we suggested for innovation.

The fourth factor which we shall consider is learning curves. Learning curves describe the widely observed effect of people repeating given actions gradually improving their performance. This is why athletes undergo rigorous training programmes, actors rehearse and it is why experienced construction teams are more highly valued than those new to the particular type of work. The existence of learning curves in construction has been established in many different countries and in many types of repetitive projects[5]. Very broadly in favourable conditions construction teams can achieve learning curves of between 90% and 80%. This means that for each doubling of the number of repetitions of similar work the time taken reduces by between 10% and 20%. This performance depends on teams having continuity of work. The work should be identical and carried out by the same teams without breaks. These circumstances are difficult to achieve in construction and depend on designers providing considerable repetition of construction details, projects being large enough to allow for narrow specialization and sufficiently competent management to give teams continuity of work.

Projects which match these demanding criteria are likely to benefit from the emergence of learning curves. Their effect is to gradually shift the range of productivity to improved levels. There is no evidence in the available data that learning reduces variability. So we see that the effects of the four factors vary somewhat. Innovation and intricacy increase the range of variability. Increased quality reduces it but increases the general level of times and costs around which that reduced variability centres. Learning curves probably have little effect on variability and gradually reduced the general level of times and costs.

This discussion of the four factors of innovation, quality standards, intricacy and learning curves suggests that in modelling construction projects a judgement must be made about the likely general level of costs and times and separately about the variability in productivity likely to be experienced. In making these judgements the four factors and others of a similar nature need to be considered. While precise values cannot be provided for the effect of each factor there is merit in making explicit judgements for each major factor. There is, however, no justification for considering very many factors since they combine in the following general form

$$D = \sqrt{d_1^2 + d_2^2 + d_3^2 \ldots d_n^2} \qquad (2.7)$$

where D = variability in productivity and d_i = variability in productivity due to factor i.

As more factors are added, their effect on the total range of variability rapidly becomes very small. Given the general nature of the data there is likely to be no benefit in considering more than four or five factors in order to select the likely level of variability on any given project.

Types of project

Having now established the general nature of variability we can use the concept to calculate important features of different types of construction project. Legard[4] provides some results based on manual calculations but they ignore the effects of interactions between teams. This simplification is necessary unless computer simulation is used to speed the calculations. Bennett and Fine[6] made many calculations of the costs and times of various configurations of the idealized model using computer simulations. These are freely drawn on in the following descriptions of the consequences of size, complexity, repetition, speed and variability in construction projects.

In these descriptions the following concepts and relationships are used

A = number of roles requiring different kinds of work = complexity,
R = number of repetitions of roles requiring similar work = repetition,
S = size of projects = number of roles,
T = number of teams,
D = variability in productivity, all values within the range D are equally likely,
ω = standard unit of time,
p = standard unit of costs,
B_n = buffer of n standard time units,
$\omega d(A, R, D, B_n)$ = mean increase over standard unit of time for project of A roles, R repetitions, D variability and buffer of n time units,
$pd(A, R, D, B_n)$ = mean increase over standard unit of costs for project of A roles, R repetitions, D variability and buffer of n time units,
Md = mean time for projects with variability in which $T = A$,
Nd = mean time for projects with variability in which $T = S$,
Vd = speed of projects with variability,
Cd = costs of projects with variability.

$$S = AR \tag{2.1}$$
$$Md = (\omega + \omega d(A, R, D, B_n)) (A + R - 1) \tag{2.8}$$
$$Nd = (\omega + \omega d(A, R, D, B_n))A \tag{2.9}$$
$$Vd = \frac{S}{Md} \text{ or } \frac{S}{Nd} \tag{2.10}$$
$$Cd = (p + pd(A, R, D, B_n))AR \tag{2.11}$$

We first consider a 100-role project with no buffers in which $A = 10$, $R = 10$, $T = 10$ and $D = \pm 50\%$. the likely results are:

Case 1
Md = 23 standard time units,
Vd = 4.3 roles per time unit,
Cd = 123 standard cost units.

We can double the size of the project either by increasing $A = 20$ and $T = 20$ or by increasing $R = 20$. Doubling the complexity produces the following:

Case 2
Md = 35 standard time units (approximately 50% increase),
Vd = 5.7 roles per time unit (approximately 33% increase),
Cd = 265 standard cost units (approximately 115% increase).

Doubling the repetitions produces the following:

Case 3
MD = 35 standard time units (approximately 50% increase),
Vd = 5.7 roles per time unit (approximately 33% increase),
Cd = 240 standard cost units (approximately 95% increase).

Before we draw any conclusions from these results which are generally the mean of 32 simulations, it is worthwhile considering the same three projects but with a buffer of one standard time unit between each team.
For $A = 10$, $R = 10$, $T = 10$:

Case 4
Md = 26 standard time units,
Vd = 3.4 roles per time unit,
Cd = 105 standard cost units.

For $A = 20$, $R = 10$, $T = 20$ (a more complex project):

Case 5
Md = 48 standard time units (approximately 65% increase),
Vd = 4.2 roles per time unit (approximately 20% increase),
Cd = 210 standard cost units (100% increase).

For $A = 10$, $R = 20$, $T = 10$ (a more repetitive project):

Case 6
Md = 39 standard time units (approximately 33% increase),
Vd = 5.1 roles per time unit (approximately 50% increase),
Cd = 215 standard cost units (approximately 105% increase).

These six cases are based on an idealized model which, inevitably at this stage, appears to be remote from actual construction projects. However, the characteristics which they illustrate clearly do exist in the real world. Construction projects vary in size, complexity, repetition and speed. The six cases provide some insights into the effects of these characteristics which will help us to understand the behaviour of live projects. For example, the results suggest that on projects subject to levels of variability likely to be experienced with work which is within the normal competence of the local construction industry, an increase in size leads to a proportionally smaller increase in the overall time (cases 2 and 3 compared with 1 or cases 5 and 6 compared with 4). It follows that the average rate of production increases as projects get bigger. There are considerable variations in these effects depending on whether the increase is achieved by adding more different kinds of work making the project more complex, or by repeating similar work using the same teams. The effects also depend on whether a time buffer is allowed between the planned starting time of the teams.

The same increase in size leads to a roughly proportional increase in costs. Depending on how the increase in size is accomplished and whether the planned start times for the teams include buffers the average costs may remain the same (case 5 compared with 4) or fall slightly (case 3 compared with 1) or rise (case 2 compared with 1 or case 6 compared with 4).

The same results suggest than an increase in repetition produces an increase in the average rate of production. Where a time buffer is introduced the increase is very significant (case 6 compared with 4 and 5).

Generally, increased repetition leads to reduced unit costs (case 3 compared with 1). However, this effect may be reversed where buffers exist because the larger number of repetitions tend to allow variability to close the buffers so that delays are likely to be caused by slow teams. This effect is shown in the form of a line of balance diagram in *Figure 2.4* where the points at which teams are delayed are circled. Such clashes are more common in the second half of the $A = 10$, $R = 20$ project than elsewhere. However, as the buffers are closed by the effects of variability, further repetitions will tend to reduce unit costs. That is the effects in case 6, which increases costs more than in proportion to size, will be replaced by those in case 3, which increase costs less than size.

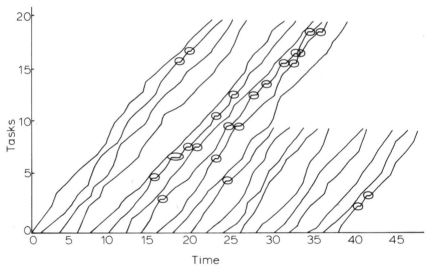

Figure 2.4 Line of balance for projects $A = 10$, $R = 20$ and $A = 20$, $R = 10$ with one time unit buffers

Complexity tends to produce the opposite effects to repetition. Where an increase in complexity is accompanied by a proportional increase in overall project size the average rate of production improves (case 2 compared with 1 or case 5 compared with 4). However, this effect is dominated by the increase in project size which, on average, enables more teams to work simultaneously. When we compare projects of the same size, an increase in complexity tends to reduce the average speed of production (case 5 compared with 6). It also tends to increase unit costs.

Finally, from these results we can consider the effect of slowing the speed of construction by introducing buffers. This strategy increases the total time, reduces the average rate of production and reduces total and unit costs (cases 1, 2 and 3 compared with 4, 5 and 6). In the real world of course, a longer total time resulting from slow construction may produce increased time-related costs for site management, major items of plant, site accommodation and other similar items. These costs may more than offset the reduction in direct unit costs produced by slow construction work. For the moment these effects are ignored in order to build up a clear picture of the behaviour of the idealized model of standard roles and teams. In later chapters we will need to elaborate the model but as we do so the direct effect of changing size, repetition, complexity or speed of projects will remain as described in this chapter. The effects may be dominated by other characteristics but they will, nevertheless, still be present.

In order to examine the effect of variability in productivity we need to recalculate the three projects used to illustrate the first four important characteristics. In recalculating we will increase variability to the level likely to be associated with innovative or intricate work. That is -50% to $+300\%$. *Table 2.8* lists the results and compares them with those obtained from assuming the variability of $\pm50\%$ likely to be experienced in work within the normal competence of the local construction industry.

TABLE 2.8. Various projects with $D = -50\%$ to $+300\%$ compared with equivalent projects with $D = \pm50\%$ in brackets

	$A = 10, R = 10$ (*case 1*)	$A = 20, R = 10$ (*case 2*)	$A = 10, R = 20$ (*case 3*)
Md	45 (+95%)	65 (+85%)	64 (+82%)
Vd	2.2 (−50%)	3.1 (−45%)	3.1 (−45%)
Cd	220 (+80%)	500 (+90%)	400 (+67%)

The new results clearly show that increasing variability produces a significant increase in time and costs and an equally significant reduction in the rate of production. They also accentuate the different effects of repetition and complexity. The complex project with high levels of variability is likely to cost 25% more than a repetitive project of the same size with the same pattern of productivity. So increased variability has important consequences. It follows, if the model is a reliable guide to the behaviour of real projects, that innovative and intricate work are likely to have a high cost. Conversely, we may hope for relatively low costs by aiming at consistently good quality work and creating conditions which enable learning curves to develop.

Strategic descriptions of projects

The five important characteristics which we have identified, size, complexity, repetition, speed and variability in productivity, provide a sufficient basis for strategic management decisions. In other words different combinations and different values of these five characteristics provide significantly different management tasks. There are no other equally significant characteristics. This means that at the strategic phase project organizations need to concentrate on defining values for size, complexity, repetition, speed and the likely variability. These values should be chosen so that in combination they meet the client's objectives.

If Pete James had thought in these terms he would have recognized that the project he had just finished was larger and more complex than either of the two new ones. It provided as much repetition as the factory and more than the refurbishment project. It had not been as fast as the factory project was likely to be but as they had been finishing their work it had shown clear signs of speeding up. The refurbishment project would certainly be slower than either of the others. As Mike and Doug had said, the whole atmosphere was very relaxed and there was no sense of speed or urgency about the work. Pete would be the first to accept that their rate of production on the 13th project had been extremely variable. He had often felt as they walked home after a days work that for all that they had achieved they might as well have stayed in bed all day. On other occasions, like this morning, the work had gone much quicker than they expected. Variability on the factory project was likely to be lower. The work was simple, straight-forward brickwork. The refurbishment project was likely to result in low and very variable productivity. Much of their work could not be clearly defined until the internal finishes were removed. As the existing brickwork was uncovered there would inevitably be some surprises leading to unexpected work. Pete and his team enjoyed the challenge of solving brickwork problems. It made their work more interesting. Provided they knew what the end result was to be like and what standards were required, they preferred to plan and control their own work. The uncertainty of refurbishment tended to push responsibility down to the construction teams.

If he had thought in these terms, Pete would have known that his team was best suited to relatively simple projects, constructed fairly slowly, and in which factors like innovation and intricacy were likely to result in variability in productivity. They did not mind whether or not projects provided repetition. However, Pete had noticed that on large projects they tended to have more problems than on small ones. He was not sure why this was so although he had once heard someone say 'small is beautiful'.

The model of construction projects described in this chapter helps managers to understand and measure this effect and all the others caused by various combinations of the five important characteristics.

Summary

We have now identified the important characteristics of construction projects from a management point of view. These have been expressed in terms of roles which are a standard size and require the work of a standard team whose productivity varies about a standard quantity of output. A standard quantity of output has a standard cost when it is produced in a standard time. Costs and time vary directly with output.

Size is the number of separate roles in any project. Complexity is the number of roles requiring different kinds of work. Repetition is the number of times the roles are repeated. Speed is the number of roles completed per time unit assuming standard output. Variability is the range of output around the standard level of productivity.

These five characteristics in combination provide a sufficient strategic description of construction projects for managers to make their strategic decisions.

References

1. RAY-JONES, A. and CLEGG, D., *CI/SfB Construction Indexing Manual*, RIBA Publications (1976)
2. A regular pattern of teams working through a project is discernible in the records of work actually carried out in: RODERICK, I. F., *Examination of the Use of Critical Path Methods in Building*, Building Technology and Management (March 1977)
3. See especially Chapter 2 of: BENNETT, J. and ORMEROD, R., *Construction Project Simulator, Final Report of SERC Research Grant*, Department of Construction Management, University of Reading, Occasional Paper No. 12 (1984)
4. LEGARD, D. A., 'Probabilistic analysis of an idealised model of construction projects', *Construction Management and Economics*, **1**, No. 1, 31–45 (Spring 1983)
5. Many examples of learning curves are described in: *United Nations Committee on Housing, Building and Planning Effect of Repetition on Building Operations and Processes on Site*, United Nations, New York (1965)
6. BENNETT, J. and FINE, B., *Measurement of Complexity in Construction, Final Report of SERC Research Grant*, Department of Construction Management, University of Reading, Occasional Paper No.8 (1982)

Chapter 3

Project environments

Red McGregor leaned back in his chair in the site office. He had just read the medium-term weather forecast. It threatened four weeks of low temperatures and rain with the possibility of snow. As he looked through the window at the site below white flakes began to fall. He cursed as the snow got thicker and the men started to troop into the site hut. The morning had been bright and clear and so Red had started the excavation on the second factory unit. Wet weather would rapidly turn the clay subsoil into a quagmire and the heavy machines could all too easily get bogged down.

Red was a big man with a great bushy beard. He looked and could sound rough and fierce when he needed to get things done in a hurry. Behind his fierce exterior he had one of the sharpest minds in the local construction industry. These two attributes had combined to give him the deserved reputation of being the toughest and best site manager in the town. He usually dealt with more difficult projects than the present one. It was a fairly straightforward factory project made up of three identical units. The units were highly serviced in the hope of attracting high-technology industry into the town. The client was a local developer who had particularly wanted Red to act as site manager and had offered an attractive bonus in return for a quick completion of the construction work.

Red had found the chance to earn a large bonus impossible to resist. He was now beginning to think that he was going to earn it. His initial reaction had been that this was an easy project but the last couple of weeks had raised doubts in his mind. The local newspaper kept reporting the project and hinting at irregularities in the granting of planning permission. Apparently the developer and the chairman of the planning committee were suspiciously friendly. Permission had been granted against the strong recommendation of the planning officer. According to the newspaper the leader of the Labour group on the local council was demanding a full inquiry into the work of the planning committee. Red could not see how all this would affect his work but he wondered if the need for a quick completion was somehow linked to the way planning permission had been granted.

Red had also begun to recognize that the buildings were not as simple as they had first appeared. The services were awkward to fit together and in a number of places interrupted work on the fabric of the buildings. He was working on the strategic plan for the later stages of the construction and trying to find some way of identifying separate zones for each service. Just at that moment the telephone rang. It was Pete James to say that they would not be taking the work Red had offered them. This was a nuisance, Pete and his team were good bricklayers. They would have been rather slow for this project but reliable. Now he would have to use Tim Smithson's team. They would work faster than Pete but there was always the danger that their work would be rejected by the architect. Red felt that if he watched him carefully Tim could do well enough, given the client's need for speed. However, the main problem with Tim, as far as the project was concerned, was that he could not start the work for another two weeks. Red was fairly certain there was no one else suitable who would be available sooner.

As Red flicked through his book of names and addresses in case he had forgotten someone who might be able to start earlier than Tim, he saw that the reporter from the local newspaper was down by the excavator with a photographer. Red had told him the previous week not to come on site without getting permission first. He would enjoy telling him again. Red started to yell at them to ask why they did not have hard hats on when he saw a stone wall which the excavator had just uncovered. The reporter looked excited. As he saw Red he said 'It's Roman, look at the way it is constructed. We must tell the museum'. The reporter rushed off to use the telephone in the site office, again without asking permission. Red watched the photographer take more photographs as the few stones which the excavator had uncovered disappeared under the now rapidly settling snow. The world outside seemed to be conspiring to ensure that Red would have to earn his bonus.

Project environments' influence

In the first two chapters we have considered projects in isolation. Now we must consider the influence of project environments. As Red knows all too well, the world outside is able to spring surprises which can make projects difficult to manage. This fact raises some important issues. It is now well-established in organization theory that organizations are, in part, formed by their environment. This effect is very simple and direct. Like all controlled systems, successful organizations tend to be strong at the points where they are most threatened by their environment. This general truth holds good for construction project organizations. There are many examples where a project organization's response to a threatening environment is clear and obvious. Clients will employ an architect who has demonstrated his ability to find imaginative responses to planning restrictions for projects where commercial success may be threatened by local planning requirements. Should the threat centre on aesthetic considerations then it is likely that the chosen architect will have an established design reputation. Similarly, where it is known that the local authority's officers are likely to subject the structural calculations for a new project to an unusually rigorous and detailed scrutiny, then it may well be prudent to include an eminent structural engineer in the project organization. When the local craftsmen and specialists are thought to be difficult to deal with or of limited competence it may be sensible to employ an experienced local site manager early in the project to advise on all construction communications and decisions. If the supply of materials and components is likely to be unreliable it may be sensible to employ a very experienced buyer and give him responsibility for negotiating special arrangements with key suppliers. In these and other similar ways, project organizations are, in part, shaped by their environments, or at least by their managers' perception of the environment.

In practice, a balance has to be struck between the certain additional costs of making contingency provisions to deal with a potential threat of interference and the risk of incurring the costs likely to result from an actual interference at some time in the future. That balance must take account of the nature of the project and of the client's objectives. A risk which might be accepted on a small, repetitive project using well-established traditional construction may be totally unacceptable on a large, complex, innovative project. Equally, clients' willingness, and indeed their ability to accept different levels of risk, varies[1]. All these factors need to be taken into account in construction project management. Before considering how this may be achieved we need to distinguish clearly between projects and their environments.

Project boundary

In practice the boundary between projects and their environments varies. For Red McGregor the boundary of his project is defined by the construction work which takes place within the physical boundary of the factory site. Everything not included in that definition is for him the project environment. On the other hand, the developer on the same project regards the whole of the client, design, management and construction responsibilities as defining the boundary of his project. Therefore, factors which Red regards as part of his environment form part of the developer's project. This illustrates the interesting point that construction project management means different things to different people on different projects and indeed on the same one project, depending on the specific allocation of responsibilities.

However, this is not merely an interesting aside. It is a part of the management responsibility to define the boundary of projects. This is essentially a process of deciding whether each particular action or influence should be managed directly or whether it is better if it is simply allowed to happen. For some factors the choice is clear.

The weather cannot be managed. We can, of course, make predictions about it, but at our present state of knowledge we cannot change it. We have simply to allow it to happen. It is possible that this restriction will be removed as science and technology advance at some time in the future. Also, it is often sensible to take actions to mitigate the effect of the weather. These actions then become part of the project but it is not possible to include the weather because at present it cannot be managed directly. It follows that one component of the environment of every construction project is the weather.

Equally clearly the necessary design and construction actions fall within at least the client's normal definition of all projects. To take a very basic example, the activity of excavating and moving soil clearly falls inside the boundary of all projects in which it occurs. There are, however, many activities which can be brought inside the boundary of projects or left in their environments. A good example is the manufacture or prefabrication of materials and components. Thus, on a major extension to O'Hare Airport in Chicago a ready-mixed concrete manufacturing plant is included in the project. This is because the construction managers, Schal Associates, recognized that the volume of concrete required by the project would, at times, place excessive demands on the local ready-mixed concrete suppliers. Many, indeed most, smaller projects in Europe and North America can safely regard the manufacturing of ready-mixed concrete as part of the environment. Concrete is ordered as and when it is needed, but the project participants do not manage its manufacture. In doing this they accept the risk that the manufacturer will fail to deliver on time. They do so because it is cheaper to accept this risk than set up a separate manufacturing plant. In much the same way most construction projects developed in the Western World regard the provision of homes for their workers and their families as part of the environment. Whereas on large projects in remote locations it may be necessary to provide such accommodation. The construction workforce on Sullum Voe oil terminal was, at times, limited by the number of beds it was possible to provide.

Similarly many major construction projects in the Middle East start by building a village for the construction workers. Within the UK in the early days of each of the new towns and in the new city of Milton Keynes a high proportion of the houses were reserved for the construction workers building the rest of the town or city. These examples merely illustrate the range of activities in respect of which a conscious decision may be made either to include or exclude them from the definition of the project.

An interesting example of a decision to extend the physical boundary of a project is reported by Holt[2]. In a project to design and construct a large chemical processing plant in north-east England it was decided to set up a staging warehouse. This was used to bring together all the design information and materials needed by each separate construction team. In addition, the warehouse was used to prefabricate particularly intricate parts of the pipework. Information and materials were delivered to site only when everything needed by a construction team was available and assembled together in the warehouse. Then everything the team needed was delivered. In this way the construction tasks were simplified and, to a large extent, insulated from uncertainty. The decision to enlarge the project by using the staging warehouse is considered by Holt to have been a major contributory factor to its success.

The last example nicely illustrates the importance of making a careful decision on the position of the boundary between projects and their environments. It can and, as in the case of the chemical processing plant, often does have a decisive effect on the project outcome.

Interference

The actions which form part of a project need to be managed in accordance with the principles described in this book. However, those which are regarded as part of the environment cannot be ignored. They, or at least some of them, have the potential to interfere with the progress of projects. This effect needs to be included in our model of projects. Essentially interference causes work to stop. The effect may, in practice, be disguised by allowing work to slow down or by working in an inefficient sequence or some other expediency. This does not alter the essential effect of external interference which is to add time and consequently, extra costs to projects. It is the essential effect we need to model. Therefore, the influence of the environment is modelled by assuming that teams make no progress in a proportion of the time units in which they are participating in any project. This has a direct effect on the duration of projects and on the time-related costs. Thus, the greater the proportion of time units affected by interference, the larger the increase in time and costs is likely to be.

The introduction of interference can be included in the model developed in Chapter 2 by means of the following additional concepts and relationships:

E = percentage of time units in which teams make no progress,

$\omega e(A, R, D, E, B_n)$ = mean increase over standard unit of time for project of A roles, R repetitions, D variability, E interference and buffer of n time units,

$pe(A, R, D, E, B_n)$ = mean increase over standard unit of costs for project of A roles, R repetitions, D variability, E interference and buffer of n time units,

Me = mean time for projects with variability and interference in which $T = A$,

Ne = mean time for projects with variability and interference in which $T = S$,

Ve = speed of projects with variability and interference,

Ce = costs of projects with variability and interference.

$$Me = (\omega + \omega e(A, R, D, E, B_n))\,(A + R - 1) \tag{3.1}$$

$$Ne = (\omega + \omega e(A, R, D, E, B_n))A \tag{3.2}$$

$$Ve = \frac{S}{Me} \text{ or } \frac{S}{Ne} \tag{3.3}$$

$$Ce = (p + pe(A, R, D, E, B_n))AR \tag{3.4}$$

The effects of the environment can be illustrated by assuming 10% interference in the projects used in Chapter 2. This is illustrated in the line of balance diagram in *Figure 3.1* which may be compared with the similar diagram in *Figure 2.4*. In *Figure 3.1* interferences are marked with double lines. They produce an average increase in time of 10% and in costs of 16% over similar projects without interference. Both results are slightly larger

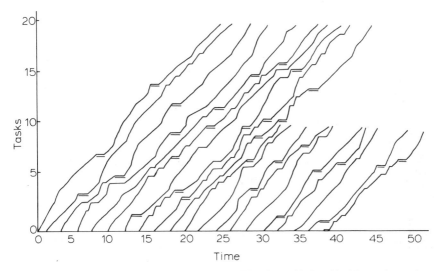

Figure 3.1 Line of balance for projects $A = 10$, $R = 20$ and $A = 20$, $R = 10$ with one time unit buffers and 10% interference

for a repetitive project than a complex project which suggests, not surprisingly, that interference from the environment is more damaging in an efficient project than one already making slower progress. These results in general terms reflect the effects we would expect. We can therefore, say that assuming that teams make no progress for a stated proportion of time units provides an effective means of modelling the influence of project environments. The immediate practical problem in using this approach is to find some means of selecting the appropriate proportion to represent the interference in specific projects and environments. Bennett and Ormerod[3] in an extensive review of published material and current practice, found no data in an entirely suitable form. However, they found wide recognition of the influence of the environment on construction projects. Also, in particularly hostile environments such as that experienced in the development of the North Sea oil fields, they found the effects of weather and sea conditions being modelled by construction managers.

Bennett and Ormerod were attempting to find data to help model direct construction work on building projects. They hypothesized that late design information, procurement delays and the weather account for a large proportion of interference. They therefore proposed and tested the relationships shown in *Figure 3.2*. Design and procurement were modelled

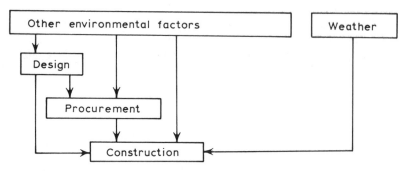

Figure 3.2 Components of interference on direct construction

as roles undertaken by teams with variable productivity. Each direct construction role was assumed to required design information and materials and components and therefore to be susceptible to delay from these two sources. In other words, design and procurement were modelled as if they were part of the project. Weather had to be treated differently.

Weather models

Weather is clearly part of the environment. Also good data are available to describe its effect on construction. First this tells us that weather has significant effects. Indeed Baldwin[4] found that in the USA contractors tend to regard it as the most important cause of delay. While Clapp[5] found that on five building sites in the UK, working time lost due to weather accounted for 5.6% of the total man-hours. On trades working in the open and therefore exposed to the effects of weather, the percentage was higher, e.g. 12% for bricklayers. Bennett and Ormerod[3] found the time recorded as lost due to inclement weather varied between 10% and 13% on four case studies of building projects.

The Meteorological Office have records of the historical weather patterns in each part of the UK. Similar records exist for many other parts of the world. Thus, the historical weather pattern for any particular construction site is very likely to be available. There are also reasonably good data on the likely effect of particular weather conditions on various types of construction work. Thresholds have been identified for combinations of weather conditions likely to affect construction[6]. The most practical approach uses threshold values for three distinct weather types:

Rainfall – during the working day (0700 to 1700 GMT) work will be interrupted when the total rainfall is greater than or equal to 0.1 mm and the rainfall rate equalled or exceeded 0.3 mm/h for at least part of an hour.
Wind – work will be interrupted when the mean wind speed is greater than or equal to 10 m/s (20 knots) during the working day.
Air temperatures – during the working day work will be interrupted if the air temperature is less than 2°C and the mean wind speed is greater than or equal to 4 m/s (8 knots). This is a combined effect to account for the wind chill factor.

Three separate sets of data can be obtained, one for each of these categories, from the Meteorological Office. Then each construction role likely to be affected by weather can be designated sensitive to one or more of the categories. For example, constructing internal blockwork walls would not be affected by rainfall, but would be affected by air temperature, it could also be sensitive to wind if the materials are handled by crane or if the structure were sufficiently open so that walls may be blown over. To reflect accurately the nuances of the weather it is necessary for each role to be labelled weather sensitive or not, and for the sensitive ones to be identified as being affected by a particular combination of weather types. However, constraints of cost, computer time and software development are likely to militate against such a very detailed approach in most construction projects.

A simpler method is to produce, for those operations designated weather sensitive, a single data plot from historic records which combine the three weather types identified on an EITHER/OR basis. For example if the wind speed were 15 m/s from 0700 to 1000 and it also rained more than 0.3 mm/h from 0800 to 1000, then, as illustrated in *Figure 3.3(a)*, the weather interference that day would be 3 h.

(a) Overlapping interference

(b) Separate interference

Figure 3.3 Weather interference

If the wind speed were 15 m/s from 0800 to 1100 and it rained 0.4 mm/h from 1300 to 1500 then, as illustrated in *Figure 3.3(b)*, the weather interference that day would be 5 h.

In this way a single combined plot of the working hours above the threshold values can be produced for every day where relevant meteorological data exist. Such data can be obtained from the Meteorological Office for specific geographical areas of the UK in the form of a tabular computer printout detailing the number of hours per week for specified years when adverse weather conditions were experienced.

The weather data can then be used in a computer simulation by choosing a single value of weather interference randomly from the weekly distribution, weighted by the relative frequencies of the adverse weather conditions. The chosen value is then applied to those activities occurring during that week which are weather sensitive and their duration extended accordingly. In this way over the course of a number of iterations of a simulation, the incidence of weather interferences will match the pattern and range of that likely to affect a specific project in a specific location[7].

By changing the start data of the project and resimulating, the benefit, or penalty of having those roles affected by the weather occurring at different times of year can be considered. This may be particularly relevant in severe climates like the North Sea, where weather effects are extremely important.

Construction environments

Bennett and Ormerod's method of dealing with the environment in modelling direct construction work was to incorporate design, procurement and weather into their model and then sweep everything else into a factor called 'other environmental factors'. They applied this approach to four case studies which covered a new hospital, a speculative office building, a repetitive housing project and the refurbishment of two Edwardian office blocks, all constructed in south-east England in the early 1980s. The projects' costs ranged from £1.5 m to £6 m and their construction times from 78 weeks to 148 weeks. The results from the case studies suggest that increasing the interference factor by about 2% for 'other environmental factors' produces realistic time and costs results. This relates to building in the UK where the three environmental factors modelled directly produce an effect equivalent to an interference factor of about 13%. In other words, a total interference of about 15% produces robust results for the construction phase of Bennett and Ormerod's four case studies. These results are specific to the projects which formed the subject of the case studies but they do suggest that at least as far as direct construction work is concerned, the influence of the environment can be modelled.

Client and design environments

We need, however, to consider whole projects including the client and design as well as the construction stages. Clearly, the flow of design information, delays in the delivery of materials and components and the weather do not influence earlier stages in the same way nor to the same extent as they do the construction work. Different environmental factors are likely to be important. In others words, the environment effectively changes as projects move through their various stages and different factors interfere with or threaten to interfere with progress.

Hall[8] describes in qualitative terms the complexity of the environments faced by major construction projects during their early formative stages. He identifies three groups who have the capacity to interfere. They are politicians, government bureaucracies and special interest groups within the local community.

As Red McGregor's experience shows, the influence of these groups is not restricted to the early stages. They can have significant effects during construction.

Red in the past has observed the influence of local politicians on his projects as they appear to support all new developments when in power but to criticize and attempt to frustrate them when in opposition. The bureaucracy has a direct influence on Red's work in the shape of the building control officers who must approve various stages of all construction work. As the discovery of the Roman remains on the factory site becomes public knowledge, Red will gain first-hand experience of special interest groups in action. He will also see how these groups work together as the Labour members on the local council align themselves with the heritage and conservation societies to try to prevent construction going ahead. Similarly the Conservative members and the local trade unions will both want the factory to be built without interruption. One to protect their own financial interests and the other because it will create new jobs. The politicians and special interest groups all attempt to manipulate the bureaucracy which in any case has its own interests. The museum's department in particular sees the new discovery on Red McGregor's site as an opportunity to increase its budget and influence within the council.

As these examples illustrate, politicians, bureaucracies and special interest groups may have an influence at any stage of any project. We therefore need to know something of their nature.

It is useful first to remember that the groups are groups, not individuals with a single viewpoint. Important actors within each are likely to have different values with respect to issues raised by any major construction project. These values can and often do change over time. This arises since in many cases actions which influence construction projects result not from rational value judgements but from conflict, compromise and confusion amongst powerful local actors. Each struggles for outcomes which advance his perception of his own or his group's interests. While each group thinks of itself as being rational and indeed usually tries to behave rationally, its concepts of rationality vary, which of itself generates conflict. Thus, decisions tend to depend on the relative power of the key actors.

However, as power also tends to change over time no decision can ever be regarded as decisive. It may be allowed to wither away or be reversed. As Hall describes with great clarity, the history of London's third airport is littered with decisions which have not been and may well never be translated into a real airport. His description also provides many examples of how individual politicians and special interest groups established especially for the purpose have influenced events decisively at various points in the story. However, in this particular case it appears to be the bureaucrats who are winning. They have consistently favoured Stanstead as the site for London's third airport and by promoting events favourable to that choice and by frustrating any productive action when the balance of advantage lay elsewhere are likely to achieve their objectives. In all events the British Airports Authority have recently commissioned Norman Foster to prepare a design for a major new passenger terminal at Stanstead which, if constructed, would establish the third London airport.

It is clear that in the early phases of construction projects, especially large and controversial ones, the client's responsibilities are decisive. He must champion the project to defeat objections and maintain progress against all opposition. He must build a committed lobby to persuade powerful local interests of the advantages of supporting his project. He needs, therefore, to identify powerful bodies who see personal advantage or public good in the project and persuade them to support it at critical stages.

These demanding requirements are caused not by construction projects themselves but by their environments. While it may well be unpractical to find objective data which would enable us to model the influence of environments at the strategic phase of projects, we cannot ignore it.

A large part of the difficulty of allowing for the influence of project environments is simply the uncertainty of the future. In looking at large projects which inevitably take a long time from inception to completion, we find that they often go wrong because they depend on forecasts based on a mechanical extrapolation of current trends. Such forecasts tend to produce substantial errors. These often include errors in the predicted demand for the product provided by the project. Common examples include misjudging the number of children when planning schools, misjudging the size of aeroplanes when calculating the number of air movements which an airport will need to handle, misjudging the capacity of city centres to cope with cars when planning new office accommodation and many other similar errors. Generally we tend to underestimate the rate of technological change and to overestimate human capacity to cope with this change. Some examples will serve to illustrate this important point[9].

A committee organized by King Ferdinand and Queen Isabella spent four years studying Columbus's plan to sail to the Indies and reported it was impossible because

(1) The Western Ocean is infinite,
(2) If he got to the Antipodes, he couldn't get back, and
(3) There are no Antipodes because Saint Augustine says so.

In 1591, Colonel Sir John Smyth advised the British Privy Council to abandon 'modern' firearms: "The bow is a simple weapon, firearms are very complicated things which get out of order in many ways . . . a very heavy weapon and tires out soldiers on the march."

In 1835, Thomas Tredgold, a British railroad designer, announced: "Any general system of conveying passengers – at a velocity exceeding 10 mph or thereabouts – is extremely improbable."

Arnold Morley, British Postmaster General, argued in 1895, "Gas and water are necessities for every inhabitant of the country. Telephones are not and never will be. It is no use trying to persuade ourselves that the use of the telephone could be enjoyed by the large masses of the people in their daily life . . ."

Rudyard Kipling predicted soon after the Wright Brothers' first flight that airspeeds would reach only 300 mph by the year 2000.

H.G. Wells predicted in *The Shape of Things to Come* (1933) that only 1000 cars would be built in the USA in 1955 and that the first round-the-moon voyage would not take place until 2054.

In 1945, Vannevar Bush, then President of the Carnegie Institution in Washington, advised President Truman on the atomic bomb: "The bomb will never go off, and I speak as an expert on explosives."

On the other hand, forecasts about social developments seem to exaggerate the rate of change. H.G. Wells (*The Shape of Things to Come*) predicted that before 1960 all national governments would collapse and be replaced by a World State. Rudyard Kipling predicted that war would go out of fashion by 2000, and that all nations would abdicate sovereignty to an 'Aerial Board of Control'.

These examples should not serve to persuade us to ignore the future but rather to teach us that we must proceed cautiously. Hall suggests that we need creative forecasting to trace the likely future evolution of the economy, of technology, of society, of culture and of values. He suggests that there is merit in having two or more teams working independently on wide-ranging evaluations of possible project outcomes. This is likely to help avoid the too easy acceptance of a single orthodox interpretation especially if each team submits the others' work to intense critical scrutiny. Beyond this strategies should remain flexible for as long as possible. This means seeking the minimal commitment at each stage where a decision is needed. It also suggests an essentially cautious approach to design which builds on existing established answers where the probable outcomes are reasonably certain rather than relying on major new developments. However, it is a part of the fascination of construction that sometimes a leap in the dark – a new technology – is what is needed. Innovation, however, raises new problems for construction project managers.

On innovative projects there is merit in setting up a preliminary project study to examine the scientific and technical problems which will need to be solved for the project to be carried out. The results should be incorporated in a plan for the design and development expressed in time, costs and the degree of risk attached to each of these forecasts. This preliminary study should pay particular attention to the problems of putting new technologies together into a system. This is because it often takes as long to resolve difficulties which arise when innovative components are assembled together as it did to develop the separate components.

The preliminary project study should include explicit consideration of the environment formed by political, bureaucratic and special interest groups using creative forecasting to take account of future change. Clients would be well advised to use such a study in making decisions to go ahead or not to go ahead throughout the life of the projects. On projects with a long time scale it is sensible to review the study periodically to check whether events have invalidated the overall project strategy or perhaps suggest the need for some change of direction.

As we discussed earlier, as projects develop over time, different features in the environment become important. This in turn is likely to lead to different teams playing leading or crucial roles at the various stages of projects. This is one of the main reasons why project organizations need to remain flexible during their strategic phase. The environment tends to ensure until the later stages of projects that any rigid or fixed organization structure will become inappropriate.

Environmental effects, particularly those which influence construction stages, are likely to be more marked in developing countries than in those in the West. An interesting study by Farzad[10] suggests that coarse economic indicators provide a good guide to the extent to which the environment will allow projects to proceed sufficiently predictably to justify the use of sophisticated management controls. He found that gross national product per capita, proportion of employment in services and the proportion of exports comprising machinery provide good indicators of national and regional environmental interference.

Variations

Before we leave this discussion of environments we need to consider one particular aspect of projects – variations or change orders. That is a formal decision to alter a previous decision which affects the work or objectives of other teams. Formal variations tend to occur during the construction stages because they have financial effects under construction contracts. However, many design offices have procedures to maintain a record of changes in their decisions and objectives which in effect give rise to formal variations.

Given that projects move through a flexible strategic phase which brings objectives, end product and organization into balance and produces the set of clearly defined roles required to complete the project, then variations should arise only from changes in the environment. The effect of variations tends to be an interruption to planned progress. Therefore, in terms of the model of construction projects which we are developing, it is consistent and convenient to regard variations as an environmental effect. The practical effect of this is to keep the model simple which is important provided that it adequately represents all important factors. It also means that in planning construction projects the effect of variations should be taken into account when the influence of the environment is considered. This implies that variations generated entirely from within project organizations represent a failure. This view is maintained despite the widely reported occurrence of hundreds of variations on many building projects in the UK. Except where they arise from changes in the environment or formal changes ordered by the client, variations should be seen as a failure.

The reason for this view of variations is that, as the model demonstrates, interference is expensive and therefore where it is self-inflicted is simply wasteful. The high incidence of variations and the relatively poor performance of the UK building industry as shown in *Table 2.7* (p. 39) are almost certainly directly related.

Support for this view is provided by the experience of the Department of Health and Social Security (DHSS) the UK government department responsible amongst other things for building new hospitals. Faced with substantial cost and time over-runs on many new hospital projects they introduced a policy of requiring the design consultants to sign a certificate stating that all design work was complete before construction contracts were let. The results as reported to the author are significantly faster construction, the virtual elimination of those matters which give rise to claims for extra payments from contractors and lower costs. This evidence suggests that controlling and indeed seeking to eliminate variations is an important part of construction project management. It is for this reason that they should be seen as, and only as, an environmental effect. That is, as an interference imposed from outside projects.

Summary

The boundary of projects should be chosen with care since it distinguishes between actions which will be managed directly and those to which the project organization may have to respond. Everything not included within the boundary definition is the environment.

Project environments interfere with planned progress and so their influence can be modelled by assuming that teams make no progress for a proportion of time units. The causes of interference change as projects move through their separate phases. In the early stages political, bureaucratic and special interest groups are important, while in the construction stages weather, design information and procurement problems tend to dominate environments' influence. Variations should be considered with the environmental factors.

References

1. An excellent review of the factors and the way they interact in decision making is provided in: HOLLOWAY, C. A., *Decision-Making under Uncertainty*, Prentice-Hall (1979)
2. HOLT, L., 'A case study of the construction of a terephthalic acid plant for Imperial Chemicals Limited at the Davies Works, Wilton, Cleveland, UK', *Construction Management and Economics*, **1**, No. 1 (Spring 1983)
3. See especially Chapter 2 of: BENNETT, J. and ORMEROD, R., *Construction Project Simulator, Final Report of SERC Research Grant*, Department of Construction Management, University of Reading, Occasional Paper No. 12 (1984)
4. BALDWIN, J. R. *et al*, 'Causes of delay in the construction industry', *ASCE J. of the Construction Division*, **97**, No. CO1, March (1971)
5. CLAPP, M. A., 'Weather conditions and productivity: a detailed study of five building sites', *Building* (14 October 1966)
6. See for example: LACEY, R. E., *Climate and Building in Britain*, HMSO (1977)
7. The development of a computer system which simulates the effects of weather in the manner suggested is described in: BENNETT, J. and ORMEROD, R., *Construction Project Simulator, Final Report of SERC Research Grant*. Department of Construction Management, University of Reading, Occasional Paper No. 12 (1984)
8. HALL, P., *Great Planning Disasters*, Weidenfeld & Nicolson (1980)
9. The examples are taken from the unpublished papers of a seminar on *Strategic Planning for the Computer Revolution*, organized by Yourdon in London (September 1983)
10. FARZAD, F., *An Investigation into the Influence of the 'Level of Development' of the Location of a Construction Project upon its Duration, its Cost, and its Use of Critical Path Techniques of Network Analysis*, PhD thesis, University of Reading (1984)

Chapter 4

Project organizations

Red McGregor, for the first time in his career as a site manager, was in danger of losing control of a project. His site had become the centre of much local interest. Officials from the town museum supported by a famous archeologist were insisting that the stone wall recently uncovered on Red's site was the first indication of an important Roman settlement. The developer who owned the site had enlisted the help of other experts who seemed equally certain that what the excavator had uncovered was probably a medieval field wall of no real interest at all. The argument had moved from the local newspaper to the local radio and television programmes and on to the national media. Red was being interrupted several times a week by reporters and camera men. He was developing into a media personality as his striking appearance and clear descriptions of the problems caused by the find provided excellent television material.

While he was faced with these new and totally unexpected pressures his task was complicated by the developer who now wanted Red to complete the first factory unit as quickly as possible. This was becoming increasingly difficult as the wet, cold weather continued, Tim Smithson was late finishing his current project and so the brickwork could not be started and the council's building inspector was being especially careful. Red was fairly sure that the inspector was under instructions to delay the work. It was difficult to think of any other reason for his insisting on extra deep excavations and then wanting the foundations to be reinforced. Certainly the newspapers and television gave the impression that the Council were uncertain what should be done about the discovery that the town might have been the site of a Roman settlement.

Red looked at his construction programme for the next three weeks' work. It was in the form of a bar chart which showed the planned work of each team. He looked at the site hut wall where the strategic programme already showed ten days delay. The programme was too long mainly because the method of construction depended on load-bearing brickwork to carry the roof. Red telephoned the structural engineer and asked if it would be possible to build reinforced brickwork columns to carry the roof trusses. This could save several weeks by getting the roof on earlier and allowing the rest of the brickwork to be carried out under cover. It might also be possible to start the services earlier.

Ten days later when Tim Smithson and his team reported for work the revised method of construction had been agreed and approved by the building inspector. Red briefed Tim in the site hut. He began by showing him the drawings on which he had marked the brickwork with red ink. Red described the sequence of the work and how the brickwork related to the steel-fixers work. He told Tim that the brickwork would be set out by his assistant and that all queries and problems were to be referred to the assistant. Red then called in his assistant and introduced him to Tim. Together they showed Tim the specification which told him the bond and type of mortar he must use. Then the three men walked around the site. Red reminded Tim that his team must wear hard-hats whenever they were working. He also told him the site working hours and the times of the lunch and tea breaks. They had worked together on one previous project where Red had been using a rather complicated computer-based progress reporting system. Tim asked if this was being used and Red grinned and said in uncompromising terms that it had been a total waste of time and that he was better off without such expensive toys. As they completed the circuit of the site they agreed the position for the mortar mixer and where bricks would be unloaded and stored. They also agreed that the brickwork ought to be finished by the second week in June. Red offered an extra bonus if that date were achieved and if none of the brickwork was rejected by the architect.

When they reached the site hut they noticed the architect's car parked just outside the site. Red had arranged for him to be on-site that morning to agree a quality standard for the brickwork with Tim. They went into the site hut and Tim was introduced to the architect. Red with his assistant then left them to their negotiations. He would be involved only if Tim and the architect were unable to agree. Red watched the two men walk across to where Tim's team were waiting to start work.

In this way Tim and team were introduced into the project organization. As we have seen, their work was related to that of the other teams involved in the factory project by means of various devices.

Coordination devices

All project organizations seek to coordinate the work of separate teams so that together they achieve agreed objectives. In order to understand how this is done we need to know the coordination devices available to construction project managers. We also need to consider how the full range of such devices relates to construction projects and their environments in terms of the model developed in Chapters 1, 2 and 3.

We start the description by assuming that all the roles needed to carry out the primary work in a project have been identified. We also know from

Chapter 1 that all the interactions between teams comprise either communications of information or transactions of values. It follows that coordination devices must either improve the project organization's capacity to communicate and to transact or they must reduce the need for information and things of value. It also follows if we are to relate the available coordination devices to our model that they must modify teams, their roles or the relationships between teams.

Galbraith[1] provides a good review of the coordination devices available to managers generally. This is freely drawn on in the following description which reinterprets his analysis in order to relate it to construction and to the model developed in earlier chapters. This new interpretation also draws on Mintzberg's important synthesis of the published literature on the structuring of organizations[2]. Both sources provide important insights into general management but construction project management requires a different emphasis. This is mainly because project organizations must be set up from scratch and accomplish their work in a relatively short period of time. Also their tasks and the teams which comprise the organization tend to change from week to week. These characteristics are in marked contrast to permanent organizations undertaking long-term tasks in which most management research is carried out.

Richard Halpern of Schal Associates, at a conference in 1983 in London on the management of construction organized by the University of Reading, Department of Construction Management and the Building Group, received considerable support for the suggestion that in construction project management the three most important factors are people, people and people. We will accept his judgement at least to the extent of starting our description with the coordination devices which modify teams. First we will consider how teams may be modified so that the need for communications and transactions can be reduced. This suggests that we are looking for some means of ensuring that teams already have most of the information they need before they join project organizations and can be trusted to make the decisions needed during the course of their work.

Professionalization

The device of equipping teams with prior knowledge and experience needed to make good decisions is usually called 'professionalization'. Construction employs people with many different levels of education and training. Pete James's labourer Tony Bronoski mixes mortar and carries bricks and mortar to where Pete, Doug and Mike need them. He has no educational qualifications and has had no formal training in his work. He has picked up what he knows from Pete and the others in an essentially informal manner. He would generally be categorized as an unskilled labourer.

Next there are semi-skilled workers. Typically, crane or excavator operators have some formal training in their work. Most major manufacturers run short courses to train operators in the use and maintenance of specific large items of construction plant. Also, industry training boards often run short courses for plant operators which in addition to dealing with plant operation teach operators how to organize their work effectively. However, a large proportion of what an experienced plant operator knows is based on direct experience of using plant in many construction projects. Much specialist construction work is undertaken by semi-skilled workers. These are people who have been trained to carry out a limited range of activities required by some specialized form of construction or unusual construction materials. Often, to help ensure proper use of their products, firms marketing new constructions or materials will train their own workforce.

The next category of workers is an important one in construction. It comprises craftsmen and skilled workers who undergo a long formal apprenticeship. This involves many years of working alongside an experienced craftsman learning from him and gradually undertaking more and more skilled work. The learning on the job is usually supplemented by education at a technical college. The education covers the theory and practice of particular trades and leads to a formal national qualification awarded on the basis of written examinations and practical tests. A properly qualified craftsman is rightly highly respected in the construction industry. Pete James and Tim Smithson and the other bricklayers in their teams, like all craftsmen, are expected to understand their materials and a wide range of the forms of construction in which they can be used. They are expected to know which tools to use and indeed they are normally expected to provide these tools and to look after them properly. They are expected to know how to plan and organize their own work effectively and to be able to estimate how long a particular piece of work will take and what resources it will require. They are expected to understand the inspection criteria for particular activities and to agree quality and performance standards appropriate in individual projects.

The final group of construction workers comprises the professionals, the architects, builders, engineers and surveyors who have professional qualifications. These require long education culminating in a university degree or an equivalent academic qualification. In addition it requires several years of practical experience under the supervision of a qualified professional. This is usually tested by an examination conducted by the appropriate professional institution. Beyond this it is becoming increasingly common for professional institutions to require their members to keep up-to-date with relevant new knowledge and new developments in, for example, legislation, codes of practice, national standards and other matters which have a direct bearing on their professional competence.

Qualified professionals are expected to have a deep understanding and considerable practical experience of their particular subjects. That is, they must know the established conventional wisdom and also know how to apply it to particular situations likely to arise in construction projects. They can therefore be trusted to make good decisions when faced with complex problems.

There are, however, two different kinds of professional work. We need to understand them both since they give rise to very different kinds of project organization. But first we need a clearer understanding of the essential nature of professionalization.

Professionals learn a repertoire of established skills. Mintzberg[2] calls them 'standard programs' which the professional stands ready to use. He further suggests that these programs are like pigeonholes. The profession-al's task is to put the particular problems he is required to deal with into the right pigeonhole. That is, to match his repertoire of established skills to practical problems. Thus, we see that the professional has two basic tasks; first to categorize problems in terms of standard programs, a task usually called 'diagnosis', and secondly to apply that program.

The process of pigeonholing achieves great economies. It greatly reduces the decisions which have to be made because it would take enormous resources to treat each case as unique and therefore requiring individual analysis. Thus, architects in the main, design buildings comprising floors, walls and roofs. They allow for access through these elements by means of windows, doors, rooflights, stairs, lifts, flues and other well-established answers. Structural engineers tend to use steel and concrete in beams, columns and slabs. Similarly, services engineers use a limited range of well-established technologies.

The process of fitting project problems into standard program pigeonholes not only reduces the effort required from professionals it also makes it possible for each task to be undertaken separately from other professional work. Part of the professionals' education and training is devoted to ensuring that their work fits into the pattern formed by the work of related professionals. Thus, architects, structural engineers and various kinds of services engineers can be situated in different firms in different physical locations and yet work effectively on the same project. Provided that each sticks to standard programs their work will fit together without the need for conscious coordination.

The built-in coordination provided by professionalization is clearly seen in craft work in traditional construction. Thus, for example, the bricklayer leaves window openings in the form expected by the carpenter; who provides timber fixing grounds in the form expected by the joiner; who constructs the window in the manner expected by the glazier and the plasterer. Both of these craftsmen leave their work in the form expected by the painter who finishes the work. None of these separate craftsmen need know anything about the others. The work of each is coordinated by their craft training. In exactly the same way, as long as the work of professionals stays within the scope of their standard programs, it can take place independently.

Describing professional work as the application of standard programs is not intended to denigrate it. Professional work is complex and uncertain. It is often extremely difficult and demanding both physically and mentally. There is often great doubt as to which pigeonhole a particular problem properly belongs. An incorrect diagnosis can have very serious consequences. It is important, however, to recognize the link between the application of standard programs and independent professional work.

There is a second kind of professional work which causes the professionals undertaking it to be interdependent. This arises where the problems to be tackled do not fit into any of the established pigeonholes. It may be that the problem requires an answer which falls on a boundary between standard programs or it may need an entirely new answer outside the range of established answers. In other words the problem does not fit neatly into the work of any one profession. It requires innovation.

Typically innovation requires highly qualified professionals to work together in small teams. There is need for frequent consultations, discussions and communications. In innovation existing knowledge and skills provide bases on which to build new answers. It often requires the combination of several bodies of knowledge and skills. Thus, an electrical engineer may be able to suggest an answer to a mechanical problem simply because he does not know the conventional wisdom. It is of course likely to need a very experienced and confident mechanical engineer to recognize the relevance of the electrical engineer's contribution. Thus, in innovative work the professionals must amalgamate their efforts.

The choice between independent and interdependent professional work is an important one. It clearly requires a conscious decision since the composition of the teams is very different. By sticking to standard programs projects can safely rely on professional teams working independently. Each team is likely to comprise members of a single profession and their support staff. Each is likely to be a well-established unit and to have worked together before. In contrast, as described in Chapter 1, projects like the Sydney Opera House which involve innovation, require multidiscipline teams. It may well be necessary to create a team specially for innovative professional work. The members may need to be assembled from a number of separate firms and brought together just for one project.

There are obvious dangers in deciding to use independent professional teams since they may adopt standard programs when the project requires an original answer. Conversely it is very difficult for an innovative team to recognize and accept that an established answer will solve their particular problem. Having been set up to find a new idea they are likely to see the adoption of an old one as a failure. Therefore, in the choice of professional teams it is particularly important to match their knowledge and skills to the specific project problem. This matching is important with all teams. When the choice is well made it serves to minimize the need for communications of information and transactions of values. It is in this sense that professionalization provides the first coordination device which construction managers have available.

Slack resources

The second coordination device is also concerned with teams. It is the creation of slack resources. The concept is best illustrated by means of an example.

Complex construction activities involving a number of teams and drawing on common items of major construction plant are extremely difficult to organize so that all the resources are used efficiently. A large multi-storey reinforced concrete frame may involve separate teams for the vertical formwork, horizontal formwork, bar bending, vertical reinforcement, horizontal reinforcement, making concrete, transporting concrete and placing concrete. It may require concrete mixing plant, a number of dumper trucks, tower cranes, hoists, bar bending equipment and a carpenter's workshop for modifying the formwork. To calculate the size of teams for such a complex activity to ensure that all are working efficiently is, for all practical purposes, impossible. The number of possible combinations of resources if far too large for them all to be considered. Yet in practice, construction managers decide such matters easily. They do so since, because it is not possible to calculate a perfect answer, all must settle for answers which do not utilize resources efficiently. In other words slack resources are provided.

In practice the competitive market for construction determines the costs and times which are acceptable. Individual construction managers need to find an answer which matches the performance determined by the local market. All can remain competitive despite under-using resources for as long as the market remains stable. Therefore, managers are usually unaware of slack resources. They accept the market determined normal performance and believe that they are being efficient as long as they achieve that norm. The results can be seen by comparing performances achieved in different construction markets. The University of Reading, Department of Construction Management's comparison of the USA and UK building industries[3], found in the late 1970s that the construction cycle per storey for reinforced concrete buildings in the USA was three days while at best in the UK it was 21 days. They also found that equivalent buildings in the USA required fewer resources. In other words, the UK building industry was providing more slack resources. It was doing so not as a conscious decision but simply in response to a market-determined norm.

Slack resources is not simply an unconscious response which indicates inefficiencies. The provision of slack resources can be a rational and efficient coordinating device. It may have benefits in simplifying the work of other teams. In the example given above, the construction managers do not have to undertake long and complex calculations in order to find an optimum answer. They merely have to find one which matches the market norm. This is likely to be a quicker and less expensive task. Also a team provided with slack resources is more likely to achieve planned performance. Thus, it is less likely to delay other teams. Consequently there will be less need for information about delays to be communicated and fewer decisions about transactions of values to be made. Also teams with slack resources are more likely to have time to communicate and make decisions properly thus further reducing their tendency to delay others. These consequential benefits may more than offset the extra costs. Thus, the provision of slack resources may well be a good decision. In all events it is a coordination device which construction project managers should consider explicitly.

It is worth noting that if project organizations are not properly matched to their tasks, then slack resources will arise by default. Projects will be delayed, will incur extra costs or will achieve poor performance, all of which are signs of unplanned slack resources.

Modification of roles

We can now consider the coordination devices which modify roles. As with teams we will deal first with those which reduce the need for information and things of value.

The definition of roles is in itself a coordination device. In defining roles we must specify the actions to be carried out by the team occupying the role. If we fully defined all the roles required by a project and they all fitted together exactly then we would have a complete coordination framework. Mass production assembly lines occasionally approach this level of role definition and, where the work is carried out by robots, it is fully achieved. Construction rarely, if ever, provides the degree of repetition needed to justify the great expense of fully defining roles. It is therefore necessary to make a judgement as to how far roles are defined and conversely how far they should be left to the discretion of the teams occupying them.

It is normal in construction to define roles in terms of their objectives. That is to describe the end product. The teams occupying these roles are usually given complete discretion in the choice of actions to produce the defined end product. However, the degree of definition does depend on the nature of the end product. In this matter the important characteristic is the extent to which a standard answer is to be used or looking at the subject from the other end of the range of possibilities, the extent to which innovation is required.

With a standard answer the role definition may well specify in some detail the actions to be taken by the team occupying the role. As an example the installation of a widely used passenger lift may well be described in a standard installation handbook produced by the manufact-urer. Typically this will describe all the separate components, suggest an assembly sequence, specify the fixings to the fabric of the liftshaft and describe, often with the aid of detailed drawings, how the components fit together. It will finally describe the tests to be carried out at each stage to ensure that the lift is installed properly. Similarly a decision to use a standard system of construction is likely to mean that the designer's role definition includes a design manual. It will describe in careful detail the procedures the designer should use and specify the constraints he must work within. The costs involved in producing such detailed descriptions is justified because they will be used many times on different projects.

Roles requiring teams to produce innovative answers cannot, by definition, have their end product prespecified. The role description can at best define the required performance. This is particularly so for design and management roles. It can, however, apply equally to construction roles. A role with responsibility for constructing the formwork for an unusually shaped roof may well merely define the shape, the required finish and weight of the concrete. The role occupant will have to decide the materials and method of construction to be used to provide formwork with the required performance. When an innovative answer is required the role definitions usually have to leave the team occupying the role considerable discretion.

Between the extremes of roles requiring completely standard and wholly innovative answers a wide range of role definitions occur in practice. There are costs associated with the production of specific and detailed role descriptions whether they define the actions to be taken or define the performance to be achieved. The costs must be balanced against the risks of an unsatisfactory answer resulting from a poor role description. The decision, however, is not a single simple one. In practice, role descriptions are built up as roles are acted out. While formal role descriptions provide definitions of work to be done in the various ways and levels of detail described above, further information usually has to be provided as teams carry out their work. This may be to deal with problems within the original description or to deal with the effects of variability in performance or interference from outside the project. Such problems are likely to cause arguments and disputes. This is especially likely when one team is delayed by another or by an environmental factor and the particular type of event is not covered in their role description. Thus, the balance which construction project managers must consider in forming role descriptions needs to take account of the likely costs of resolving issues not specifically covered in the initial formal statement.

In the main, role descriptions are concerned with the work of individual teams and rather less so with coordinating the work of several teams. There is, however, one component of role descriptions which is primarily a coordination device aimed at reducing the need for information and decisions about valued things. This is the use of goals.

Goals

Goals provide a powerful means of coordinating the work of teams within construction projects. Goals specify a level of performance which teams will attempt to achieve. They, in effect, provide formal predictions of the end product of teams' work. In doing so they allow the work of separate teams to be fitted together while leaving each to carry out their work independently provided that they meet their goals. An example of this device is a team responsible for the design of the steel frame of a building which has included in its role description goals which specify the loads to be carried, the specific points at which these loads will be transmitted, the required clear heights and spans, the maximum load to be transmitted by the frame to the foundations, fire protection requirements, the planned life of the building, maintenance criteria, maximum costs, construction times and any other matters which may influence other elements or the performance of the total building. Provided that all these goals are met, other teams designing the foundations, walls, floors, roofs, services and indeed, all the other elements, can work independently of the steel frame team. The other teams must have goals which are consistent with those established for the frame. Thus, a team designing the roof would have in their role description goals which specify the maximum loads which the roof can transmit to specific points on the frame. In this way goals serve to coordinate the work of all the teams who can then work independently and in parallel on the individual elements.

It is difficult to set goals which will be achieved, which fit together exactly and provide efficient answers. Obviously it is easy to set and achieve goals which include large safety factors. The result is inefficiency which provides an example of the use of slack resources. This may be acceptable, for example, in projects with demanding technical requirements needed quickly. Where inefficiency is unacceptable and demanding goals are set it is likely that some will not be achieved. In the example used above it may happen that to achieve the performance required in the roof it must be fixed to the frame at closer centres than originally envisaged, no design for the external walls which meets all the other criteria can be constructed quickly enough and deflections in the frame invalidate the floor design. In these circumstancess either the teams must search further for better answers or the goals must be changed.

In practice, for some aspects of construction management there are well-developed methods of setting broad strategic goals and then developing them in more detail as projects move through successive stages. *Figure 4.1* illustrates the procedure recommended by Bennett *et al*[4] for setting and achieving goals in respect of construction costs through the design stages of building projects. Similarly well-developed methods exist to coordinate the scheduling of design and construction work[5].

Certain general principles emerge from practice. Goals which are set in agreement with the team who will carry out the work are more likely to be

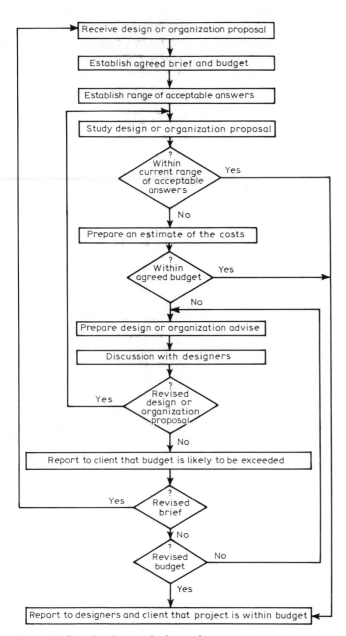

Receive design or organization proposal

Establish agreed brief and budget

Establish range of acceptable answers

Study design or organization proposal

? Within current range of acceptable answers — Yes

No

Prepare an estimate of the costs

? Within agreed budget — Yes

No

Prepare design or organization advise

Discussion with designers

? Revised design or organization proposal — Yes

No

Report to client that budget is likely to be exceeded

? Revised brief — Yes

No

? Revised budget — No

Yes

Report to designers and client that project is within budget

Figure 4.1 Cost planning standard procedure

achieved than those which are imposed. This is true even for goals which are equally demanding. The sense of commitment engendered by formally accepting goals appears to have a direct and beneficial effect on subsequent performance. It also appears generally to be beneficial to suggest a fairly tough goal to a team, to provide some supporting evidence for the fact that it is capable of achievement and then negotiating the specific goal to be used. The development of quality circles in Japanese manufacturing industry where teams accept responsibility for achieving ever tougher goals is a further development of this approach. Construction does not often provide the degree of repetition which would enable quality circles to be used. However, the principles of involving teams in setting their own goals and challenging them to seek higher performance do apply to construction. Beyond this teams need to be reminded of their goals frequently and with enthusiasm. Unless they believe their work is important and is making a real contribution to a worthwhile project they are unlikely to meet tough goals. When these conditions are met then goals provide an effective coordination device in construction projects.

Management roles

We now move on to consider devices which increase the capacity of roles to communicate and make decisions about transactions. This involves creating additional roles. They are normally called 'management roles'. Their purpose is to deal with the uncertainty generated within the client, design and construction responsibilities. Management teams exist to resolve problems preferably before they arise. They provide information and make decisions about values required by teams in the other areas of responsibility. There are two distinct types of management role.

The first type form management hierarchies. *Figure 4.2* illustrates this type of role by means of a simple hierarchy. The basic design and construction roles are represented by the sequence at the bottom level.

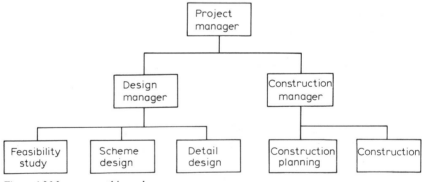

Figure 4.2 Management hierarchy

Ranged above them are three management roles forming two further levels in a hierarchy. The design manager's responsibility is to deal with the uncertainty generated in the design roles. The construction manager's is similar but relating to the construction roles. The project manager's responsibility is to deal with uncertainty generated by the other two management roles. Thus, a problem in detail design caused by the scheme design should be referred to the design manager. However, a problem in construction caused by the scheme design will have to be referred to the project manager because his is the only role whose responsibilities cover the whole problem.

Red McGregor's team have a management role within a hierarchy. Above his team is the developer while below it is Tim Smithson's team and others undertaking direct construction work. We observed that the developer had been instrumental in employing Red and in agreeing his conditions of employment. Red in turn had taken the decisions needed to employ Tim and beyond this he has the power amongst other actions to offer Tim a bonus for improved performance or to threaten to dismiss him unless his performance improves and if necessary to carry out that threat. That is each higher level has the authority to grant rewards in return for satisfactory performance and usually they also have the authority to withold rewards or apply sanctions when a team's performance is unsatisfactory.

Authority is central to the work of hierarchies. In the context of construction projects it is safe to regard its basis as being the power to provide financial rewards. This is not to argue that workers can be successfully motivated by money alone. The need to involve and enthuse teams with the task in hand has already been described. In suggesting that power over money is the essential source of authority in construction projects we are simply affirming that fact and in no sense suggesting that it provides a sufficient basis for management. Indeed good construction managers will make explicit use of their authority only as a last resort, rightly preferring to work through negotiation and agreement if at all possible.

Red McGregor's ability as a site manager rests primarily on his clear planning and his skills as a communicator and negotiator. He would, of course, admit that his role is possible only because as a last resort he has authority over the teams who undertake the construction work. That is he has the power to control the flow of rewards which the construction teams receive.

While authority describes the superiors' side of relationships in management hierarchies, at the same time subordinates acquire responsibility. Authority and responsibility are the two sides of the same one type of relationship. Responsibility is the obligation to perform in an agreed manner as a condition of receiving rewards. Hierarchical relationships raise a number of issues which construction managers need to understand. We shall deal with these in Chapter 7. For the moment it is sufficient to recognize that management hierarchies and the roles which form them are coordination devices.

Lateral coordination

The second type of management role provides lateral coordination. *Figure 4.3* repeats the management hierarchy of *Figure 4.2* with the addition of a lateral coordination role between detail design and construction planning. Its purpose is to deal with interactions between the two basic roles.

We have seen examples of lateral interactions in the work of Pete James and his team. The bricklaying on their 13th project interacted with that of steel fixers and plumbers. In the main this was dealt with directly by Pete and the other team leaders. However, when they were unable to resolve

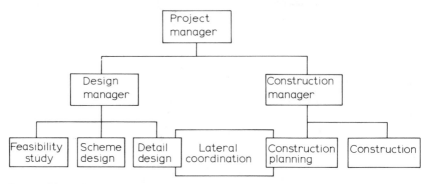

Figure 4.3 Lateral coordination role

problems a member of the site manager's team was called in. In some cases, as when Doug suggested a means of eliminating the delays in the bricklayer's work, the architect was involved. It is possible that the communications and transactions arising from the lateral interactions between the bricklaying team and others could become so numerous and time consuming that it was worthwhile creating a new role to deal with them. This would have allowed Pete's team to concentrate on laying bricks and would have released the site manager's team to deal with other matters.

In much the same way we can envisage a number of design teams whose work interacts. Thus, we might have a structural engineering team, several services engineering teams and teams responsible for various elements of the fabric of a building design. Interactions between their work could all be referred to a design manager to determine the detail design. Alternatively, lateral coordination roles of various kinds could be used. A common approach is to hold regular design team meetings where problems arising from interactions between separate teams are discussed and answers or, more usually, methods for finding answers are agreed. Where there is a great deal of interaction between teams there may well be a case for creating a separate coordination role. This often arises for example in modern 'hi-tech' buildings where the external walls and the mechanical services are often closely integrated. An example is provided by the new Lloyd's Building in London designed by Richard Rogers and Partners where warm air is to be circulated through triple-glazed window units. Given the close interlocking of the external wall system and the heating system there is an obvious need for a lateral coordination role to handle the multitude of communications and decisions between architects, structural engineers and the various service engineers whose work interacts closely in the external envelope of the building.

In practice, lateral coordination takes a number of different forms. In some cases it modifies basic roles, in others it leads to the creation of additional management roles. The arrangements selected in any particular situation should depend on the amount of information to be communicated and the number of decisions about transactions of values which arise from lateral interactions. It is sensible, therefore, to describe the possible arrangements in sequence of increasing capacity to deal with communications and transactions.

The simplest form of lateral coordination is simply to require the team leaders involved to discuss problems as and when they arise. This is likely to be very effective since they are likely to know all the directly relevant information and, in most cases, will be motivated to find a mutually satisfactory answer. It does, however, take them away from their direct responsibilities which may suffer as a consequence. Also it is by no means certain that they will find an answer which is best for the project as a whole. Even at low levels of interaction the costs of relying on direct contact can easily exceed the benefits. Then it is worthwhile considering the creation of liaison roles.

Liaison roles usually involve an individual in having a place in two teams who interact frequently. A common example occurs in the design stages of major chemical processing plants. It is normal for the costs and schedule teams to be represented in the design teams. These individuals are members either of the costs or the schedule team and of one of the design teams. They are responsible for ensuring good communications between their two teams, for identifying problems and seeking to persuade the teams to find answers. The role carries no formal authority. However, because it sits in the interaction channel and often provides the occupant with a unique set of information and understanding of the two teams, an energetic and talented individual can acquire considerable informal power. He can gradually come to represent the project interest and so may be seen as an unofficial spokesman for the client or project manager. Liaison roles work best when two teams are involved. Where lateral interactions concern more teams then it may be worthwhile establishing a task force.

A task force is a group of individuals drawn from a number of teams brought together to find an answer to a problem arising from the interactions between them. Task forces may include full-time members or only individuals who share their time between team and task force. They may be set up to solve one specific problem or meet regularly to deal with continuing problems of coordination. Holt[6] reports a case where the construction teams working in each area of a large chemical processing plant met each week to agree which team should have priority in access to workplaces during the following week. He regards these regular meetings as an important factor in reducing the number of men required on site at any one time which in turn helps industrial relations and contributes to high productivity.

A task force may face a large intractable problem and so meet regularly for long periods of time and in effect become an extra team. While the new team could be regarded as a coordination device it seems more straight-forward to accept that it is a team undertaking a basic role and that its creation effectively redefines the responsibilities of other teams. The emergence of a new team may of course create new coordination problems. However, it does not raise additional types of issue nor identify an additional type of coordination device.

When the coordination devices described above, direct contact, liaison roles and task forces, are insufficient to deal with lateral interactions, an integration management role may be created. This is a lateral coordination role with formal authority. It has authority over some aspects of the primary roles but does not have formal authority over the team members. In effect, a lateral coordination role has authority over decisions. Typically this includes the power to authorise costs, schedules, performance levels, resource usage or other aspects of the primary work. The role can work in three essentially different ways which provide different degrees of authority. First, such roles can simply have the right to agree proposals put forward by the basic teams. Secondly, they can take the initiative in proposing answers for the teams to consider and agree. Thirdly, they can have the authority to make decisions which the primary teams must then accept. In practice all three approaches are likely to produce very similar behaviour most of the time. This is because problems should be discussed and answers sought from all those involved whichever pattern of authority is adopted. So there will usually be real efforts to obtain agreement on answers. Indeed there is considerable evidence that those who are effective in lateral coordination roles tend to work through persuasion and negotiation. It is only at a final stage when a decision must be made and a concensus has not emerged that the differences between the three patterns of authority become significant.

The authority carried by lateral coordination roles is essentially that of the client or project manager in respect of some specific aspect of the project. The client or project manager would carry the responsibility himself if he had the time. Creating a separate role is intended to relieve him of a mass of detailed work. Obviously the more such work arises the more likely it is that there will be benefits in using this device. Consequently lateral coordination roles are most frequently found on large projects. *Figure 1.8* indicates the kind of relationships required in such projects. Responsibility for the project objectives in the second level of the system illustrated in that diagram could well give rise to a lateral coordination role. Examples often arise on chemical processing plants. Such projects typically comprise a number of distinct physical locations usually clustered around a major item of plant. Flowing through and around these are various systems usually of pipes or wires which carry various gases, liquids or electricity between the items of plant. Each item of plant must be designed and constructed as a coherent whole and so must each system. Therefore, work can be organized around physical locations with lateral coordination roles to represent the system interest. Alternatively work can be organized around systems with a lateral coordination role for each separate area of the project. Both approaches, as Holt describes[6], have been used in practice. When these devices are used it is necessary to specify which manager has the authority to make the final decision over each subject where conflict of interests may arise. Thus, on one project, lateral coordination roles responsible for systems may have the final authority in respect of technical performance and quality in the end product but the team leaders responsible for each separate area be given the final say in all other matters. On a different project perhaps with different objectives the lateral coordination roles may have authority over all scheduling matters.

The allocation of authority is worth considering carefully because it can reinforce the project objectives. Matters which are made the responsibility of a lateral coordination role which has considerable authority will be regarded as important. Clearly there is potential in these devices for confusion and conflict when managers with overlapping responsibilities disagree. They may disagree over possible answers to problems but equally, and more damagingly, they may disagree over the nature of the problem and therefore over who has authority. It is therefore sensible to select individuals and teams for lateral coordination roles who are tough enough to stand between teams without being absorbed by them. They should be problem-solvers rather than dogmatic personalities wedded to established answers. They have a difficult role to play and perhaps, above all, need to be good communicators and negotiators. They need, for example, to be able to present engineering problems in costs and schedule terms and vice versa without distortion so that different disciplines came to a common view of the questions to be answered. The aim is to achieve coordination without eliminating the differences in attitudes, language and style which make for good performance in primary roles.

It is easy to see how such demands can overload a lateral coordination role. When this happens, responsibility must be given back to the interacting teams. However, in such circumstances it is likely that the uncertainty is such that a simple management hierarchy will be unable to cope and therefore, a different form of structure is required. This is the last of the lateral coordination devices available to construction project managers. It is called a matrix structure. An organization which matches the information system in *Figure 1.8* can be drawn in the form of a matrix structure as illustrated in *Figure 4.4*. This shows that the project manager has divided his project into a number of sub-projects and into design, management and construction responsibilities. A separate role is created for each of these divisions and all have equal authority. Separate teams are

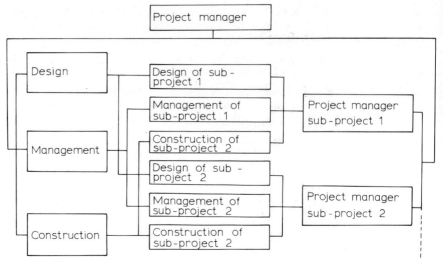

Figure 4.4 Matrix structure

established for the design, the management and the construction of each sub-project. Each team is equally responsible to two different managers.

At first sight the matrix structure appears confusing. It breaks the well-known principle of unity of command. It undoubtedly creates problems and we shall discuss these in a moment. However, before we do that, it is worth observing that duality of command is much commoner than the classical management writers generally recognized. We all have two parents and most of us were raised in the dual authority system of the family. This probably goes deep into human nature. Our brains which are clearly divided into two tend to divide the world into pairs of opposites. In resolving problems it is useful to have both sides of the argument stated as in the classical pattern for debate or in criminal trials. As Townsend[7] argues in a passage on two-man teams, it is extremely valuable to work with another person who asks the awkward, obvious, crucial questions that we may have overlooked. In building projects as we have seen with Pete James' team it is normal for construction teams to be responsible to the site manager for most matters but to have to satisfy the architect over quality standards. This does not in fact, usually create a formal matrix structure but the work of the construction teams would be little changed if it did. Indeed, it might well provide a more effective organization if the two sets of interests were put on to a clearly equal footing. Formal matrix structures are common in the design stages of large construction projects where the separate design professions form one axis of the matrix and major elements of the project the other; the one representing professional standards and the other the requirements of the various elements. While this creates problems which we shall now describe, matrix structures for some projects may well cause less uncertainty for the occupants of primary roles than the alternatives.

The first and fairly obvious problem is that teams responsible to two different managers who have different objectives and interests are likely to experience a sense of confusion and conflict. The matrix structure does not cause this but it does tend to bring ambiguities to the surface. Managers used to having undisputed control over a given area of work may well find it uncomfortable to have to argue their case, to defend their decisions and not be able to allocate blame or credit to individuals or even to teams. This can easily create stress. There are likely to be more meetings and more discussions than with other organizational forms which can easily create too many demands on managers' time. This adds to the stress which is often observed in practice to be characteristic of matrix structures.

A further problem is the difficulty of maintaining a balance between the different interests within the matrix. An emphasis by the project manager on quality or on professional standards can easily cause a reversion to a traditional single chain of authority. On the other hand, an exact balance could easily produce complete stalemate with no decisions being made. In practice the power tends to vary with the subject matter of the question under consideration. A balance is achieved by the different interests each winning the argument on these issues of greatest concern to them. It requires considerable interpersonal skill and maturity for managers to recognize when to lose gracefully and when to insist that their own view should prevail. A final problem with matrix structures is the extra cost of management. There tend to be more managers, more time spent discussing work and more negotiation between specialist interest teams than in single-authority structures. This is often erroneously seen as a symptom of inefficiency. In the right circumstances matrix structures provide the appropriate answer.

Matrix structures are particularly well suited to problem-solving projects. They tend to force important questions to the surface where they must be dealt with. They provide a balance of points of view and of authority which means that all decisions are open to challenge and so must be robust if they are to be adopted. The key advantage of a matrix structure is that once accepted, decisions tend to be widely understood and therefore implemented with enthusiasm.

Galbraith[1] and Mintzberg[2] regard the lateral coordinating devices as forming a continuum. This idea is illustrated in *Figure 4.5* in terms of professional and project interests. It is useful in illustrating how the various possibilities change the balance of authority and consequently help to determine the effective objectives within projects.

Procedures

We have now completed the description of coordination devices which modify roles and can now consider those which modify relationships between teams. As with teams and roles we will deal first with devices

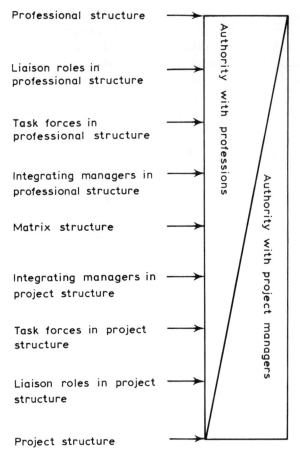

Professional structure

Liaison roles in
professional structure

Task forces in
professional structure

Integrating managers in
professional structure

Matrix structure

Integrating managers in
project structure

Task forces in project
structure

Liaison roles in project
structure

Project structure

Figure 4.5 Continuum of lateral coordination devices

which reduce the need for information or things of value. The first of these is the use of procedures.

Procedures are sets of rules which teams should obey. They can and do relate directly to roles. Thus, when Red McGregor establishes a rule that everyone on his site must wear a hard-hat he is creating a procedure which influences the role description of all the construction teams. However, the procedures which are of more interest in construction are those which modify relationships.

Essentially procedures establish the correct response to given situations. They tell teams what actions to take when certain circumstances arise. In doing so they reduce the need for communication between teams since each knows what to expect from the others. With a well-established procedure this is true irrespective of who actually occupies any given role. Thus, where procedures are established, teams can more easily move from project to project since the rules they have to work to remain the same. A good example of well-established procedures is provided by the standard methods of measurement used by quantity surveyors in several countries. A standard method of measurement establishes rules which tell quantity surveyors which items of work to measure and how to measure and describe them in preparing bills of quantities. Then when bills of quantities prepared in accordance with a standard method of measurement are sent to construction firms to price in competition they all know what each item means without further communication with the quantity surveyor. Without the established standard procedure there would be ambiguity over whether particular work was included in particular items in the bills of quantities. At best there would be many questions for the quantity surveyor at worst misunderstanding, dispute and litigation. The existence of an established convention helps to avoid these problems.

Procedures are limited to those project-related situations which can be anticipated in advance and for which the appropriate actions can be identified. In construction there tend to be relatively few such situations. However, where they exist procedures provide a powerful means of reducing the flow of information and the need for decisions about transactions of values between teams.

Sub-projects

A second way in which relationships between teams can be modified to reduce the amount of interaction is to subdivide projects into self-contained sub-projects. In effect dividing projects into a number of separate smaller projects. There are a number of ways in which this can be done in construction.

It is common to separate the design stages from the construction stages of projects by arranging for them to take place at different times. Where this can be done it results in a great reduction in the interaction between design and construction compared with projects where they are carried out at the same time. Separate stages of the project requiring different knowledge and skills are often separated. Thus, on major shopping centres the organization responsible for the main fabric often has no responsibility for fitting out the individual shops. These each become a separate project. Similarly, small areas of complex work which would normally require the work of many specialist teams are often made the responsibility of a team with generalized talents. Thus, in alteration work a new cloakroom may be constructed by a small team who place concrete, lay bricks, plaster, fix tiles, lay floor screeds, install sanitary equipment, fix pipes and plumbing fittings and make connections to the drainage system. They are almost certain to be very much less productive at each of these kinds of work than specialist teams but by eliminating the complicated set of interactions between the six or seven teams who would otherwise be required the generalist team may in total be more efficient. On the other hand, it is likely to be more difficult for a generalist team to find a steady stream of work which matches its particular combination of knowledge and skills than it is for a more specialized team. Thus, a generalist team may have higher costs to allow for the greater risks of being unemployed. Therefore, once again there is a balance to be struck, in this case between the benefits of reduced interactions between teams and the probable costs arising from a slower project and less productive workers. When this results in a net benefit then sub-dividing the project into self-contained sub-projects provides a useful device which reduces the need for communications and transactions.

Information systems

The final type of coordination device increases the communication capacity of project organizations. It is the use of information systems. That is, the systematic gathering of information about a project and its distribution to those in the project organization who need to know in a convenient form at appropriate times.

Modern computers have reduced the costs and increased the value of information systems. This in turn is likely in the near future to make construction project organizations simpler, yet more effective than they tend to be in practice at the moment. These benefits will arise as computer-based information systems deal with routine matters and so enable managers to concentrate on important decisions. The computers will carry out routine monitoring of progress, calculate the probable effects of variability and interference and involve the managers only when a significant deviation from planned progress is found. It remains to be seen whether this leads to more sophisticated buildings and civil and heavy engineering products or to greater speed and efficiency in construction.

Manual information systems are useful but they have not had and are almost certainly incapable of producing the same dramatic effects as those based on computers. Since their use is becoming common the ensuing description assumes computer use. It also tends to look ahead of current practice in the construction industry to what is now technically possible because this provides a clear description of the principles of information systems.

We described the main components of construction project information systems in Chapter 1. They are project objectives, a description of the end product, a model of the project organization and definitions of the roles required by the project. In addition managers need feedback on their project's behaviour. The list of main components appears to imply five separate descriptions of projects each expressed to some extent in different terms. In current manually based practice the situation tends to be more complex than this. Whilst the statement of the client's objectives tends to be reasonably well integrated, design information for example is often very fragmented. Thus, even on a small building, project design information is likely to be produced relatively independently by three or four consultants and perhaps ten or a dozen specialist contractors. Similarly, descriptions of project organizations tend to proliferate. They may include organigrams, bar charts, networks, budget statements, cost plans, flow charts, responsibility allocation charts, statements of policy and other models of the organization. Role descriptions tend to draw on relevant parts of the design and management information and add yet further information including particularly statements of specific role objectives. This further information may include standard conditions of engagement or forms of contract, project specific modifications to these standards and formal role descriptions such as those provided by bills of quantities. The complexity of real world project information is compounded by feedback which tends to be extremely fragmented. This is because in the main each team produces feedback to suit its own work independently of the others. The overall effect in current, manually-based practice is that information systems are over complex and of limited value.

Project information like the projects they represent does not exist in a vacuum. Its preparation requires teams to draw on general information sources. That is information about construction which is not specific to any one project. This includes information on regulations, procedures, methods of construction, properties of materials and components, general studies of user needs, maintenance problems and feedback on the performance, costs and schedules from past projects. It is contained in a multitude of books, reports, standards, trade literature and increasingly on microfiche and computer-based general information systems.

Project information also draws on and feeds into private information concerned with the management of firms and organizations. This includes information on the costs and schedules of teams, their availability, use and performance on projects and other information which is usually regarded as confidential. It is contained in formal records and accounts owned by separate organizations.

Information systems bring a degree of order to construction project information. This is their purpose whether they deal with whole projects or single aspects of projects and whether they use manual methods or advanced information technology. However, as we noted earlier, the main principles are clearer if we assume computer-based systems and also it is most helpful to describe a system which deals with whole projects.

An ideal construction project information system would enable the teams which make up the project organization to record all their decisions and progress. At the same time they should all be able to select and examine what they need to know from the current total set of project information. All this should be achieved economically and efficiently. Obviously if this were possible most of the coordination needs of construction projects would be satisfied since each team would be fully informed on all project matters. Unfortunately, such an information system is impractical because it would, in fact, have to duplicate the real world project expressed from the viewpoint of each of the teams involved. It would be cheaper to construct the project.

The practical compromise appears to be to construct a common description of the end product in neutral terms. This is likely to take the form of a three-dimensional computer model using widely agreed symbols and terminology. There seems to be merit in structuring the model so that in addition to representing the various elements of the end product, it reflects the separate roles within the particular project. The model will be more concerned with defining the interfaces between roles than with the content of individual roles. In recognition of its central role in providing coordination, responsibility for maintaining the common description should normally rest with the project manager's team. Clustered around the common description will be workstations for individual teams. They can examine information obtained from the common description, use it, make decisions and record them in their own information stores. When such activity results in a need to alter or extend the common description this decision is communicated to the project manager's team. They will have their own workstation which will help them to evaluate the proposed decision and either accept or reject it. When such a decision is accepted it is incorporated into the common description and communicated to all the teams whose role is affected by it. When decisions are rejected the team concerned must search for a different answer. Thus the project manager's team retains overall control.

Teams frequently need access to information stored within another team's workstation. This needs to be in a form which the first team or its workstation can understand. There need to be agreed conventions to determine the form of such information so that inter-team communication is effective. Ideally this would allow direct communication between workstations. This is likely to be extremely expensive to achieve and in most projects in the near and middle future, will require human interpretation of information passed between teams. However, in situations where particular types of communication are common, agreed conventions will be developed which allow direct computer-based communications between teams. Obviously it should not be possible for anyone to modify information belonging to another team. Teams may well need to sound a warning that there appear to be errors in information held by another team or to suggest changes but each must remain responsible for its own information. With these safeguards and facilities built into the system the amount of computer-based communication will gradually increase over time as information technology develops and as the construction industry produces the essential standard conventions.

An important part of each workstation is the ability to access catalogues of general information. These will contain regulations, standards, descriptions of materials and components and all the other types of general information described earlier in this chapter. Ideally this will be in a computer accessible form. There is obvious merit in such information being published and kept up-to-date in a suitable form by its originators. Such developments would, over time, provide a major step towards the standardization of symbols, terminology and data structures which computer-based information systems require.

In addition to using general catalogues, individual teams are likely to build up their own catalogues of the information which they tend to use frequently. This will tend to reduce the costs of computer-based information systems on any one project and so make their use more likely.

Figure 4.6 illustrates the main components of the construction project information system described thus far. It allows teams to develop their own use of computers independently and at their own pace. It allows the originators and publishers of general information to continue to contribute to project information as fully as they wish. At the same time it provides for central coordination by project managers.

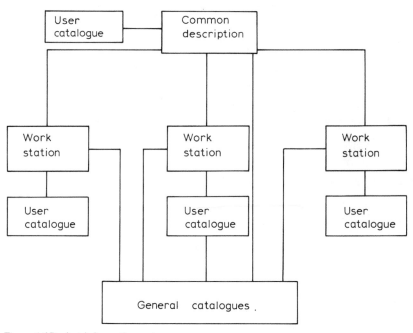

Figure 4.6 Project information system

In large projects the common description could be divided into descriptions of sub-projects or even sub-sub-projects. Each level would have its cluster of workstations around it coordinated by the appropriate common description controlled by the appropriate manager. Thus, the information system can match the project organization no matter how complex it is. It can incorporate manually-based components alongside computer-based ones. A team which works in a manual mode will receive information in the form of computer-produced hard copy, carry out its work and provide its decisions and progress reports in a manually-produced hard copy form. The implications on the common description will need to be abstracted and processed to retain the integrity of the system. However, apart from that additional process it is incidental to overall project coordination whether or not any team works through a computer-based workstation.

The crucial decision in designing a construction project information system is the level of detail stored in the common description. The more detailed it is the greater the costs of monitoring it but the more effective the coordination. Research and development work is needed to establish the appropriate levels for various projects. It seems likely that at present a very coarse common description will suit all except very demanding projects. This will change over time as the use of such systems becomes established and is supported by agreed conventions and as information technology develops yet further. As more detailed common descriptions become feasible, so an increasing proportion of the coordination burden will be lifted from the devices described earlier. It is in this way that computers will have a major effect on construction project organizations. For the moment, information systems provide one of the coordination devices available to construction project managers. They can be very expensive to set up and maintain. They can, however, in the right circumstances, free managers from an otherwise overwhelming mass of detailed information and so allow them to concentrate on major strategic decisions.

Checklist of coordination devices

We have now considered all the coordination devices available. They are set out in *Table 4.1* in a form which relates them to the model of construction projects described in Chapters 1 and 2. This provides a useful checklist. Project organizations are made up of teams undertaking basic

TABLE 4.1. Coordination devices

	Reduce the need for information and things of value	Increase organizations' capacity to communicate and transact
Modify teams	Professionalization Slack resources	*
Modify roles	Goals	Management roles
Modify relationships	Procedures Sub-projects	Information systems

* Professionalization and slack resources may also increase organizations' capacity to communicate and transact.

roles coordinated by some, or in difficult projects, all of these devices. The choice of coordination devices for specific construction projects is obviously crucial to their success and is the subject of the next chapter.

Summary

Project organizations consist of teams whose work must be coordinated so that their combined actions achieve agreed objectives. The coordination devices available either reduce the need for information to be communicated and values to be transacted or else they increase the organization's capacity to communite and transact. A device which modifies teams is professionalization which encompasses the knowledge and skills of unskilled workers, semi-skilled workers, craftsmen and professionals working either independently or interdependently. A second device which modifies teams is the provision of slack resources. In considering devices which modify roles we first noted that the definition of roles is, in itself, a coordination device. Beyond this, devices which modify roles are the setting of goals and the creation of management hierarchies and lateral coordination roles. Management hierarchies work on the basis of paired sets of authority and responsibility. Lateral coordination may be provided by direct contact between teams, liaison roles and taskforces, by creating integrating management roles or by using a matrix structure. Devices which modify relationships between teams are procedures, dividing projects into self-contained tasks and information systems.

References

1. GALBRAITH, J., *Designing Complex Organizations,* Addison-Wesley (1973)
2. MINTZBERG, H., *The Structuring of Organizations,* Prentice-Hall (1979)
3. Department of Construction Management, University of Reading, *UK and US Construction Industries: a Comparison of Design and Contract Procedures,* Royal Institution of Chartered Surveyors (1979)
4. BENNETT, J., MORRISON, N. L. and STEVENS, S., *Cost Planning and Computers,* Department of the Environment (1981)
5. See for example: LESTER, A., *Project Planning and Control,* Butterworth (1982)
6. HOLT, L., 'A case study of the construction of a terephthalic acid plant for Imperial Chemicals Limited at the Davies Works, Wilton, Cleveland, UK', *Construction Management and Economics,* **1,** No. 1 (Spring 1983)
7. TOWNSEND, R., *Up the Organization,* Hodder Fawcett (1971)

Chapter 5

Patterns of project organizations

Work had stopped on Red McGregor's site. First, severe weather had delayed them for two weeks. When the snow had cleared the developer had instructed Red not to reopen the site until he had resolved what was to be done about the Roman villa. There was now no doubt that the stone wall was part of a very important archeological site. The developer faced with the real possibility of a long delay and perhaps a messy and very public dispute with the council over the planning permission they had granted, needed to find an answer quickly if he was not to lose a lot of money.

Red was aware of all this background as he entered the developer's office for a meeting to discuss what should be done. He expected to be dismissed on the grounds that the work could not go ahead. In preparation for this eventuality he had talked to one or two people about the possibility of another project. He was fairly sure that he could find another job reasonably quickly. Both the developer and the project architect were already in the office. They were looking over a pile of drawings. Red saw that the drawings portrayed several long, low buildings with ornamental brick columns and pitched roofs ranged in front of two large rectangular blocks. One of these seemed to be completely enclosed and entirely devoid of windows while the other looked like an orthodox multi-storey office block with alternate bands of windows and brickwork.

The developer explained that this was to be the town's new Roman Leisure Centre. It would incorporate the newly discovered villa and provide a luxury sports and entertainment complex complete with a hotel for the visitors likely to be attracted by a combination of culture, sport and top entertainment. The architect explained how the new design incorporated the work already done on the first of the factory units. Both men suggested to Red that there need be no further delay to the construction work. The developer had done a deal with the council and work could start immediately.

They sat down to discuss what was needed to be done. Red discovered that the six drawings on the table were all that existed of the design. He could see that the architect was excited at the prospect of creating the Roman Leisure Centre. There was much discussion of the appropriate atmosphere, of the need to capture the essential decadence of Rome and of recreating a circus for major sporting battles. There was no discussion of the form of construction, the flow of design information, the quality standards or any of the matters which were crucial to the construction.

Red waited for a pause in the discussion. When he was sure he had the other men's attention he explained that the organization he had set up to build three factory units to a fully developed design could not cope with the new project. He further explained that it would take him at least a week with the drawings evaluating the new project before he could begin to discuss what he would need if he was to manage its construction. The developer and the architect were clearly irritated by this turn in their discussions. They argued that the new project was not really very different from the old. They pointed out that it was on the same site, apart from the hotel and the large sports hall it was the same size on plan and used many of the same materials as the original project. Red explained that the difference in size was significant, that the buildings were much more complex individually and in total than the factory units and the lack of design information would pose an entirely different and more difficult management task. Taken together these changes would mean a much larger and more sophisticated organization. He confirmed that he needed at least a week to evaluate the new project.

Red, of course, was right. The new proposals would need a different kind of project organization. That is a different set of the coordination devices described in Chapter 4 as well as different teams to undertake the basic construction work. However, the developer and architect's response was fairly representative of many clients and indeed of many people in the construction industry. They appear to believe that there ought to be one best answer which suits all projects. One of the reasons for producing this book is to establish that project organizations have to be chosen to match individual projects and their environments. The basic components which need to be considered in making this choice have been described in the earlier chapters. Now we need to consider how these separate components fit together.

Productivity and uncertainty

In Chapters 1, 2 and 3 we described a simple model of the task posed by individual construction projects. The model consists of patterns of roles occupied by teams subject to uncertainty. Uncertainty was seen as having two components; one internal caused by the effects of variable levels of productivity on the interactions between teams; and the other caused by interference from outside projects. The task of the coordination devices described in Chapter 4 is to reduce uncertainty, that is, to create a situation in which, as far as possible, each team arrives in the project as soon as their work is available and accessible knowing what they must do and the performance standards and schedules which apply; all the materials, components, tools and equipment they need are available; the work is within their normal competence; and they are motivated to complete it properly. This perfect situation which does not occur in the real world, is assumed to relate to the minimum level of costs and times. Uncertainty adds to both as we saw in Chapter 2. We can, therefore, envisage a relationship between productivity and uncertainty for any given team as illustrated in *Figure 5.1*. It shows that, given complete certainty, productivity is high. As teams are faced with growing uncertainty their

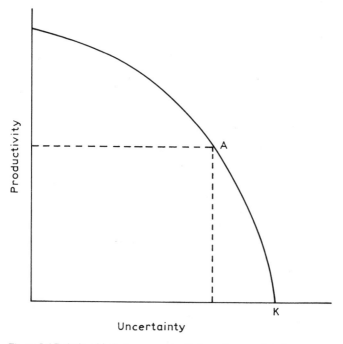

Figure 5.1 Relationship between productivity and uncertainty for any team

productivity reduces, slowly at low levels of uncertainty and much more quickly at high levels. This relationship holds good whether the team in question is undertaking primary work or coordination work. In practice as we have described in Chapter 4, most roles necessarily involve some combination of primary work and coordination responsibilities. However, in the main, teams are specialists in one or the other and we can therefore expect to find that the relationship between primary and coordination work actually accomplished by any individual team is of the kind shown in *Figure 5.2*. This suggests that a team which undertakes high levels of primary work is unlikely to have the capacity to cope with very much coordination. The reverse also applies. However, teams faced with roughly equal primary and coordination work are significantly less productive than those which specialize. This accords with common experience which tells

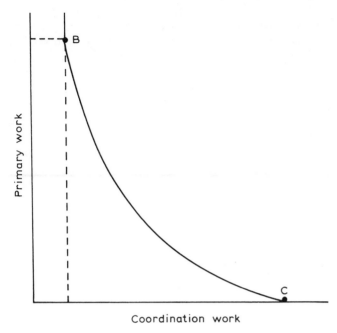

Figure 5.2 Relationship between primary work and coordination work for any team

us that high productivity occurs where there is sufficient, clearly defined work for a specialist team to be fully occupied. The diagram also suggests that teams do not specialize completely in primary work. Certainly it is hard to think of an example of a team undertaking basic construction work which has no coordination responsibilities. It is easier to envisage the converse in, for example, teams maintaining information systems or drafting standard procedures. This distinction is reflected in *Figure 5.2*.

Project organizations

In choosing an appropriate organization for any project we need to define sufficient roles to undertake all the primary and coordination work required. We might, for example, envisage a project in which teams are likely to experience the level of uncertainty indicated by point A on *Figure 5.1*. This equates with productivity of about 60% of that likely to be achieved under conditions of complete certainty. We might then select sufficient roles to be occupied by teams represented by point B on *Figure 5.2* working at 60% productivity to undertake the primary work required by the project. These primary roles would have some coordination capacity which may fall short of the coordination required. We might then complete the project organization by adding sufficient roles to be occupied by teams represented by point C on *Figure 5.2* working, again, at 60% productivity to make up the short-fall in coordination capacity.

To select an organization in the way described in the previous paragraph we need to know the level of uncertainty likely to be experienced and the requirement for primary and coordination work in the project under consideration. We saw in Chapter 3 (Equations (3.1), (3.2), (3.4) p.53) that uncertainty is in part a function of the number and pattern of roles which make up any particular project organization. Therefore, we cannot calculate the likely level of uncertainty until we know the roles which will make up the project organization and, as we have just seen, we cannot choose the roles until we know the level of uncertainty they will face. The calculation is further complicated if we accept that the purpose of coordination work is to reduce uncertainty. The circle of relationships is

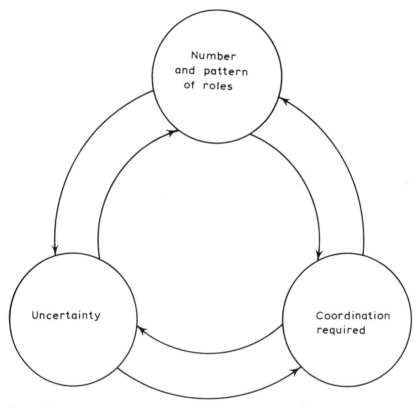

Figure 5.3 Relationships between three key factors in the selection of project organizations

closed since the coordination required is in part a function of the number of roles which make up the project. Therefore, we have three factors each of which, to some extent, is dependent on the other two. *Figure 5.3* illustrates this set of completely circular relationships. Add to this that in practice the relationships in *Figures 5.1* and *5.2* and the absolute values they represent are likely to be different for each team and we must conclude that selecting appropriate project organizations is unlikely to be reduced to a simple calculation. The factors to be considered are too numerous and the relationships between them too complex for that to be possible.

The problem just described exists even if we have a complete description of the end product so that all the primary roles required can be identified. In practice, decisions about project organizations have to be made before that complete description exists. Given this further requirement the task of selecting appropriate project organizations begins to appear impossible. This is probably why practitioners tend to want to adopt a single established approach to organization. Given the difficulties we have just described, it is obviously tempting simply to adopt a standard answer. However, we have seen that projects and their environments vary considerably and it is inconceivable that any one standard answer can provide the best possible organization or even a satisfactory organization for every type of construction project.

Structural configurations

The way forward is indicated by Mintzberg[1]. In his important synthesis of the management literature he identifies five, and only five, structural configurations. That is five types of organization each best suited to a particular kind of work. They are idealized types in the sense that real-world organizations are unlikely to fit exactly any one of the configurations. However, the idealized configurations do define the boundaries within which real organizations are to be found. More importantly for our purposes, by locating the work required by specific projects within the boundaries, we can obtain guidance which helps to identify the appropriate type of organization.

Mintzberg's synthesis relates to the whole of management literature on organization structure which, in the main, relates to permanent organizations. The result is not directly applicable to construction projects. However, the concept of a small number of consistent idealized patterns or kinds of construction project and matching organizations provides the key idea for the rest of this chapter. Assuming that the patterns exist, then the selection of project organizations is greatly simplified. Once a project is identified as belonging to a particular type the general nature of the appropriate organization will be determined by reference to the matching idealized pattern. There are, from a construction project management view point, three distinct types of project and matching organization. Each is described in the following paragraphs in sufficient detail to enable it to be recognized.

Programmed organizations

We shall call the first idealized type 'programmed organizations'. It provides standard answers to common recurring needs. These include basic housing, simple warehouses and factories, standard systems of construction capable of providing a range of simple buildings and routine road building. Typically the standard answer is marketed by a single commercial firm. Such firms search for clients, agree project objectives, carry out any necessary design work and construct their standard answers. In order to maintain the flow of work for their project teams such firms often construct speculatively and sell the completed buildings. A large proportion of basic housing and simple warehouses and factories are provided in this way.

Like mass production organizations in other industries the construction work of firms providing standard answers is routine, simple and repetitive. It tends to consist of simple assembly tasks which can be learnt in a matter of weeks, or at the most, a few months of on-the-job experience. To achieve the degree of standardization which allows construction work to become routine requires very competent and careful detail design.

This is undertaken independently of individual projects because it often requires several years of development work to produce new standard answers. Such careful design is likely to involve professionals drawn from a number of different disciplines. Their work often includes a careful analysis of existing designs in terms of performance, costs, work content and speed of construction. They may range widely in a search for better answers. The work may involve research and development. New designs emerge as a result of teamwork, much discussion and wide consultation. Often prototypes are constructed, tested and re-designed until a satisfactory answer is found. The agreed answer is then very carefully documented. Each component is drawn and specified in detail. Each construction role is described in terms of the components involved and the way they are to be handled, the plant, machines and equipment to be used, the number and skills of the workers required and the standard time for the work. Thus, the pattern of construction roles is an essential part of the design which is normally expressed in standard procedures. The long time scale and the complexity of development work means that programmed organizations need to spread the costs of their designs over many projects. Therefore, the firms providing standard answers tend to be large. The remarkable growth of volume house builders in Britain in recent years illustrates this. The commercial success of firms providing standard answers depends on their construction efficiency. This in turn depends on the routine execution of coordinated and standardized roles. This is why we have chosen to call them programmed organizations.

Procedures permeate programmed organizations. They are essentially bureaucratic, depending on tough, experienced site managers to organize the construction work in accordance with standard procedures. Communication is formal and depends mainly on written formalized documents. Standard order forms call up standard components in a standard sequence. Production rates are built into computerized bonus systems to help motivate the operatives to achieve rapid construction. Regular and frequent progress reports in a standard and often very detailed format keep head office in the picture. There is considerable obsession with control. This in turn leads to attempts to eliminate all possible uncertainty so that the machine-like programmed organization can run smoothly.

Uncertainty can be reduced by building up land banks on which speculative building can take place and by negotiating large long-term contracts with major clients. It can be further reduced by negotiating long-term contracts with suppliers or by manufacturing key components inside the firm. All these strategies tend to require ever larger and ever more bureaucratic organizations.

The insistent demands of the bureaucratic head office for formal control data is often resented by the site managers. The insistence on sticking to procedures, keeping to budget, working to the programme all tend to generate conflict between site-based managers and the central technical experts and staff. The pressure on site managers inevitably spills over into tough demands being made on the operatives. The resulting conflicts seem to be an inevitable feature of programmed organizations caused, no doubt, by treating human beings rather as though they were machines or rather as replaceable cogs in a large machine. The fragmented and temporary nature of construction in the main prevents the conflicts becoming serious. However, on large projects where the organization exists for several years it is not at all uncommon for industrial problems similar to those which beset many mass production industries to fester and erupt. As in the automobile industry many of the problems on large projects, are rooted in dehumanizing, repetitive, simple but efficient technical systems. Programmed organizations are not designed to serve their members social ends but to serve the ends of efficiency.

It follows, from the nature and size of programmed organizations, that they need stable, predictable environments. Their work, and with it their commercial viability, depends on a steady demand for their standard answers. Many excellent systems of construction, especially housing systems, were developed in Britain between 1950 and 1970. The vast majority failed commercially because there was insufficient demand to support them all and because of sudden and largely unpredictable changes in the level of demand. In much the same way unpredictable external control creates problems for programmed organizations. Planning requirements which vary from district to district and building or fire regulations which depend on the interpretation of local officials, make it difficult to rely on standard answers. Much of the basic housing in Britain today is provided as a standard internal structure of prefabricated timber components which can be clad with non-standard external skins, selected to meet the requirements of local planning officers. Such non-standard elements severely inhibit the efficiency of programmed organizations. Non-standard elements require individual design and craftsmanship. These are alien forces which corrupt and destroy the standard programme and the standard work processes. They break the rules and do not observe the procedures. So programmed organizations need stable environments which do not pose unpredictable or variable demands which need individual answers. Typically, programmed organizations are large, commercially-orientated firms operating in stable, predictable environments.

The clients of programmed organizations need to be sufficiently experienced to ensure that their needs will be met by the standard answer. They need to ensure that the activities they wish to carry out can be accommodated fully and efficiently and that the end product will be available when they need it and for as long as they need it. They will need to know the financial implications including not only the size of the initial capital investment, but the timing of payments and the likely running and maintenance costs throughout the life of their new facility. Clients of programmed organizations need to examine the nature and extent of their liabilities in the event of possibly changed circumstances in the future. They also need to be sure that they have full and proper guarantees of the performance of the product which they are buying. These checks represent normal prudence in making any major capital investment. Looking at the other half of this basic relationship, programmed organizations require clear and decisive clients who will state all their requirements at the outset and who have no second thoughts which lead to demands for changes to the standard end product.

Programmed organizations lead to the simplest of all project organizations. The experienced client whose objectives lead to a standard answer and who operates in a stable, predictable environment simply places a contract for a complete package with a single competent firm. The single firm assumes responsibility for agreeing the project objectives, design, management and construction.

In practice the brief and scheme design are often combined. Drawings showing the client's space requirements in terms of the standard answer, a standard description of the performance provided and an agreed cost and schedule provide the essential basis for a standard contract which is usually drafted by the firm. The client's role is simply to ensure that the complete package meets his needs, to monitor progress and pay the bills as they are presented.

The firm will obtain all necessary approvals and agreements from local authorities and other statutory bodies. This is usually handled by a team of tough, experienced negotiators whose aim is to ensure that the firm's projects go ahead on schedule and that they are permitted to use standard answers. Once the approvals and agreements are obtained the firm carries out standard ordering procedures to call up the required materials and components in accordance with the agreed schedule. Much of this work is likely to be virtually automatic and almost certainly computer based. A site management team will be selected to take responsibility for the project. Specialist construction teams will be scheduled to arrive in the project at the right times in much the same way as the components. Work which is necessarily non-standard including ground-works and the provision of main services to the end product are often sub-contracted to local teams. This work is too variable to be programmed and so it is usually excluded from the firm's own work.

Progress is clearly monitored against budgets and schedules. Again this is increasingly computer based with standard reports from site automatically generating bills to the client and bonus payments to the construction teams. The site management team is expected to solve all problems so that planned progress is achieved efficiently.

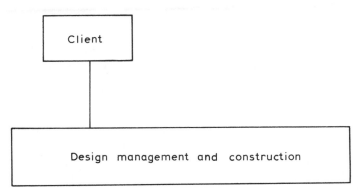

Figure 5.4 Package deal

The features described here serve to identify the first idealized project organization configuration. We have called it programmed organizations which exist to provide standard answers. Its essential features are illustrated diagrammatically in *Figure 5.4*. In practice, commercial organizations operating in this manner are called 'package deal' or 'design-and-build' firms.

Professional organizations

The second idealized type is called 'professional organizations'. It uses traditional construction to produce a wide variety of buildings and civil and heavy engineering products. As we saw in Chapter 4, the essential nature of professional work is the application of a repertoire of standard programs which have been learnt in professional education and training. The professional needs first to categorize client's needs in terms which indicate which program to use. This stage is normally called 'diagnosis'. It is followed by the application of the chosen program.

A recent development in many professions, including those in the construction industry, is formal recognition of the need for continuing professional development. This is caused partly by changes in the construction environment and in clients' needs which call for changes in diagnosis procedures and partly by the emergence of new programs.

The new programs may emerge in response to new problems, they may result from new knowledge, or be a response to opportunities provided by new technology. For example, the cost planning systems developed by quantity surveyors in the 1950s provided new programs in response to client's needs for more reliable cost control during design. Computers, especially microcomputers, provide the basis for more sophisticated cost and schedule prediction and control programs. Professional institutions need to ensure that their members are aware of new developments of this kind and are competent in their use. Hence the need for continuing professional development. This growing knowledge base also leads, in time, to new professions emerging.

In construction many separate professional specializations have emerged. They can conveniently be regarded as clustering into the three broad groups of design, management and construction. Thus, for example, the design of the fabric of buildings, their structure, each separate service, the acoustics, landscaping and indeed other elements all give rise to separate professional skills. Similarly management may be divided into the work of budgeting, scheduling, contracting, surveying, estimating, planning, purchasing, accounting and man management specialists. Construction is shared amongst specialist teams based on various craft skills. As with professional work the essential coordinating device in craftsmen's work is provided by their education and training. This provides a range of standard skills which can be applied in response to the needs of individual projects. In well-established forms of construction the work of the separate craftsmen fits together without the need for elaborate or detailed communication. Each craft leaves the work in the state expected by the next group of workers. Craft training enables each man to cope with minor variations in the preceding work and still allows him to select and apply the appropriate program from his repertoire.

Professionals also tend to form small separate firms each concentrating on the work of one profession. Provided that designers use traditional construction, professionalization provides the primary means of coordinating their independent work. Traditional construction means any established method of construction in which the functional performance of the end product is understood, the pattern of roles is reasonably consistent, the materials, components, plant and equipment needed are readily available and local construction teams are well-practiced in the skills required. Essentially, traditional construction provides a range of construction details which are well known. Indeed they are usually incorporated in textbooks and taught to craftsmen and professionals alike as part of their basic education and training. In most parts of the world the established traditional construction allows a wide variety of shapes, sizes and styles of end product.

In addition to established methods of construction, professional organizations tend to use formal procedures which are often carefully negotiated by professional institutions. In Britain a body called the

Coordinating Committee for Project Information has been set up by professional institutions representing architects, builders, structural and services engineers and surveyors[2]. Its task is to produce detailed procedures which control the form and content of drawings, specifications and bills of quantities. It is intended that these procedures will help coordinate the work of all the separate professions involved and reduce the need for further coordination devices.

In much the same way professional institutions and similar bodies representing craft and trade interests publish standard forms of contract or conditions of engagement. These set down the normal responsibilities and powers of their members when they are employed by clients. The published standards usually state the basis of remuneration and include provisions to deal with changes or disputes and various other matters which may influence the performance of the work. While some of these forms of contract and conditions of engagement are negotiated, in the main they are produced by the professions unilaterally. That is, without reference to clients or their representatives. Predictably the result is often that clients' interests are not protected or at least not protected very well. Also there are often conflicting provisions in the documents produced by separate professions. As a simple example most forms of construction contract used in Britain assume that construction teams will make no design decisions. The conditions of engagement used by services engineers assume that detail design will be produced in collaboration with the construction teams. This has arisen because the construction contracts are drafted essentially with the approach adopted by architects in mind. Their conditions of engagement envisage a complete design being produced and fully documented before construction teams are involved. The bodies concerned are aware of the conflict and are attempting to agree a consistent approach.

Clients who decide that their needs can be met by the use of traditional construction need to establish a professional organization. On all except the smallest and simplest of projects the use of traditional answers requires clients to accept a major and demanding responsibility for the outcome. First they must establish the overall objectives and then create an organization to carry out all the necessary roles within a framework of properly balanced authority and responsibility which ensures that these objectives remain paramount. That is they must create a management hierarchy with themselves at the top.

In setting up a management hierarchy, clients need to ensure that there is a clear allocation of responsibility for design, management and construction. In practice this can be organized in several different ways. The main patterns are illustrated diagrammatically in *Figures 5.5, 5.6* and *5.7*. The one used in any specific project depends on the extent to which the client can fully define his objectives, the levels of uncertainty likely to be experienced in the project and the normal patterns of working in the local construction industry.

Separate trades approach

Figure 5.5 illustrates the separate trades approach. This is the traditional approach. It existed as the normal pattern for building projects in England up to the early part of the 19th century, in Scotland until just after World War II and still exists today in, for example, large parts of West Germany.

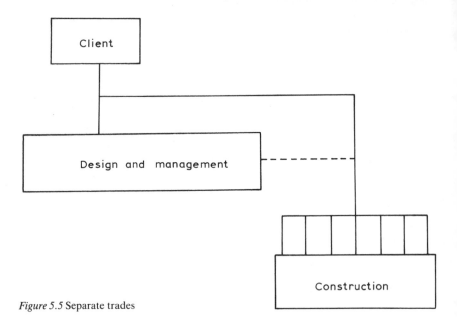

Figure 5.5 Separate trades

Its continued existence in West Germany appears to depend on unusually rigorous standards of education and training for craftsmen and on architects' work being differentiated into separate design and management specialisms. This is reflected in schools of architecture where it is common for students, after completing a common first three years, to specialize either in design or in management. Where these circumstances do not exist, as for example in Britain, the traditional approach to organization has been swamped by the increased sophistication and complexity of modern building and so has been replaced by other patterns.

Where the separate trades approach exists, clients using it as the basis of their project organizations need to define their objectives. They then employ a firm to produce a suitable design and coordinate the work of the construction teams needed to produce the end product. The client enters into a separate contract with each construction team which requires it to accept instructions from the design and management firm. Under this arrangement the client's statement of objectives is not so critical as with the package deal approach since he is not committed to the construction work until he enters into the separate construction contracts. Nevertheless, as the design is developed, the client is responsible for ensuring that it meets all his needs. The major weakness of the separate trades approach is that it is difficult for the client to be certain that his performance objectives are being achieved. Thus, for example the possibility of cost or time overruns is likely to be a source of concern. In principle the design and management firm are responsible for the end product but the multiplicity of contracts makes it difficult to avoid divided responsibilities. The approach tends to produce good-quality results but it requires clients to accept considerable risks and responsibilities.

General contractor approach

Figure 5.6 illustrates the general contractor approach which represents one attempt to provide more predictability for clients. Here one firm takes responsibility for all the construction work. It may directly employ construction teams, or more usually nowadays, it may sub-contract the basic construction work.

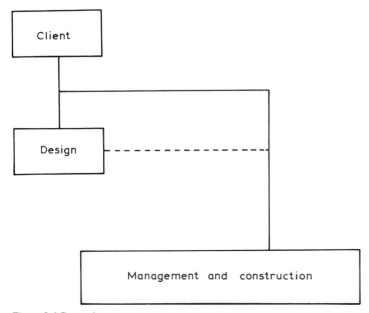

Figure 5.6 General contractor

Clients using this approach have essentially the same relationship with the design team as with separate trades. However, once the single construction contract is entered into the client is committed to the whole of the construction. The approach works well where the design is complete before the general contractor is appointed. Provided that the design is not subsequently varied, clients have reasonably good assurances about costs and time before they are committed to the construction work.

General contractors' contracts usually require work to be completed to the satisfaction of the designer and give him the right to reject work which falls below the standards specified. However, the designer is one stage removed from the construction teams and good-quality work is more difficult to achieve. The right to reject work appears to provide an adequate safeguard but in practice it often aggravates quality problems. The work may well turn out to be worse when it is redone and the construction teams will be alienated if they are led to expect that their work is likely to be wasted. Good-quality work seems to require the design team to cut across the formal contractual relationships and establish direct communication with the construction teams. There is obviously scope for conflict between designer and general contractor in these circumstances. This is considerably aggravated when clients or designers vary the design on which a general contract was based.

The orthodox quantity surveyor's role with its use of bills of quantities has developed in the UK largely to deal with the problems which arise between designers and general contractors. It is essentially a lateral coordination role rather than being part of the management hierarchy. However, in recent years it has tended to grow into a full management role. This has happened as building projects have become larger and more complex and more subject to government regulation and control during the design stages. Clients have been unwilling to wait until the design is complete before knowing their financial commitments. Quantity surveyors using their knowledge of construction costs have developed cost budgeting, planning and control methods which enable them to predict general contractors' prices with a fair degree of confidence during the design stages.

The orthodox quantity surveying role provides clear benefits in the general contractor approach but it has been widely misused in two ways. First, bills of quantities with their unit rate methods have been used to provide an administratively simple but essentially inequitable method of valuing substantial changes to designs. This has led to contracts being let on the basis of incomplete design and the proliferation of variations. Both effects undermine the fundamental basis of the general contractor approach which essentially depends for its efficiency on a firm price in return for a given quantity and quality of well understood construction work. Secondly, the orthodox quantity surveying role has been used in projects which use innovative rather than established traditional construction. The profession's quantity related methods of predicting construction costs depend on a large data base of similar projects using similar methods of construction. That is they depend on established local traditional construction. The essential requirements of the general contractor approach are undermined when innovative answers are used. The costs and time consequences of innovation are extremely difficult to predict and it is clearly unrealistic to expect general contractors to be held to a firm price for work in which the effects are uncertain. Equally, innovation undermines the quantity surveyor's orthodox role. This is not to suggest that individual quantity surveyors have no role to play in respect of innovative design. Some are capable of making an excellent contribution but within a different form of project organization from that implied by the general contractor approach.

Responsibility for ensuring that project organizations and the related end products match each other rests with clients. The general contractor approach appears to be especially demanding in this respect. In particular, clients need to ensure that designs use well-understood traditional construction and are complete before they enter into contracts with general contractors.

Construction management approach

Figure 5.7 illustrates the construction management approach. It gives separate expression to each of the major responsibilities. Construction management firms offering management as a separate professional service have emerged in recent years notably in the USA but also in the UK and elsewhere. They have tended to emerge from multi-discipline design firms,

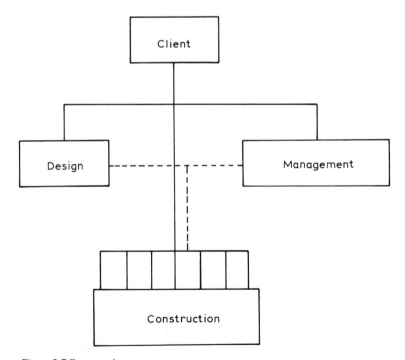

Figure 5.7 Construction management

quantity surveying practices and general contractors. They work alongside a design firm. The two firms jointly design and then coordinate the work of the construction teams needed to produce the end product. The client enters into a separate contract with each construction team which requires them to accept instructions on design matters from the design firm and on management matters from the management firm. This approach allows clients who do not have clearly defined objectives to use the construction industry successfully. The two professional firms provide a balance between design and management objectives which allows clients to examine alternatives and gradually determine their objectives without the pressures and distortions which would arise if they had employed either separately. The approach also allows the client to use traditional construction or innovative answers when that is appropriate. The flexibility arises from the use of separate trades contractors to undertake the construction. The implications of using this approach with innovative answers will be considered with the third idealized type of project organization. For the moment we will concentrate on projects using traditional construction.

When so used the construction management approach can combine the benefits of the separate trades and the general contractor approach. The direct contact between design and construction teams helps to ensure good quality standards. The management team generally can provide clients with reliable predictions of their costs and time commitments. These results depend ultimately on clients managing their projects in the sense that they must decide their own objectives and ensure that they are being met.

Coordination in professional organizations

The three approaches briefly described here are the main representative types of management hierarchy used in professional organizations. In practice there are many modifications and hybrid versions of these representative types. In particular the major responsibilities are frequently subdivided into many further roles in addition to those mentioned above. However, the basic requirements, strengths and weakness described tend to hold good.

One important consequence of the subdivision into more separate roles is that a further coordination device tends to be used. This is the setting of goals. As we described in Chapter 4, goals can provide a powerful means of coordinating the work of independent teams. At the same time they help ensure that clients' objectives permeate project organizations. Clients can fairly easily monitor their projects by checking that the goals set accord with their requirements. In large projects which adopt a professional organization the setting of goals is likely to be reinforced with an information system. The development of computer-based information systems described in Chapter 4 are likely to be used widely and, indeed, to have significant effects on professional organizations. The general nature of these effects will be to allow project organizations to be relatively simple even for large and complex projects. Initially, however, this, like practically everything else said about professional organizations, depends on the use of traditional construction. In stating this caveat we must remember that traditional construction means whatever method is established locally. In one place at one time it may mean simple forms made from clay and timber while elsewhere it may mean the use of sophisticated highly-industrialized components. The essential requirement is that the local construction industry understands the method and can provide all the required resources as a matter of course.

Weaknesses in professional organizations

Professional organizations work most effectively when they are given a clear statement of objectives and are left to diagnose and apply the appropriate program. They are well-practiced in established professional programs which, almost without exception, will have been well tested and implicitly approved by their professional institutions. As a result, clients are safe in the knowledge that professionals can draw on a vast store of recorded knowledge and experience and will not be adopting experimental procedures. These virtues are accompanied by some important weaknesses.

The first concerns the diagnosis stage. Professionals are concerned to identify the appropriate program to suit an individual client's needs. For clients whose problems fall between the professional pigeonholes, this ensures that the professional solution fails to satisfy their real needs. The professions are inherently conservative, adopting new programs only when innovation is unavoidable. So problems which do not fit the standard programs are generally not solved but distorted. Construction projects are likely to be forced through standard procedures even when other approaches would have served clients better. The second weakness concerns the professional ownership of specialized bodies of knowledge. This exclusive access to knowledge places everyone outside the profession at a disadvantage in all matters falling inside the professional competence. At a simple level this creates problems for clients who are unfortunate enough to employ professionals who are either incompetent or unconscientious. At a more subtle level it requires very experienced clients to be sure that they are receiving competent professional service. Attempts at direct control tend to be counter-productive because complex work cannot be performed well unless it is under the direct control of the operator who performs it.

It is in part to deal with these two problems, that the management hierarchies described in this chapter tend to be based on twin primary responsibilities in order to create a system of checks and balances to direct professional effort to the client's ends. The matching of equal and complementary roles in design and management achieves this more effectively that any alternative arrangement. Given this safeguard then, professional organizations play, and will continue to play, an important role in the construction industry being responsible for many of its most important and famous products.

Problem-solving organizations

The project situations described so far in this chapter are capable of being dealt with satisfactorily using established methods of varying degrees of complexity. All other project situations pose, or are likely to pose, original and difficult problems which are outside the normal range of programmed or professional organizations. Such projects require the third idealized type which is problem-solving organizations.

Organizations capable of sophisticated innovation are very new. The classic example remains the Manned Flight Centre of the National Aeronautics and Space Administration (NASA) in the USA. Such organizations rely on problem-orientated teams which bring together all the disciplines needed to tackle a specific task. The teams have a highly-organic structure which avoids the trappings of bureaucracy. Such organizations are the most appropriate for difficult construction projects and there is a growing number of examples of their use. Coordination between teams relies on liaison roles and sophisticated systems to create matrix organizations. That is, as we saw in Chapter 4, organizations which do not have a system of direct line management and do not provide unity of command. Instead they superimpose management structures to create a matrix of roles and responsibilities.

Managers abound in problem-solving organizations. Each team has its project manager and lateral coordination managers provide liaison between teams each responsible for self-contained sub-projects. Such organizations employ many professional specialists but they are not professional organizations. They do not pigeonhole clients' problems in order to apply standard programs. Instead they aim at innovation, they concentrate on the unknown and the puzzling and seek to solve problems. Such organizations are designed to cope with difficult, complex and dynamic environments. They are ideally suited to the production of sophisticated, innovative technical systems.

Problem-solving organizations are most likely to be appropriate on large projects of national or even international importance. The client's role is crucial to the success of such projects. As we described in Chapter 3, the environment is likely to provide substantial problems in large and important projects which tend to have major political implications. Successful outcomes depend on clients steering their projects past or through all obstacles. The client's role is made more demanding by the difficulty of defining precise objectives at the start of projects which can, in fact, be achieved. Objectives emerge as projects develop. Almost by definition any initial statement of objectives except in the most general of terms must be speculative if their achievement requires innovation. Therefore, clients will need to be closely involved with their projects at least in the initial stages. Their role at this time will be to accept proposed answers or to authorize further research or development work aimed at finding better ones. Unless they understand the issues under consideration, which means they must be fully involved in the decision-making processes, they will have no proper basis on which to make their strategic decisions.

It is common in problem-solving organizations for design teams to be drawn from large multi-discipline firms. An important exception is where the project has demanding aesthetic requirements. Great architects tend to work in small firms. In these circumstances it is sensible, as happened with Sydney Opera House, to supplement their aesthetic contribution with specialist designers drawn from a multi-discipline firm. In the example mentioned Ove Arup's multi-discipline firm worked alongside the architect Utzon. The management teams in problem-solving organizations are likely to be drawn from major construction, quantity surveying or project management firms. Strategic project teams in such organizations need to take account of all the major responsibility areas and so will include client, design and management representatives especially during intensely creative phases of their work. This helps to ensure that all the requirements and objectives and a wide range of answers are considered.

It is often valuable for such strategic project teams to be isolated for short intensive problem-solving periods. During these sessions it is not uncommon for members to be working up to 15 hours a day since the involvement has to be total in order to find good answers. Joint working needs to continue into the detailed stages so that, for example, the management teams should be involved in all key design teams to ensure that the total technical system is capable of being constructed within such time and cost constraints as the client has agreed.

In problem-solving organizations construction is almost always best provided by means of separate direct contracts with specialist contractors. Almost by definition the professional role and standard approach of the general contractor are inappropriate for the construction of designs which are likely to break new ground. The implicit assumption of a normal sequence and pattern of trades may well severely inhibit the project if a general contractor were employed to undertake the construction work. Also the flexibility of employing specialists direct allows construction firms with a relevant expertise to be involved in design when this is likely to provide benefits.

The management teams are likely to exercise strategic control through simple, flexible manually-based budgets and schedules. These will become more elaborate as projects develop and on large, complex projects may well justify computer use. The uncertain nature of the work means that detailed predictions of costs or times are not worthwhile. It is more important to model the overall structure of the end product and the project organization. This will provide the basis for realistic predictions of the order of costs and times. As firm decisions are made the models can usefully be refined by including more detailed data. However, by definition innovation is uncertain and as we saw in Chapter 1, again using Sydney Opera House as an example, an initial prediction of construction costs of $A 7 m related to a final cost of $A 102 m. By concentrating on the overall structure of the project and explicitly recognizing uncertainty, it is reasonable to expect that the initial prediction could have informed the clients that the costs were likely to be between $A 50 m and $A 100 m. It is, of course, a matter of conjecture whether such advice would have caused the client to decide to go ahead and build an opera house or not. However, an implicit assumption underlying much of this book is that clients of the construction industry have the right to make their decisions on the basis of the best possible information. When they decide to set up a problem-solving organization they are accepting large risks. It is best that they do so with their eyes open.

One way in which clients can minimize the risks implicit in innovation is to ensure that their project organizations include the appropriate coordination devices. The major formal coordination devices in problem-solving organizations are lateral coordination roles which will rely on much direct communication on a day-to-day basis. This is especially true early in the life of large sophisticated projects. At the outset no one can be quite sure of what needs to be done and so there is much discussion. Once the overall shape and nature of the technical system begins to be defined so more formal organizational arrangements can be established and more formal coordination devices become effective.

Formal coordination will largely emerge from the management team's responsibility for ensuring that the project can be constructed efficiently. The need for advice on the construction implications of alternative technical systems is essential especially in an unpredictable environment. The most effective way of ensuring that this is given due weight is for the management teams to be responsible for monitoring design decisions against agreed budgets and schedules. They should be produced in step with the scheme and detail designs as an essential part of the definition of the total project. On projects which tend to be repetitive it may well be worthwhile to use the goals emerging from budgets and schedules as the basis of formal information systems. On large, innovative and essentially complex projects the inherent uncertainty is likely to make it impossible to use any but the simplest of information systems.

Whatever form they take the budgets and schedules, together with drawings and specifications describing the selected technical systems, provide the basic information framework for the specialist construction firms. They will be invited to tender or negotiations will be based, on sets of project information which describe the programme and construction method constraints in addition to providing orthodox drawings, specifications and bills of quantities. The management team's responsibilities, therefore, include selecting the construction method strategy and coordinating the work of the separate contractors.

The organization in the most difficult of construction projects will need to be tough and dedicated to absorb the uncertainty of original designs and a complex, dynamic environment. Conflict is inevitable in problem-solving organizations as committed professionals search for better answers and it is part of the client's task to channel it towards productive ends. Answers emerge from the anxieties and frictions which, in more structured organizations, tend to be bottled up. Such constraining efforts in problem-solving organizations stifle creativity. So conflicting views must be encouraged, exposed and then resolved in the search for new answers.

An important characteristic of problem-solving organizations is that a matrix organization is likely to be formed with design responsibilities on one axis and management responsibilities on the other. As described earlier, these separate responsibilities are commonly allocated to separate firms. The commercial separation of these responsibilities serves to ensure that the client's interests remain paramount rather than the project being dominated by either design or management views. The responsibilities are merged in project teams drawn from the two organizations. In small projects a single team may well be able to undertake all the design and management work. In large projects many teams will be required. It may well be sensible to divide such projects into self-contained sub-projects. As we saw in Chapter 4, sub-project teams' work will be defined and coordinated by a strategic team concerned with the whole project. So we see that in the most difficult of projects all the coordination devices are likely to be brought into play.

In the case of large, sophisticated projects in difficult environments for inexperienced clients it is extremely difficult to achieve high levels of efficiency. A number of arrangements have been used in attempts at improving performance levels. These include appointing a project manager to play the client role and appointing a single design and construct firm to take total responsibility for the project. These arrangements are essentially a gamble on the part of a desperate client. In effect he has handed responsibility for his project to someone else and must just accept the outcome. He may be lucky and win a good project. Equally he may lose and be given a very unsatisfactory and expensive project. The arrangements described earlier provide the best hope for inexperienced clients on very difficult projects. The design firm's role is to decide what is to be built and to produce complete and fully documented descriptions of the technical systems. The management firm's role is to ensure that the project is finished within the agreed budget and programme. This involves responsibility for the total management function at all stages of the project. It includes advice on costs, time, construction and contracts; developing schedules and budgets; cost planning and cost control;

selecting construction method strategies; the identification of specialist work packages; organizing the production of project information and contracts; selecting specialist construction firms, inviting and evaluating tenders; managing the construction site; coordinating specialist contractors and certifying payments. The role requires many separate specialists and in practice, the management role has been played by firms based on general contracting, architecture, engineering and quantity surveying. In each case the firm has employed a much richer variety of skills and disciplines than its parent company. In many cases the construction management firm has rapidly outgrown its original parent company in size and turnover. Construction management has emerged over the past decade in the USA as the normal approach for large and difficult projects. This experience is already being repeated in Britain and many other parts of the world.

In many industries problem-solving organizations are seen as the organization structures of the future. They suit educated specialists who understand the need for a systems approach and see the world as an integrated whole rather than as a collection of separate parts. There is much construction which requires simpler, less demanding arrangements but for the technology of the late 20th century, problem-solving organizations are essential. They are demanding and rewarding. The need for individual responsibility within multi-discipline, multi-firm teams working within a total framework of design schedule, cost and legal coordination, is challenging. Success brings great personal satisfaction and often rich material rewards.

Choice of structural configurations

The full range of essentially different project situations has now been described and the general nature of the appropriate idealized project organization in each case has been identified. It must be admitted that the description is couched in general and largely unstructured terms. This reflects the current level of understanding. However, some tentative patterns can be discerned. These provide the best currently available basis for selecting project organizations.

First, the three idealized types of organization relate to standard construction, traditional construction and innovative construction. These relate to the extent to which established answers satisfy clients' requirements. *Table 5.1* lists the relationships.

TABLE 5.1. Construction options

	Established method of construction	Established overall form and layout
Standard construction	●	●
Traditional construction	●	
Innovative construction		

An important strategic decision is to determine whether a particular client's requirements can be met by an established method of construction and by an established overall form and layout. This decision determines whether the project will use standard, traditional or innovative construction and, in turn, determines whether the project organization should be based on the principles of programmed, professional or problem-solving organizations. The choice of an idealized type of project organization indicates the coordination devices most likely to be used. *Figure 5.8* illustrates these relationships. The diagram is somewhat speculative but

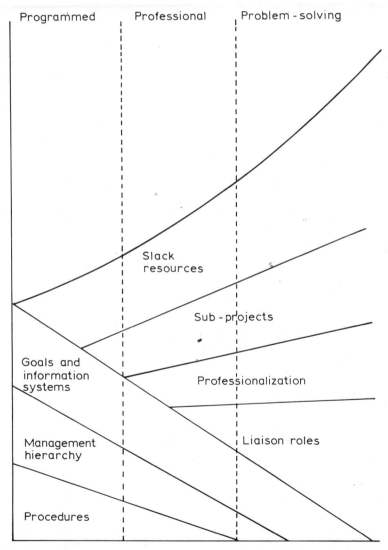

Figure 5.8 Relationship between coordination devices and idealized patterns of project organization

appears to be consistent with published management literature and, as indicated in the earlier sections of this chapter, is consistent with successful practice. It therefore probably provides the best available guide to the choice of coordinating devices. Very generally projects for which the devices listed are likely to be appropriate increase in difficulty from left to right. That is large, complex, fast, uncertain projects tend to be further to the right than small, repetitive, slow, certain ones. It is also tempting to envisage that the vertical axis represents increasing costs of coordination. This would be to claim too much since the data needed to make such a judgement simply do not exist.

The relationships illustrated in *Figure 5.8* provide the insights which enable us to break into the circular relationships of *Figure 5.3*. They indicate the type of pattern of coordination devices likely to be required. Beyond this we can describe the general nature of the calculations needed to refine the strategic decisions and so make specific and detailed choices when the necessary data become available in the future.

We saw in Chapter 4 that coordination devices modify teams, roles or the relationship between teams. Therefore, each device modifies some of the terms in Equations (3.1), (3.2), (3.3) and (3.4) in Chapter 3 (p.53). That is, they may add more roles or more teams or alter the performance data. Therefore, one approach is to make a series of attempts to find better answers by proposing different combinations of coordination devices, remodelling the project and calculating the new results. Given the general guidance of *Figure 5.8* this is likely to identify reasonably satisfactory project organizations. To go beyond this essentially controlled pragmatic approach depends on using more powerful models than those described earlier. To illustrate what is required, Equation (3.4) would need to be modified as follows:

$$C_c = C_e + \sum_{i=1}^{n} K_i - \sum_{i=1}^{n} C_e f_i \qquad (5.1)$$

where C_c = costs of coordinated projects, K_i = costs of coordination device i, f_i = factor which relates coordination device i to costs of projects without coordination, i.e. relates K_i to C_e.

The choice of project organizations requires the value of C_c to be minimized. It requires much research and development work before such calculations are possible in practice. For the near and middle future *Figure 5.8* and the generalized relationships it illustrates will provide the basis for strategic decisions about construction project organizations.

At later stages the key requirement in projects is for consistency. That is consistency between detailed decisions and the agreed strategy. It is, for example, easy to spoil a good decision to use a programmed organization by introducing alterations to the standard answers. Similarly if professional organizations begin to search for new answers they are likely to create major uncertainty which they are not equipped to deal with. Equally attempts to force a problem-solving organization to accept established answers is likely to be resented and lead to poor performance. It is only by selecting an appropriate strategy and applying it consistently that construction projects can be carried out efficiently and to high standards.

Summary

Current understanding does not allow best project organizations to be calculated. It is possible, however, to identify consistent links between types of project and three idealized patterns of project organizations. These are programmed organizations which relate to standard construction; professional organizations which relate to traditional construction; and problem-solving organizations which relate to innovative construction.

References

1. MINTZBERG, H., *The Structuring of Organizations,* Prentice-Hall (1979)
2. The sponsors of the Coordinating Committee for Project information are the Association of Consulting Engineers, the Building Employers Confederation, the Royal Institute of British Architects and the Royal Institution of Chartered Surveyors.

Chapter 6

Communication and information

In the five preceding chapters we have described a set of concepts and the relationships between them which, taken together, are intended to help us think about and understand construction project management. To go beyond this we must delve deeper to identify more fundamental concepts. The next three chapters are devoted to this next level of analysis. The first two deal with the basic interactions within and between teams which project managers use – communications and transactions. Then, in Chapter 8, we will consider the client's role. We give this emphasis because, as we have already seen particularly in Chapter 4, the client's role is crucial to the success of construction projects.

The earlier chapters provide many examples of the importance of communications and of information which is the subject of the first of the interactions within and between teams.

One such example is Pete James' reliance on communications to ensure that his team decided to work on the refurbishment project rather than on Red McGregor's factory site. Although now that the plans for the Roman Leisure Centre have been made public, Pete rather wishes they had chosen the factory site. They would probably then be involved with the new project which appears to provide the kind of work which Pete and his team enjoy. He has communicated his interest in the work to Red McGregor. Most of the communications which Pete initiates are verbal. Probably most of the communications he receives are also verbal. However, one of the skills which helps him to retain the leadership of his team is an ability to read and understand drawings.

We have seen a number of examples of the importance of drawings as a means of communicating information. The developer and architect for the Roman Leisure Centre used six outline drawings to help transfer a set of ideas in the architect's head to the developer's head and subsequently to Red McGregor's head.

Drawings, specifications, bills of quantities, conditions of engagement, forms of contract, formal procedures, schedules, variation orders and other documents make up the total set of formal project information. It relies on words, numbers and symbols to record information. It is recorded in these documents so that it can be communicated from the head of the author or draftsman to someone else's head. It is, of course, possible to keep records for one's own use but these are rarely of interest in construction project management.

Information may be stored and subsequently communicated verbally, on paper or, as is becoming increasingly common, electronically with the aid of computers. In the latter case it can then be transferred automatically on to paper or a video screen for communications with humans. Three-dimensional physical models are another transfer medium frequently used in construction. They are particularly useful in providing realistic representations of the end products of the industry.

Construction projects involve a rich variety of forms of communication but they have a single purpose which is to transfer meaning. This may be to transfer meaning between teams or within teams or between the project and its environment. The purpose of the communication may be to inform, to motivate or to instruct but it achieves all these by transferring meaning.

Meaning

It is worth considering what we should understand when we say that words, numbers or symbols have meaning. The ensuing answer to that question draws freely on Kuhn's[1] use of systems theory to unravel the logic of organizations from fundamental principles.

We all use concepts, that is images stored in our brains. How did these images get there? Our senses provide information to our brains. The human brain seems to be arranged in such a way that it searches for patterns amongst this information. Patterns which recur are stored. We learn that patterns of interest to groups of humans are given names. That is a word which means the particular pattern.

A young child will be told that a particular object is called a door. Initially he may well associate the word door with one specific example, perhaps the door of his bedroom. Just as the word mummy applies to one person, the child not unreasonably expects door to refer to one object. Subsequently he learns that several objects are called door. Some are very similar to his bedroom door but the glazed front entrance door and the metal up-and-over garage door are very different. So gradually the word door comes to acquire a complex meaning in the child's brain. The learning of images or concepts and the words which stand for them is reinforced by feedback. Thus, when the child points at a window and calls it door he learns that he is now dealing with a different concept. When he first learns the word he will try it out on every door he sees. The feedback he gets is a sense of pleasure aroused by his parents' approval. He learns that a window is not a door from the sense of pain aroused by his parents disapproval.

In later life the adult still learns with the aid of feedback. When we learn a new word we tend to try it out at the first opportunity, in which if we have misunderstood its meaning we will not be embarrassed. If it proves to be useful we remember it and use it regularly. However, if an opportunity to use it in friendly circumstances fails to arise in the few days following our initial encounter with the word and its meaning we are likely to forget.

Returning now to the child. As he learns the meaning of words he also learns how to combine their images. Thus, he will be able to imagine a red door even if he has never seen one. He does this because he knows the meaning of the words red and door and can relate them to each other to build a new image. With the example used, the image in his brain is likely to match reasonably closely with the image intended by anyone saying 'red door' to the child. However, if the same person said 'trap door' the child might well imagine something quite different from a door in a floor or ceiling. The child might well imagine a door which slammed shut as soon as anyone attempted to walk through it rather like the trap he has seen his mother use to catch mice. Indeed he may well be reluctant to walk though doors once this image has been put into his head. Until he learns better the child will have a different meaning for the words trap door from that understood by most English speaking people.

One of the tasks of construction project organizations is to ensure that teams acquire correct meanings with the minimum of effort. So if a project includes a trap door it is helpful if the teams whose roles impinge on that particular element know that it is intended to provide access rather than to trap people.

The human brain appears not to store all the information it receives but instead to relate it to the images already stored. We look for similarities. Thus, our image of door may be conjured up by a door-shaped hole in a wall, by a shadow or a noise which sounds like a door being slammed shut. That is we use the images already in our brains to classify new information. Information entering our brains may reinforce what we already know about doors or it may add something new. It is very satisfying when information does add to our knowledge. This seems to depend on the information largely falling within a recognizable pattern which calls up remembered images but also provides a slight deviation from our current understanding. A door with an arched top, when we have previously seen only rectangular doors, is interesting. It modifies our understanding of the meaning of the word door. However, when the information fails to arouse any images, it is meaningless and we are unlikely to learn anything new. However, if the meaningless information recurs we may begin to detect patterns and build up new images which are remembered and, therefore, available for future reference. The massive print-outs provided by many of the early computer-based information systems often appeared to raise just these kinds of problem. However, now that more is understood about the different capabilities of people and computers, much more attention is given to providing computer-produced information which is readily understandable by humans. The term 'user-friendly' has been coined to describe this development.

Whether information is provided by people or computers, communications which use images or concepts which are already known to the parties involved, are very much more efficient than those which require new concepts to be learnt. It is worth remembering that we cannot learn directly what concept any particular word, number or symbol produces in another person's mind. We can, however, check that it produces behaviour which is consistent with our own meaning. We could check that another person understood the concept of trap door by inviting them to describe a trap door, to point to one or to draw one. Alternatively, we could merely observe their behaviour and check that it is consistent with our expectations. If we ask a builder to construct a trap door into the roof space in our home and the first time it is used it crashes down on our head we may be right to wonder whether he, like the child, has misunderstood.

It is important in communications to check that the intended meaning is being received. This is why it is sensible in architect's drawings, for example, to include somewhat more information than is strictly necessary for any particular role. Thus, a drawing of a roof intended for a carpenter may show the roof covering and gutter details since this further information may well make it easier to understand exactly how the roof timbers are required to be constructed.

In building our images or concepts we start with direct experience of the real world. Thus, the child's image of door is initially based directly on the one in his own bedroom. Gradually and with more experience we construct increasingly abstract concepts. A child will learn about doors, bricks and books and from these images will recognize the idea of a rectangle. Later the concept of shape will be learnt from experience with rectangles, squares, circles and triangles. Later still the increasingly abstract concepts of lines, angles, circumference, radius and the other fundamental ideas of geometry may be understood.

The process of abstraction seems to depend on us selectively forgetting much of the detail of the information we receive about the real world. The idea of rectangular would be extremely clumsy if it called up all the examples of doors, bricks, books and other rectangular objects which we had ever experienced. We remember common recurring patterns which are useful to us. In looking at a door we abstract the concepts red and rectangular because these patterns are common and we find in dealing with other people that most of them behave as though they share our meaning. Therefore, we learn these concepts and ignore the many other images which the door might have conjured up in our minds.

In combining information into concepts in this way the mind builds a rich variety of relationships. Thus, seeing a red door may, in certain circumstances, remind us of bricks or books which are rectangular or at a different time or in a different place, of an apple or the lips of a beautiful woman because they are red. It is likely that the rich, freely connected set of relationships inside each human brain is unique. Culture imposes an overall pattern which ensures considerable similarities in many of the relationships understood by the people in one nation, one race, one industry, one firm or one construction project. It does not and cannot produce completely identical knowledge. Thus, we cannot be sure what reaction particular information will produce in any individual. It may call up remembered pleasures or frustrations. The reaction depends on the concepts brought to the surface of conscious thought in the individual's mind. Shared culture ensures that most of the time reactions are more or less what we would expect but without careful attention communications can prove to be a fuzzy and imprecise tool for project managers.

The rich and wide-ranging relationships which grow in human brains provide the basis for inspired problem solving and creativity. Indeed Humphrey[2] suggests that our concepts of beauty are based on the mind's habit of searching for consistency and its basic urge to classify together with its reaction to minor discrepancies which signal something new and interesting and so arouse pleasure. Thus, great architecture builds consistent rhythms but also introduces variations. No doubt architects rely also on cultural symbols to evoke appropriate reactions but the mere repetition of established symbols does not produce great architecture. Neither does a complete departure from these symbols, we need both the familiar and the surprising for beauty, learning and good communications. This combination of requirements appears to hold good in the mind's approach to problem solving. Innovations usually turn out to be a variation on an old answer or a new synthesis of old ideas. These problem-solving characteristics of the human mind are important in the early strategic stages of construction projects. The organization especially if it is a problem-solving one must allow for free-ranging thought.

However, in general and certainly to a large extent during the tactical stages, project organizations seek to ensure that the response to given information is limited to a narrow range of predictable behaviour. It is worth remembering that this, to some extent, goes against the grain of the mind's normal way of working. This is of course why at least some people find they are stifled in organizations. It is, however, hard to see how large purposes can be achieved without many being subject to an overall plan conceived by a few. Thus, we must continue within project organizations to use communications to help coordinate the work of many teams. In doing so it is helpful to understand that on occasions the response may be different from what we expect without this necessarily being due to irrational behaviour.

To summarize the points we have described thus far, we can see that communications are attempts to transfer combinations of concepts from one mind to another using signs which, in project organizations, are likely to take the form of words, numbers or symbols.

Information

We will now consider how much information must be provided to achieve a given communication. Starting from fundamental principles we can envisage a building project which includes two types of window. The two types are indicated on the architect's drawings by means of the symbols (a) and (b) in *Figure 6.1.* Assuming that the windows are closely stacked on-site so that only the ends can be inspected and the site manager wishes to determine how many of each type are in the stack, he merely has to determine whether each one has a transom in the end panel. In other words he can correctly identify any window from one piece of information. However, if the project also includes types (c) and (d) he will need two pieces of information. That is, he now needs to know whether there is a transom in each end panel. If the project also includes types (e), (f), (g) and (h), he will also need to know whether each window has one or two mullions. The three pieces of information are given in *Figure 6.1* in the

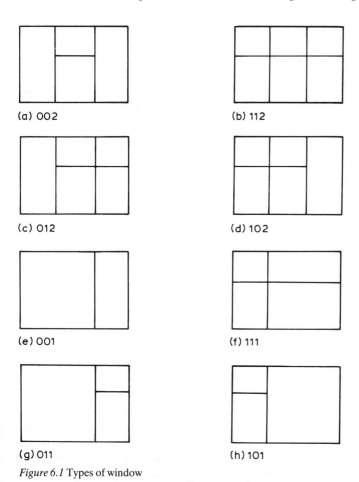

(a) 002

(b) 112

(c) 012

(d) 102

(e) 001

(f) 111

(g) 011

(h) 101

Figure 6.1 Types of window

sequence of transom in the left panel, transom in the right panel and number of mullions. These three pieces of information allow us to distinguish between eight different windows. We have arranged the windows so that each piece of information has one of only two possible values. Therefore, the number of different cases we can identify is $2^3 = 8$. The eight cases are illustrated in *Figure 6.1*. Each piece of information which allows us to distinguish between two equally probable states is usually called a 'bit'.

The site manager is able to determine how many of each type of window are in the stack because he knows the full range of windows being used on his project. That is he has learnt which patterns exist. This step is concept learning. Next he needs to identify each pattern from the sets of three bits of information which he gathers by inspecting the top and sides of each window. This step is perception. It is the calling-up of images already stored in response to information entering our brains. As we have seen, small amounts of information may call up rich sets of concepts. We can illustrate this by pursuing our example of the site manager. Once he has determined which type of window he is dealing with from the three bits of information, he is likely to be able to conjure up a mental picture of the complete window. He may also know how many panes of glass of various sizes, the types of ironmongery and the quantity of paint the particular window will require. He may know its price and have a detailed knowledge of its manufacture, the construction details surrounding it on his project and its maintenance requirements. The same three pieces of information may be meaningless to the driver of the excavating machine passing the site manager as he prepares his schedule of the windows in the stack. The driver will recognize them as windows but they may conjure up images of his own home, his honeymoon hotel or a sports car he saw in a showroom window on his way to work. He has not learnt the set of concepts required to interpret the three bits of information and he has virtually no knowledge of the particular windows used on the project. To equip the driver with the same knowledge as the site manager has about the windows would require a great deal of time and a mass of information.

Communication

The cases of the site manager and excavator driver illustrate an important characteristic of communications. This is that we cannot measure the amount of meaning provided by a given amount of information. This is because the meaning is a function of the state of the mind of the recipient at the instant he receives the information. To a large extent this is determined by the knowledge already stored there but it depends on other factors as well.

Before we consider the other factors which help determine the outcome of communications it is worth emphasizing that a decision to learn new concepts has an essentially practical basis. Pete James faced with several different types of brickwork on a project tends to choose and then cause his team to learn a different name for each. Thus, 'one brick wall in Ibstock handmade old pewter facing bricks in cement-lime mortar coloured yellow in Fletton bond' becomes for Pete and his team 'cladding'. Now one word replaces nineteen. There is an initial effort involved in selecting an appropriate name and learning its meaning. However, once learnt it allows more efficient communications within the team and indeed with the rest of the project because Pete insists on using his terminology in all his discussions. There is therefore a judgement, which is probably subjective, that the cost of learning the concept 'cladding' is justified by the benefit of increased efficiency in future communications.

Returning now to the factors which help determine the outcome of communications, we noted in Chapter 1 that all communications require the five steps of source, coding, medium, detection and decoding. Problems in any one of these steps may cause communications to fail. To understand the kinds of problem which may arise we must remember that communications within project organizations have purposes. Using the three basic interactions between controlled systems as a guide the purposes may be to inform, motivate, instruct or, more usually, some combination of these. These various and often complex purposes may lead the person sending a message to seek to disguise or hide its true meaning. This feature of human nature seems to be widely understood. Certainly it is common in conversation to look beyond the words actually spoken in an attempt to read the thoughts of other people. In written messages we try to 'read between the lines'. The ever-present possibility that a person sending a message may be disguising its meaning ensures that communications are typically beset with problems.

Source

We will now consider the main causes of defective communications in order to identify steps likely to ensure that construction project managers communicate efficiently and effectively. Problems arise at the source of communications if the sender is vague about the concept he wishes to send. This may be because he does not understand them well or often it is because he wishes to disguise his real intentions as a negotiating ploy. It is now clear that Utzon's first sketches of Sydney Opera House, which looks remarkably like the sails of yachts heeling over in the wind, were vague. Certainly they failed to communicate sufficient information to enable the design competition jury to determine whether the building could be constructed as designed or if so at what costs and in what time. On the other hand, Utzon's vague sketches served his intended purpose of winning the competition. Vague drawings are not confined to the early sketches of projects. A detailed examination of working drawings[3] produced many examples of vague information. *Figure 6.2* provides an example where,

Architect's drawing

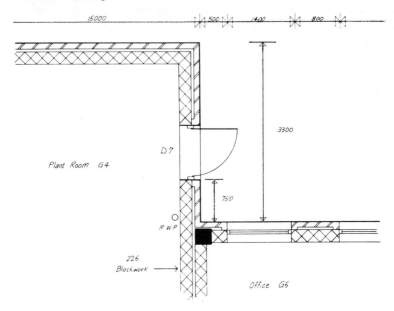

Services drawing

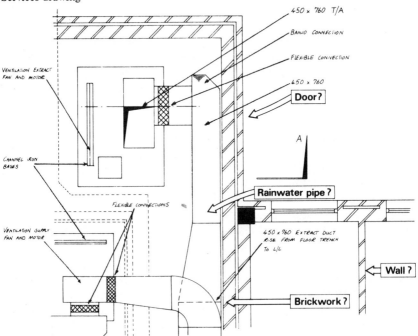

Figure 6.2 Working drawings. Examples of conflict between architect's and services drawings. (a) The trunking conflicts with the position of the door. (b) The trunking conflicts with the rainwater pipe. (c) Is the inner skin of the wall brickwork or blockwork? (d) Which office layout is correct?

presumably, the services engineer has not understood the significance of the different symbols for brickwork and blockwork, nor that for the rainwater pipe. Alternatively it may be that the architect was vague about the detailed functioning of the plant room.

Coding

These examples necessarily carry us on to the second essential step in communications. This is coding concepts into a medium. In the case of the examples in *Figure 6.2*, the concepts of brickwork, blockwork, rainwater pipes and other elements are coded into graphic symbols on working drawings. A problem which often arises with coding and with decoding is ambiguity in the meaning of a particular word, number or symbol. The numbers and letters '450 × 760 T/A' at the top right corner of the services drawing in *Figure 6.2* may well not convey a clear and accurate meaning to some recipients of the information. Words may be ambiguous. The architect's drawing in *Figure 6.2* refers to a 'plant room'. Given the accompanying services drawing we can be sure that plant means ventilation equipment, but without the second drawing some recipients may have envisaged a room full of potted palms and rubber plants. Similarly the words 'banjo connection' on the services drawing depend heavily on the context.

Medium

The next necessary step in communications is to transfer the medium from the sender to the receiver. A further study of working drawings in use[4] considered how site staff set about finding the drawings relevant to a piece of work they have in mind. The study found that searches invariably start from the general arrangement or location drawings showing the area in which the piece of work occurs. The drawing may give all the information required but usually more drawings are needed. Ideally the first drawing will contain a reference to the other relevant drawings. However, almost without exception, there are drawings which are not referred to in this way. Knowing this the user having followed all available references but still needing more information, will continue to look for relevant drawings. He may be helped by a clue which indicates the existence of another drawing. His experience of drawings may suggest that more information is likely to exist in one particular place within the set of drawings. Often, however, there is nothing to lead a user to expect that another useful drawing exists. In all these cases users have little choice but to apply their knowledge of drawing arrangement and do some guessing. It is not surprising that the researchers made recommendations on the arrangement and content of working drawings which are essentially concerned to ensure that they reach the intended recipients. Their advice was based on the best practice observed during their research.

In summary, the researchers recommended that sets of working drawings should have a systematic structure comprising separate groups of location, assembly and component drawings. Within each of these groups individual sheets should be further classified as necessary on the basis of the elements of the building which they describe. Location drawings should be contained on sheets which are large enough to minimize fragmentation of overall plans and elevations. These drawings have two main purposes: first to provide basic overall dimensions and levels, and secondly to provide a basis for references to assembly or component drawings. The location drawings should incorporate references which lead the user of drawings directly to individual sheets in the majority of his searches. However, the researchers recognized that it is unrealistic to expect referencing to meet all search requirements. Therefore, to aid search where no reference is provided, each sheet should have a title which is short and explicit. This is difficult to achieve unless the subject and contents of the sheet are selected with titling in mind. Detailed views should include information which fixes the position of each view. Grids and controlling lines representing key reference planes, for example finished floor level, are recommended for this purpose. For any set of drawings to be used effectively a brief guide to the arrangement of the set is important.

In the researchers' view, if their recommendations are followed, not only will there be an improvement in the content of working drawings but the information they contain is much more likely to reach the intended recipients.

Detection

Even when the medium is prepared with great care other problems may prevent it being transferred to the receiver. Mail may be delayed or the telephone out of order. Even in direct face-to-face discussions listeners may be distracted and simply not hear something said to them. This leads on to the fourth step in communications which is the receiver detecting the words, numbers or symbols. A particular problem in this step is that they may be obscured in some way. A structural engineering drawing on gridded paper containing design grid lines, dimension lines, lines showing the edges of reinforced concrete elements and lines representing reinforcement all densely interwoven with no variety of line thickness, may be extremely difficult to read especially if it is folded and dirty. Things which are random and take the same general form as the message are generally called 'noise'. Thus, a conversation in a crowded room, a telephone conversation using a defective instrument or reading a badly copied document may all suffer from noise. This may well prevent the recipient from detecting the whole message.

Decoding

The final necessary step in communications is for the receiver to decode the message. This step, like the others, may be subject to problems which prevent communications being successful. A simple and common problem is that the receiver is too busy to read a document which could have provided vital information. Assuming that he does attempt to decode the message he may have less knowledge than the sender assumed he had. Serious examples of this type of failure surround attempts to build better houses in Britain over the past 40 years. The Goverment sent a number of messages to the building industry which in essence asked for houses to be warm and comfortable. The industry responses by reducing ventilation and adding insulation to external walls, roofs and floors. The results, to say the least, have been unfortunate. The 8 to 101 of moisture produced by a typical family each day and which previously had escaped up the flues of open fireplaces, through cracks in suspended ground floors and round doors and windows now had nowhere to go except to form condensation on the internal surfaces of the external envelope. The result is often damp, unhealthy and virtually uninhabitable buildings.

That is not the full extent of the problems because the thermal insulation in walls and roofs has increased the temperature range to which the outer faces of buildings are subjected. The results include cracked bricks, spalling concrete, loose joints, flaking roof tiles and leaking roofs. The designers did not have the knowledge needed to avoid these problems, while the Government, which sent the original messages, presumably expected that architects and builders would make houses warmer and more comfortable in ways which would not render many of them uninhabitable and destroy their fabric. It is safe to say that the Government's communications aimed at providing homes fit for heroes failed. They failed because the recipients, the house-building industry in total, had less knowledge than the sender assumed.

A further problem which can influence decoding is that the receiver misunderstands the context of the message. This can happen in a meeting, especially one which is run badly, where several subjects are under consideration at the same time. An individual comment about subject A may be interpreted as referring to subject B and result in a complete misinterpretation of the speaker's views. In much the same way a builder asked by a manufacturing firm to provide a handrail from drawings of a staircase which he takes to be in a factory is likely to provide an unsuitable product if the staircase in fact leads to the board room and the managing director's suite of offices. The builder has misunderstood the context and so the communication fails.

Effective communications

We have considered a rich variety of ways in which communications can fail in order to understand how construction project managers may avoid, or at least minimize, such failures.

The first and most obvious way of ensuring good communications is to appoint teams who understand and are experienced in the role they are to occupy in the project. This is likely to ensure that they put a correct interpretation on the information they receive but also may well mean they know what information is needed. Then, if some necessary communications fail to arrive, they are likely to search for them rather than take action on the basis of inadequate information. Experience also tends to create an instinct for spotting mistakes, an ability to recognize what is important and so double checking it, and, in general, an understanding of what feels right. When teams have worked together previously, communications can become very efficient and at times appear almost telepathic. Experience of working together affects communications largely because it is easier for each party to judge how much credibility to attach to any given message.

Red McGregor knows that Pete is reliable. His statements about quality and time are very likely to be accurate. Red knows this because in the past, Pete's team has done what it has said it would do. On the other hand, Red knows from his previous experience that Tim Smithson is less reliable. He is not consciously dishonest but rather too optimistic about his team's performance. So, faced with identical messages from the two bricklaying team leaders, Red would receive different meanings. The different interpretations are based on, and justified by, his experience of working with Pete and Tim in the past. When he is dealing with a team with whom he has not worked before, Red takes more care over communications. He tends to repeat all his messages in somewhat different ways and to discuss them with the team leader. He also gets direct feedback on their actions at the first opportunity. While he is inspecting their work, he will discuss it with the team leader to ensure that he really understands what actions he is required to take.

Redundancy

The second way of ensuring good communications is to use the first device which Red McGregor uses with new teams. That is to provide redundancy. We all tend to do this almost instinctively. For example, it is common in arranging important meetings to give both the day of the week and also the date. It is surprising how often this simple precaution prevents a mistake from being effected. Redundancy works by providing additional clues to the intended meaning. It seems to be a fundamental characteristic of successful controlled systems. It is normal to provide a back-up electricity generator in buildings and processing plants where a failure of the main supply would otherwise be disastrous. An operating theatre has most of its systems duplicated and even triplicated when it is expected that it will be used for long and difficult surgery. Even more fundamental is that our own survival is more assured because of nature's use of redundancy. At the level of reproduction there are thousands of sperm for each egg to be fertilized and scores of eggs for each child that is to survive. Human organizations also depend on redundancy in communications for their survival. We tend to accept information which comes from several sources much more readily than that emanating from one.

Figure 6.2 illustrates nicely the benefits and problems of providing redundancy in communications. The site manager would have been helped by having the two drawings if they had been consistent. He would then have been sure of the need to construct a door, a rainwater pipe, a partition wall between the two windows and the inner skin of the cavity wall in blockwork. As it is a probably inadvertent, unplanned provision of redundancy has created a problem. In doing so the benefit of redundancy is also demonstrated. Armed with the architect's drawing, the site manager may well have constructed the door and the rainwater pipe only to discover later that they were no longer required. Given both drawings he is led to seek further information by having the discrepancies resolved.

It remains a mystery as to how we can find the optimum balance between economy and redundancy. Since construction projects are likely to require design teams, for example, to provide information for construction teams who are not yet appointed, it seems best to risk providing too much redundancy. In practice, this means that when information is repeated in separate documents there seem to be advantages in providing strong clues as to the intended meaning. It is common for construction work to be described on drawings and in either specifications or bills of quantities. Some approaches use all three documents. There seems merit in deciding which types of information are best conveyed by each document. Thus, drawings are efficient at providing descriptions of shapes and relative locations. Specifications are efficient at describing the quality of the end product and the materials, components and workmanship which make it up. Bills of quantities are efficient at describing the cost significant characteristics of the required materials, components and work and the contractual framework within which they are to be provided. The separation of information about individual elements caused by using these three conventions is best mitigated by coordinating the separate documents. This can be achieved by adopting the same overall arrangement and sequence in all the documents and by providing clear cross references between separate pieces of information which relate to the same elements.

We might imagine a project which includes three different types of brickwork which are fully described in the specification. They can be given a coded reference which ensures that information about them comes in the same sequence and the same position relative to information about other elements in all documents. They can further be given a brief name which describes their important characteristics. In the case envisaged we might use 'red facing brickwork', 'blue facing brickwork' and 'common brickwork' to identify the three types. The codes and names could be linked to the full descriptions in the specification and both used whenever the brickwork elements are referred to in other documents. This is broadly the approach being adopted by the UK Coordinating Committee for Project Information[5].

Structure

In addition to using controlled redundancy in communications the proposed UK approach also relies on a classification scheme to structure project information. This arranges the information in a manner which is intended to help each team involved in a specific project find all which relates to their responsibilities. The classification scheme uses elements of the end product to coordinate design work. It uses work sections, that is the work of separate trades or specialist contractors, to coordinate construction work. In addition, the proposals rely on ad hoc location references identifying significant areas, blocks, floor levels or other similar major divisions of the project which, particularly in the construction stages, are likely to generate separate roles. The implicit aim of the Coordinating Committee for Project Information is to produce standard conventions which will aid communications within professional project organizations. It is this implicit assumption of professionalization which justifies, and indeed makes possible, the use of a standard classification scheme to identify the information relating to separate roles. Programmed organizations could use a more direct approach to project information. On the other hand, problem-solving organizations are likely to adopt many innovative answers which fall outside any standard classification scheme.

However, the principle of structuring project information so that it matches the responsibilities of the separate teams is of general value and is the third way of ensuring good communications. It is extremely helpful for each team to be able to identify a package of information and know that it contains all the formal information which they need to know about the project in hand. It is this benefit which gives rise to the work package concept in construction management. This is the idea that project information should be structured around the organization of the construction work. Indeed the idea goes rather deeper than this and in essence work packages are a synthesis of roles and teams. This is given effect by deliberately designing the end product so as to provide clearly-defined roles which, as far as possible, can be undertaken independently. This same pattern is reflected in the project information and in the organization since a separate team is appointed to take responsibility for each role.

Achieving all this requires early decisions on the way the work is to be divided amongst firms and teams. Having identified separate areas of responsibility both the acting system and the information system are structured to reflect them. Ideally all strategic documents are arranged to match the same pattern. Thus, each team has its own clearly identified budget and schedule which forms one part of the overall project budget and schedule. *Figure 1.6* indicates the general form of such a document at an early strategic stage of a building project. Each of the strategic work packages illustrated is likely to be further divided into the work of separate construction teams as the project proceeds. As we described in Chapter 4, this is likely to be most effective if the resulting budgets and schedules are agreed with the teams who will have the responsibility of achieving them rather than being imposed from above.

Work packages appear to have advantages in coordinating construction work beyond the obvious simplicity of the search pattern for individual teams. Given a work package approach, strategic work tends to concentrate on defining the boundaries of each team's work rather than being concerned with its internal detail[6]. This has two benefits. First it tends to insulate teams from interruptions by others working on the same project. This is so because if designers simply allow the boundaries between the work of construction teams to occur without explicit consideration it is just as likely that a complex and closely interwoven pattern of work will result as it is that a simple and efficient one will be produced. Also, by giving explicit consideration to the boundaries throughout the project, it is much more likely that there will be a conscious and successful effort to define clearly each team's work. The second benefit is that designing and controlling the boundaries between work packages allows the work inside each work package to be dealt with in the most efficient way. Some work packages will need to be fully designed before construction teams can be involved. In other cases there are benefits in joint work by the design and construction teams and in others the detail design is best left to experienced craftsmen or specialists. All these approaches can be combined within a framework of well-defined work packages. It is difficult to achieve the same efficiency unless the boundaries are identified early in the project and properly designed. It is interesting to observe that there is a similar concentration on the boundaries between the work of separate teams by American construction managers and West German architects using the traditional separate trades approach. Both of these approaches appear to result in high productivity on site. This is in marked contrast to architects in the UK who, in the main, use the general contractor-based approach. Also, as is clear from the research described earlier[4], most UK architects structure their working drawings in design elements and, with few exceptions, do not consider the pattern of construction likely to result. They are often criticized for producing designs which are difficult to build[7]. It is difficult not to connect these different approaches and results and see them as cause and effect. The reason given for not using work packages in the UK general contractor approach is that different contractors are likely to adopt different methods of construction. Therefore, no one pattern of project information is likely to suit all those invited to bid for the construction work. This may be true in the absence of any agreed and widely used structure. It is anticipated that the Coordinating Committee for Project Information's proposals will provide a consistent work-based structure. It is further hoped that it will be sufficiently widely used to justify architects in the UK considering buildability and choosing to rely on the experience and knowledge of construction teams as a matter of course. Be that as it may, there is ample evidence for the principle that communications matched to project organizations are likely to be more effective than those structured in some other way.

Face-to-face communications

The fourth way in which communications can be made more effective is to talk direct, face-to-face. This is particularly true in negotiations where body-language messages may either confirm or modify verbal statements. Thus, the participants are likely to gain a more accurate picture of others' values and priorities than if they were to conduct the same negotiations through, for example, a series of written messages. Indeed, the style of communications is always important. Well-presented printed information is likely to have more effect than badly typed, misspelt, ungrammatical messages on poor quality paper. Style is perhaps even more important in face-to-face communications. Generally superiors need to convey a clear sense of direction by emphasizing objectives and agreed goals. A ruthless concentration on projects' objectives helps ensure that they are achieved. Ideas which do not contribute to this or lead in other directions should be quickly and quietly killed off. Concentration is one of the keys to success in construction project management. One of the important ways in which this can be achieved is to regularly remind teams of the importance of the project and of their contribution. It is useful to remember particularly in face-to-face communications that people generally are motivated more by a wish to avoid pain than by the possibility of pleasure. This leads most people to try to be agreeable in conversation.

Managers should accept this normal pattern and so tend to praise and encourage teams working on their projects. One advantage of so doing arises when a team is failing and has to be criticized. Since the manager's rebuke stands out from his other messages it is likely to be effective and to be taken seriously. An important principle is that teams breaking the rules should face sharp, clear criticism. Otherwise rules become devalued and all will think they can be broken with impunity. In much the same way it is important that grievances are taken seriously and, if at all possible, dealt with quickly. This not only serves to prevent the grievance from festering and growing but rapid attention to their problems helps teams to know that their work is valued. Indeed, one of the advantages of regular face-to-face discussions at the workplace of each team is that managers have an opportunity to anticipate problems and so prevent them.

These same principles have also been identified by Reavens[8]. He expresses them in somewhat different terms but he has no doubt that his lifetime of action research provides ample evidence for the following propositions. First, the prime motivator to the enthusiastic and successful completion of work is that what is required to be done is intelligible to the team doing it. Secondly, the prime influence in making work intelligible is the readiness of managers to listen to their subordinates and to discuss with them ways in which work can be more successfully carried out. Also Reavens is clear that team leaders pass on to their teams the treatment they perceive themselves to receive from their superiors. Therefore, the third prime influence and probably the most important condition for success amongst managers and professionals is that they shall understand how and by whom their goals are set. Given all these aids to intelligibility and improvements in communications the successful completion of work also depends on the majority of those involved with a project accepting the value system of those in command.

Reavens himself observed that these propositions are implicit in the quality circles which appear to be an important factor in the astonishing growth of the Japanese manufacturing industry. Indeed there is overwhelming evidence that the style and the content of communications are a key factor in motivating people and, therefore, the principles described in this chapter are crucial to the success of construction projects.

Feedback

The preceding description of communications is, in the main, concerned with the forward flow of information directly concerned with identifying and defining the roles required to complete projects and with motivating teams to carry out the work. There is another important flow of information which is essential in construction project management. It is 'feedback'. We saw in Chapter 1 that feedback is essential for the survival of controlled systems. This applies to construction projects and to the teams within them just as much as to any other type of controlled system.

Feedback is information about systems' actions on their environments. It is an essential part of control. The control sub-system must be able to detect the state of relevant variables in the operating sub-system. Specifically it needs to be able to determine whether the variables are within, above or below some specified range. The control sub-system needs to have some preference about the state of these variables. Normally it wishes to maintain them within the specified range. Thirdly the control sub-system must be able to take action which will move the system towards the preferred state if that does not already prevail.

Feedback does not raise new fundamental principles in communications or information, but it does pose some particular problems in practice within construction projects. We have seen in earlier chapters that feedback exists at all levels in construction.

Pete James receives direct feedback about the condition of the mortar he is using from the reaction it produces as he pushes each brick into place. This does not involve communication. The information about the mortar arrives in the bricklayer's head by means of perception. However, communication comes into play if Pete, on discovering that the mortar he is using is unsuitable, turns to Tony Bronoski, his labourer, and says 'this mortar is too wet'. Tony now has feedback on his own performance. Tony's preference is that the bricklayers in the team are happy with the mortar he makes and so he adds less water to the next batch. Much of the feedback which Pete uses to manage his team is provided by perception rather than communication. He will make sure that the next batch of mortar is suitable by checking it himself. Pete is aware also of Doug and Mike's progress because several times a day he looks at their work. He does this almost instinctively and totally naturally. He often combines this direct feedback with communications especially if they are making good progress or have a particular problem. In the first case Pete will seek to encourage by praise and in the second, will help to find an answer. At lunchtime and on the way home in the evenings, Pete uses the casual conversation of his team to provide feedback on their morale, state of health and any other factors which may influence the team's performance. Using this rich mixture of perceptions and communications Pete keeps himself informed on the state of his team.

Red McGregor, particularly on a large and complex project such as the Roman Leisure Centre, has to rely to a great extent on feedback obtained by communication. He likes to walk around his projects at least once a day but on large projects he has to delegate much of the direct observation of progress to members of his team. When they tell him of a problem, he likes to look at the part of the project causing the difficulty, but in the main he must rely for his feedback on progress charts, cost statements, complaints from architects or engineers responsible for designing the product and approving the construction work, promises from suppliers of materials and components, newly issued drawings and variation orders and other communicated information. Red knows that all this information is not equally reliable. Materials suppliers may make optimistic promises in the hope of obtaining an order, cost statements may be distorted because one of Red's team wishes to hide failure or to provide insurance against failure in the future, or a lack of variation orders may simply indicate that the architect's secretary has resigned. Red seeks to avoid being misled by checking for consistency in the information from different sources and by direct observation of progress.

The developer on the Roman Leisure Centre relies almost totally on communications for feedback on his projects. He may at the most, visit an architect's office or the site of a project under construction once a week. Inevitably his knowledge of progress is based on broad summaries of costs and schedules and formal reports on progress and problems requiring decisions.

At this level those providing feedback face a real temptation to report steady uneventful progress in accordance with the agreed plan irrespective of actual progress. There are other potential problems at this level. Faced with a difficult problem Red McGregor, like other effective managers, concentrates on finding an answer. At such times the completion of feedback reports has a low priority. As a consequence, either required information is not provided for the developer or it is prepared hurriedly and therefore is likely to contain errors. A further problem as feedback becomes increasingly remote from the activities it is intended to describe is that the information may represent characteristics which differ from those assumed by the recipient. Thus, a project manager who uses cash expended or man–hours worked as an indication of progress may be badly misled. Only by obtaining independent evidence on progress can he be sure that the consumption of resources in accordance with an agreed plan really does indicate a successful project.

Feedback is most likely to be reliable when it is provided as a necessary product of carrying out the project. That is, when it emerges naturally from the design, management and construction processes. Thus, records of design meetings at which teams responsible for separate but interacting elements of the end product formally hand over coordination drawings may provide a better record of progress than a specially produced statement by the design manager. Similarly, a record of changes to the master schedule and budget may identify problems more reliably than a formal report by the construction manager. During construction the level and type of adjustments made in calculating bonus payments may suggest a different picture from that provided by a monthly cost statement prepared by the company accountant for a board meeting.

The need for feedback can be used to concentrate managers' attention on important issues and at the same time help to ensure that its provision is an integral part of projects. Thus, checklists of necessary actions which are filled-in at regular intervals to indicate which actions have been started and which finished, can be useful. They do not necessarily ensure accurate reporting but at least serve to remind managers of what needs to be done. Checklists are likely to be useful provided that they include only a small number of items, comprise clearly identifiable stages and the reporting periods are short, say once or twice a week depending on the size and complexity of the project. Closely related to checklists is the use of the project schedule to record actual performance. A bar chart marked to show the project status at the beginning of a reporting period and the planned activities during the period can be marked to show each day's work. Similarly in the finishing and fitting out stages of complex building projects of the progress of various construction teams is usually marked room by room on floor plans. This is necessary to allow the site manager in planning ahead to ensure that all teams have a clear working space and it also records progress accurately.

A technique which deliberately seeks to improve performance on construction projects is foreman-delay surveys. This requires team leaders to report time lost by their team due to delays, variations or re-doing defective work at the end of each working day. A common approach is to carry out the survey for one week each month. Team leaders are informed at a short orientation meeting in advance that the purpose of the survey is to identify problems which they do not have the power to solve. It should be emphasized that the intention is to help remove difficulties and the results will not in any way be used to criticize them. When the survey is complete and the results analysed a further meeting should be held with the team leaders to try to find ways of avoiding delays in the future. This in itself provides obvious benefits. The meetings also provide good opportunities for the team leaders and project managers to discuss the project openly and so provide valuable feedback. Also, by examining the trend in several months' summary reports a picture is built up of whether the project is settling down and running more smoothly or is deteriorating. This, combined with the records and discussions of the causes of delays, provides feedback which is sharply focused on problems. There are reports of the use of foreman-delay surveys on construction projects leading to improved productivity[9].

Many other methods of obtaining feedback are used in construction projects. These include the use of progress photographs, activity sampling by direct observation and, increasingly, by monitoring electronic detectors in construction plant. Whatever form it takes the recipient should consider how reliable feedback is likely to be; whether there are pressures on the source to distort the information; whether it is corroborated by information from other sources; and whether it fits into current trends on the project.

Feedback in control

To be useful in controlling construction projects, feedback needs to be compared with the expected values of the variables it describes. This means that the the project plan and the feedback collected must match. Both should reflect the project objectives. Thus, if completion on time is important, the schedule should provide frequent deadlines which can be closely monitored. When costs are important detailed budgets, regular estimates of future costs and rapid accounting for expenditure and financial commitments are likely to be justified. Similarly, if the quality and performance of the end product are given high priority it may be sensible to establish clear standards, perhaps by using specially prepared samples of workmanship and to measure and evaluate the work continuously as it is produced.

An important part of monitoring construction projects is to manage allowances included in budgets and schedules as contingencies. These may be allowances for possible changes in the scope of the work, for poor ground conditions, for bad weather, for errors in estimating, for inflation, for elements not yet designed, for innovative designs or simply to reduce the chance of an over-run. The total contingency allowance can easily amount to 10% or 15%, or even more, of total costs and schedules. The project management team should be responsible for authorizing expenditure against these allowances. Such authorizations should be restricted to the factors for which the allowances were made otherwise they simply hide poor performance until it emerges as a major problem when the contingency is exhausted.

When feedback shows a deviation from the planned performance it is necessary to consider very carefully exactly what it indicates. Thus, a cost over-run may have a number of causes. Low productivity, wasted materials, variations, increased costs or poor original estimates are obvious possibilities. Only by analyzing the evidence carefully will it be clear, to take a common cause of confusion, whether the teams on site are performing badly or the buyer is paying too high a price for materials. The calculation of separate variances for each cause is dealt with in a number of textbooks[10]. The analysis of feedback to identify the factors causing problems often helps to suggest possible remedial actions.

Having identified and analyzed a problem, the control sub-system requires that action be taken to bring the project back to the desired state. It may, of course, be difficult or even impossible to do this. Irrespective of the outcome those concerned with the problem area should be made aware of the proposed remedy or if no change is proposed, they should know why no action is to be taken. The best way of doing this is to include the team leaders in discussions of possible ways of improving the project performance. However it is done, it is important that those providing feedback which identifies problems should know that it is taken seriously by their superiors, otherwise there is little chance of accurate and timely reports on performance.

Such reports are crucial to construction project management since most planning and forecasting depends on feedback. In the main this is feedback from earlier projects, although of course, feedback from the project in hand when it is available is especially useful. However, early estimates at least must be based on historical data. Thus, cost estimating depends, to a large extent, on cost feedback and cost analyses of completed projects. It also depends on the estimator's experience of having produced estimates in the past and having received feedback on their accuracy. However, it should be remembered that no two projects are exactly alike. It is therefore necessary for those using data based on old projects to understand its structure and the factors on which it depends. To make simple extrapolations from one project to another especially with large, complex, innovative, uncertain ones is to invite error. The analysis required by the model of projects and their environments described in Chapters 1, 2, 3 and 4 is likely to provide a more robust basis for estimates of performance. It therefore also provides an overall structure for feedback which is tailored to the particular needs and objectives of individual projects.

Summary

Communications are intended to transfer information between controlled systems. Information consists of meanings which comprise images or concepts in our heads to which we give names. The names are usually represented by words, numbers or symbols within construction projects. We can measure the quantity of information in bits which distinguish between equally probable states. The amount of meaning provided by given information is a function of the state of mind of the recipient.

Communications have purposes which increase the possibility that problems will arise in one of the five necessary steps of source, coding, medium, detection and decoding. Problems arise when the sender is vague about the concepts he is sending; when the meaning is ambiguous; when the recipient does not receive the whole message; when the message is accompanied by noise; when the recipient has less knowledge than the sender assumed he had; or where he misunderstands the context.

Problems in communications can be minimized by appointing experienced teams; by providing redundancy in information; by structuring information to match the responsibilities of separate teams, particularly by using work packages to structure both the acting and the information systems; by direct face-to-face discussions; and by managers adopting a style and approach likely to motivate their subordinates.

Feedback is an important form of communications. Care needs to be taken that it is not distorted by the source to mislead the recipient; that it does describe the characteristics the recipient assumes; that it is provided regularly; and that it is taken seriously.

References

1. KUHN, A. and BEAM, R. D., *The Logic of Organization,* Jossey-Bass (1982)
2. HUMPHREY, N., *Consciousness Regained,* Oxford University Press (1983)
3. CRAWSHAW, D. T., *Coordinating Working Drawings,* Building Research Establishment CP60 (1976)
4. DALTRY, C. D. and CRAWSHAW, D. T., *Working Drawings in Use,* Building Research Establishment CP18 (1973)
5. The Coordinating Committee for Project Information is jointly sponsored by the ACE, BEC, RIBA and RICS to coordinate the preparation of three agreed and coordinated conventions for the production of drawings, specifications and bills of quantities for building projects to facilitate the preparation of effective project information.
6. A good example of the care with which work packages are defined is described in: GRAY, C. and FLANAGAN, R., 'US productivity and fast tracking starts on the drawing board', *Construction Management and Economics,* **2,** No. 2 (Autumn 1984)
7. See for example: Building Unit of the Polytechnic of Central London. *Buildability – an Assessment,* CIRIA (1983)
8. REAVENS, R. W., *Action Learning,* Chartwell Bratt (1982)
9. TUCKERS, R. L., ROGGE, M., HAYES, W. R. and HENDRICKSON, F. P., 'Implementation of foreman–delay surveys', *ASCE J. of the Construction Division,* **108,** No. CO4 (December 1982)
10. A good example is: ARCHIBALD, R. D., *Managing High-Technology Programs and Projects,* John Wiley (1976)

Chapter 7

Transactions and values

The second of the types of interaction used to manage construction projects is 'transactions', that is, the transfer of valued things between controlled systems. As far as management is concerned we are primarily interested in the negotiations which precede transactions rather than in the physical movement of the things exchanged. Negotiations centre on the values placed on things by the separate parties to a possible transaction. An essential feature of transactions is that the parties involved shall have different values. That is, if we consider an exchange of two goods, X and Y, and both the owners of these goods value X more than Y, there is no basis for a transaction. It is only when the owner of X values Y more and the owner of Y values X more that a transaction is likely. An essential and fundamental problem in all formal organizations is that individuals must agree on certain values if they are to work together effectively, but the transactions which bring them into and keep them in the organization depend on there being differences in individual values. Much management effort is necessarily devoted to ensuring that the potential problems implicit in these conflicting requirements do not break out into actual conflict.

We have noted in earlier chapters signs that individuals have different values.

The discovery of Roman remains on Red McGregor's factory site was seen differently by the developer and the museum director because of their different values. Given an entirely free choice it is likely that the developer would have buried the Roman remains under the factory units, while the museum director would have taken over the site and built a new museum. Neither obtained entirely what they wanted initially because they had insufficient power to get their own way. Through negotiations both have obtained sufficient for them to be satisfied. Also neither believes that they could obtain more benefits by further negotiation. Therefore, they have agreed to the building of the Roman Leisure Centre incorporating the remains which will be looked after by the museum department. Both parties incur costs in this transaction. The museum director has given up his hopes of controlling the complete site and the developer has given up part of his building. These negotiations involved many other parties. The museum director needed the support of colleagues and councillors since, for example, he does not have the authority to commit the council to giving planning permission. However, in the event, the crucial negotiations turned out to be those between him and the developer. All the other necessary negotiations complicated the crucial ones but did not alter the basic principles involved.

Those principles were that each party had its own different set of values. Arising out of these values each had something which the other wanted. The developer had the Roman remains and the museum director had the power to persuade those with the necessary authority to allow the development to go ahead. The two parties used communications to find some agreement in which both felt that from their own viewpoint the benefits exceeded the costs and that further negotiations would not increase that net gain.

The transactions which Pete James or Tim Smithson enter into when they agree to undertake the bricklaying on any particular project are preceded by negotiations which have the same basic characteristics. In these cases the valued things are primarily money and skill in bricklaying. As we have seen, other factors enter into such transactions. Pete or Tim prefer certain types of project, they prefer work in the town where they live and they much prefer work to being unemployed. In deciding whether to employ them Red McGregor takes into account their availability, the quality of their work, how quickly they work and their general reliability.

These factors affect the value which each of these actors place on money and particular bricklaying skills in the context of any one project. They do not alter the underlying principles. It is these which construction project managers must understand and then use in their work of forming and controlling effective and efficient organizations.

Transactions

In describing the principles we shall rely extensively on Kuhn's fundamental logic of organizations[1] and, like him, we shall begin by assuming two parties to a transaction, whom we shall call A and B. A has something which B wants and B has something which A wants. They both have the authority needed to agree to an exchange and to complete the ensuing transaction. This condition is important. We may all want many things and these desires undoubtedly affect our behaviour in many subtle and various ways. However, in any negotiation we are concerned with preferences to which the participants can give effect. Thus, if A has money and wants a quantity of brickwork of a given quality it may well be the case that he has the authority to pay up to a given sum but no more for the work. Then, in negotiating with B, the leader of a bricklaying team with the required skills, A's effective preference is the maximum sum of money he is authorized to spend on the brickwork. It is also likely that B's team will refuse to work for very much less than the normal rate for bricklaying and, therefore, his effective preference is limited to this minimum sum. These relationships are shown in *Figure 7.1* which shows that A is authorized to pay up to £20 000 for the brickwork while the least that B will accept for providing it is £10 000.

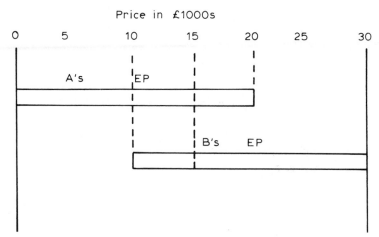

Figure 7.1 Effective preference of two parties negotiating over one good

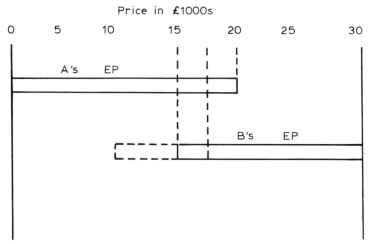

Figure 7.2 Modification of one party's effective preference

A number of things are immediately apparent from the information in *Figure 7.1*. First, there is clearly scope for an agreement between A and B. Secondly, assuming equal negotiating skills, it is likely that a bargain will be agreed at about £15 000. However, if we consider *Figure 7.2* where B's effective preference has shortened so that the least he will accept is

£15 000, the situation is different. There is still scope for an agreement but rather less than in the first case and now the most likely price has risen to £17 500. *Figure 7.3* illustrates a third case in which B, perhaps having observed that by shortening his effective preference he obtained better terms, has again raised the level of the least amount he will accept. In this case B's effective preference is £21 000 whilst the most that A is prepared to pay remains at £20 000. There is now no scope for an agreement.

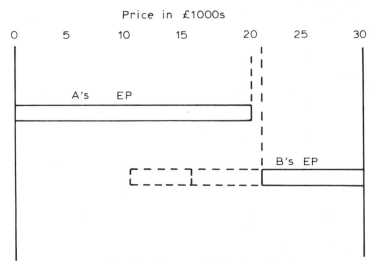

Figure 7.3 Further modification of one party's effective preference

We see from these three cases that the longer B's effective preference, the more likely he is to obtain an agreement. That is, his power is directly proportional to his effective preference. However, the shorter his effective preference the better terms he obtains. This is so even in the third case where if either party can be persuaded to modify their effective preference in order to reach agreement it is likely to be at about £20 000. So we see that B's bargaining power is inversely proportional to his effective preference. B's position is also influenced by the length of A's effective preference. Both his plain power, that is his ability to obtain things he wants, and his bargaining power are directly proportional to A's effective preference.

The relationships just described provide an adequate basis for understanding negotiation. They are therefore worth restating to emphasize the distinction between plain and bargaining power. The plain power possessed by any individual in a negotiation is directly proportional to their own effective preference and to that of the person with whom they are negotiating. Their bargaining power is inversely proportional to their own effective preference but directly proportional to that of the other party.

Negotiations

In negotiations each party seeks to discover the limit of the other's effective preference without revealing its own. Thus, taking the case in *Figure 32*, if B can learn that A is authorized to pay up to £20 000, then he is likely in negotiation to represent his own minimum price at the same figure. By doing so he will hope to improve the terms he obtains in the agreement. Also, in negotiations each party seeks to persuade the other to lengthen its effective preference. This is necessary in the case shown in *Figure 7.3* since no agreement is possible unless one or other of the parties decides to accept worse terms. Therefore, clearly in this case, and in practice in most cases, each party is likely to attempt to persuade the other to lengthen its effective preference.

Negotiations may involve all three basic forms of interaction. That is they may involve communication, transaction and organization. Agreements based on communication are generally preferred to the other possibilities. They are based entirely on discussions which continue until all those involved reach agreement. They provide each of the parties with what they prefer even if they have to be persuaded by discussion to recognize the particular outcome as their preference. Agreement by communication alone requires none of the parties to make compromises. This is true even if the agreement finally reached is different from anything envisaged by any of the parties at the outset. It may be that during discussions a new alternative is identified which all prefer once it is recognized. The outcome of agreement by communication is unanimous acceptance of the terms of a transaction irrespective of how enthusiastically or grudgingly it is arrived at.

The next preferred approach is agreement based on transaction. This essentially involves bargaining in which each party gives up some part of its preferences in return for the others also making concessions. In this approach no one gets exactly what he prefers but all come to accept a compromise because they judge that they have received sufficient concessions to justify their agreement. They may not be pleased with the outcome but nevertheless they agree.

Finally, agreement may be imposed by one party on the others. This is agreement by organization in the sense that the party imposing the agreement needs to have authority or power in order to get its own way. It is probable, but by no means certain, that the dominant party gets what it prefers but the others are likely to be unhappy with the outcome. They have been neither convinced nor compensated for having failed to achieve their preferences. Within construction project organizations the creation of such frustrations is likely to lead to poor results. The recognition that, for example, a team working for low wages is unlikely to produce good work limits the ability of dominant parties to impose agreements. Consequently even when they have the authority or power to obtain their preferred outcome, dominant parties are likely to seek agreement by discussion or bargaining if at all possible.

In practice, negotiations prior to agreements may involve a rich variety of actions. Flattery, insults, threats or lies whether real or imagined may all play a part in negotiations. Bribes, blackmail or physical force may be used to induce or impose agreements. Strikes and lock-outs are attempts to try to force the other party to agree to better terms. This list suggests that negotiations concern not only goods, that is things which have value, but also their opposite, that is things which the parties or at least one party is likely to wish to avoid and which can therefore be regarded as bads.

Bads can be used in two distinct ways. First one party can threaten to impose a bad. Then negotiations continue, if they continue at all, with the implication that if the other party does not agree to terms acceptable to the first, the bad will in fact be applied. The second use of bads is to apply them and then to negotiate on the basis that if agreement is reached the bad will be removed. Certain practical consequences flow from the use of bads. There may well be costs in applying, maintaining and removing a bad.

Once a bad is applied the party imposing it may feel compelled to seek a better bargain than they would have accepted before the costs were incurred. The longer the costs are allowed to continue to mount up the harder it will be for them to accept any agreement. On the other hand, there may be limits to the costs they can afford and in the long run they may be forced to accept terms which fall far short of those they hoped to obtain. Many industrial disputes appear to have these kinds of characteristic. Long strikes, for example, rarely produce a net benefit to either side. There may, therefore, be advantages in threatening to impose a bad rather than in incurring the costs of actually doing so. When this succeeds in producing improved terms for the party issuing the threat and as a result agreement is reached, there is no way of knowing whether the bad would in fact have been applied or not. Threats have their greatest effect when the other party believes that they will be carried out. Threats are likely to be credible when the party making them has the power to apply the threatened bad, when it can be applied at relatively small costs and the party has consistently carried out threats in the past. It is, therefore, unwise to use threats unless it is fully intended to carry them out if that becomes necessary or unless previous behaviour is likely to give them real credibility.

Bads do not introduce new principles into transactions. This is so because their use in negotiations necessarily translates into something valued by one of the parties which, therefore, can be regarded as a good. In the case of a threatened bad the good is the implied offer of not carrying out the threat. In the case where the bad has already been applied the good is the usually explicit offer of removing it. It is these goods which are negotiated over and, like any other, fit within the basic framework illustrated in *Figures 7.1, 7.2* and *7.3*.

Competition

Transactions become more complex when more than two parties are involved but again analysis of the interactions involves no new principles. A common situation in construction is that there are several different sources for a required good. *Figure 7.4* illustrates a situation in which A is seeking a good for which there are three potential suppliers, B_1, B_2 and B_3.

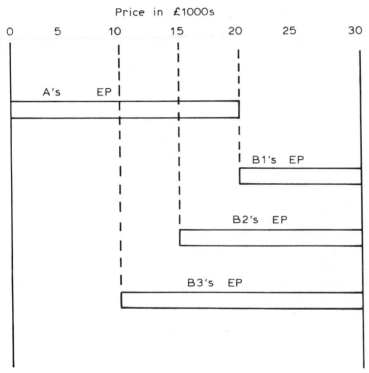

Figure 7.4 Competition

In negotiations with B_3 alone, A is likely to agree to pay £15 000. However, if he has already negotiated with B_2 and so discovered that the price of £15 000 is available to him from another source, this lower figure will become the limit of his effective preference in negotiations with B_3. In which case he is likely to secure a price of about £12 500 assuming that both parties are equally good negotiators.

In the competitive situation illustrated in *Figure 7.4*, there are advantages to all the Bs in deciding amongst themselves on the lowest price any of them will accept. Since the limit of B_1's effective preference is £20 000 this is likely to be the figure chosen. Then negotiations with any B are likely to result in A having to agree to this much higher cost. The cartel benefits B_1 by giving him a one-in-three chance of completing the transaction, whereas without the price agreement he would have little or no chance. B_3 benefits by obtaining a better price and B_2 increases both his chances and the likely price. In the long run it is likely that the weakest competitor, that is B_1, with the shortest effective preference, will be the firmest supporter of the cartel. Equally it is probable that B_3 as the strongest competitor will become increasingly disenchanted and prefer a larger share of the market even if it means accepting lower prices. In all events it is clearly in the interest of buyers that there should be competition unfettered by price agreement amongst the suppliers. Equally an agreement establishing the maximum price which competing buyers will be prepared to pay acts against the interests of their suppliers. All such restrictions on competition essentially shorten the effective preference of one of the partners. However, once the effective preferences of the parties are established irrespective of the means by which they are established the negotiations themselves are subject to the basic principles described earlier.

Future transactions

In many negotiations the parties need to take into account the effect of any agreement which they may be able to obtain on future transactions. In construction the future transactions may be at later stages of the same project or in other projects. Thus, negotiations between a client and a contractor will be different depending upon whether the client uses the construction industry regularly or just once in a lifetime. There are almost certainly differences in knowledge and experience in these two cases but beyond that there will be differences in motivation. Assuming that the negotiation is such that the contractor has strong bargaining power, in the case of a regular client he may well decide to agree to less than he could have obtained in the hopes of building up a store of goodwill for the future. Faced with an occasional client the contractor is likely to press for the best possible terms since there is unlikely to be any future benefit to offset the cost of accepting less. Similarly if the occasional client has strong bargaining power he will seek all he can get. The regular client will need to consider how far he can afford to damage his goodwill with the particular contractor or to damage his wider reputation for being fair and reasonable in his dealings with the construction industry.

Over time and many such negotiations, regular clients and a small group of contractors whom they tend to employ, are likely to build up large commitments to each others goodwill. Once this is built up, each fresh negotiation is severely constrained by the wish on both sides not to damage the relationship by exploiting strong bargaining power. In other words, both parties' effective preference is lengthened to a position where there is a comfortable and probably well-understood overlap. There is then no real need for negotiation since both know within narrow limits the agreement which will be reached. Negotiation in such circumstances can easily become merely a ritual performed for the sake of appearances rather than comprising any serious bargaining.

Many negotiations in construction are part of a series of interactions and are likely to be influenced by considerations of long-term goodwill which evokes a generous attitude. It is also possible for one party to a negotiation to feel hostility towards the other party. There are many possible causes, including previous negotiations, where one party feels aggrieved by the deal they had to accept. The effect of hostility is to shorten the effective preference of the hostile party. By applying the basic principles of transactions we can see that hostility decreases plain power but increases bargaining power. Conversely, generosity increases plain power while decreasing bargaining power. This accords with common sense in that most people would prefer to negotiate with a generous person rather than a hostile one in part at least because they might reasonably expect to obtain a better deal.

Future costs

Negotiations essentially are a search for a transaction which all parties consider provides them with more benefits than costs and which they judge will not be improved by further negotiation. It should always be remembered that the costs and benefits to be considered are those in the future. Past costs cannot be influenced by a current decision and therefore are irrelevant. This is often hard to accept and people often choose to continue to pursue a mistaken decision on which they have already spent heavily in order to avoid admitting a large mistake. This is probably common in construction where once a project is under way, especially once the construction stages are under way, there is great reluctance to abandon the work even when it is clear that the remaining necessary costs far outweigh any possible benefits. Nevertheless, it remains irrational to make decisions or to persist with the consequences of decisions when future costs exceed the future benefits. This is not to suggest that each minor decision in construction projects needs to be continuously evaluated to ensure that it provides net benefits. Decisions on the position of a mortar mixer on-site, or how many stacks of bricks are needed to ensure an uninterrupted supply, or which end of a project to begin bricklaying are often made with little or no explicit evaluation. Such day-to-day decisions are commonly made within a broad framework established by earlier decisions. This is not to suggest that there may not be advantage in some projects in careful calculation of the decisions implied by these examples. It is merely to suggest that some decisions are subject to formal negotiation and explicit evaluation and some are not. This is common place and it seems that all construction projects involve a hierarchy of decisions. It is useful to distinguish between two distinct levels of decision.

Levels of decisions

The first level establishes the structure of project organizations. This is essentially concerned with decisions about roles; in particular with deciding what roles shall exist, defining their responsibilities and appointing teams to occupy each one. The second level is more commonly referred to as 'decisions' and deals with the day-to-day implementation of a team's responsibilities. It includes identifying details of work not specified in the roles and the allocation of tasks within teams. So we have a two-level hierarchy comprising structure and decisions. This relates to two distinct stages in the contracts and conditions of engagement which establish the formal relationships between teams and project organizations. The higher level is equivalent to the conditions specified in contracts and conditions of engagement. We shall call this the 'major bargain'. Since it is usually impossible to specify all the requirements of a role in a formal major bargain there need to be subsequent decisions which we shall call subsidiary transactions. They are concerned with day-to-day interactions between teams which are necessary because major bargins have not provided comprehensive role descriptions and because unexpected events occur.

The distinction between structure embodied in the major bargains and decisions comprising subsidiary transactions is important. It is perhaps clarified by observing the difference between the end products and the organizations which produce them in construction. A building, for example, is fully described in its structure in the sense that the word is used here. That is the role of all the elements is fully specified and the bricks, beams and pipes are not expected to make subsequent decisions about their own functions. This, of course, is because they are not able to. This remains true even if we consider the computer controls now incorporated in most modern constructions which are able to respond to changing circumstances and to do so in very complex ways. The decisions they make are built into their hardware and this remains so even when the hardware carries sophisticated software. The instructions which tell the computer control what to do with input and what output to produce are in the hardware, otherwise they do not exist.

This is true even if the instructions can be changed by the user of the building or plant which houses the control. It does not decide to change itself. It merely carries out its instructions no matter how complex and subtle they may be. That is the decisions made by controls are part of their role definitions and, therefore, as with all the other elements, are provided by their structure. So buildings and all the end products of the construction industry rely solely on structure to ensure that all their elements combine together to fulfil the overall intended purpose. The same is not true of organizations.

A large part of the coordination required between teams making up construction project organizations can be provided by structure and embodied in major bargains. However, there will always be some subsidiary transactions since not all the responsibilities of roles can be specified in advance. Construction is too complex, too variable and too much beset by interference from project environments for major bargains to be comprehensive. Also, teams have to be induced to enter organizations. The negotiations needed to persuade a team to accept any given role may well change the role description to some extent.

Red McGregor knows that when he employs Pete James he must accept a slower rate of work than from say Tim Smithson. Therefore, the role description will probably need to be changed to accommodate completion at a later date. On the other hand, the often poor quality of Tim Smithson's work is likely to require additional provisions in the description of any role which his team occupies to allow their workmanship to be monitored.

Finally, of course, the teams employed may not behave as expected. This can, and does, happen with elements of the end product. Bricks may crumble, beams may sag under their load and pipes may leak. Equally teams may fail in somewhat similar ways but beyond this they may seek to move outside their role. Such initiatives can be helpful or unhelpful. A bricklaying team may help to unload bricks when the material manager's team is busy with other responsibilities. On the other hand, it may devote much of its effort towards provoking an industrial dispute in the hopes of gaining some financial, political or other advantage. Bricks, beams and pipes do not behave in similar ways. Therefore, while constructions can be, and indeed have to be, specified in advance, organizations cannot be completely prespecified. There has to be a division in role descriptions between what is contained in the major bargains and what in subsidiary transactions.

Major bargains

The division between major bargain and subsidiary transactions depends on the nature of the work required. We saw in Chapter 5 that the coordination devices used depend on the type of project. *Figure 5.8* sets out the basic relationships insofar as they are currently understood. Programmed organizations suitable for standardized work rely on procedures and goals for much of their coordination. These can be specified in advance and therefore included in major bargains. Professional organizations producing traditional constructions rely less on devices which can be described in major bargains and more on professionalization. Although professional knowledge and skills are learnt in advance of their being applied to any particular project, the process of diagnosis which precedes their application implies a degree of discretion in professional roles which precludes a detailed specification of the required actions.

Nevertheless, the role description can specify the type of professionalization required in the role occupant. This may be difficult to do in the case of problem-solving organizations providing innovative constructions. Such organizations rely on many liaison roles to make decisions at the level of subsidiary transactions. The major bargains in these cases can do little more than specify the objectives of roles leaving the choice of actions and required knowledge and skills to teams doing the work. These relationships are shown in *Table 7.1.*

TABLE 7.1. Role of major bargains

Type of work	Type of organization	Major bargain
Standard constructions	Programmed	Specifies actions, knowledge and skills and objectives
Traditional constructions	Professional	Specifies knowledge and skills and objectives
Innovative constructions	Problem-solving	Specifies objectives

The likely contents of major bargains described in *Table 7.1* apply to the early stages of projects. As projects of all types progress, the required work is more clearly identified and so can be specified, the major bargains reflect this. Thus, construction roles tend to be specified in terms of the required actions, knowledge and skills and objectives to a much greater extent than design or management roles. This is one of the features which distinguish the strategic from the tactical phases of projects.

Major bargains in construction deal with other matters besides specifying the required actions, the knowledge and skills the role occupant is expected to possess and the role objectives. Essentially major bargains establish ongoing relationships in which one party agrees to provide a service on a regular basis in return for specified rewards. Therefore, they must establish that role occupants are required to accept instructions from superiors. That is they must provide for effective authority. They do this usually by specifying the type and form of legitimate instructions which the role occupant will be expected to obey. They also provide sanctions for the non-performance of a legitimate instruction. Sanctions may take the form of terminating or suspending the major bargin or the imposition of financial penalties. Major bargains must also specify the basis of payments to the role occupant. This usually includes stating the amount, or at least the precise method, of calculating the amount, the frequency and method of payments including, as noted above, provisions for reducing or withholding part of the sums due to the role occupant. Major bargains also usually specify the method of resolving disputes. In construction this commonly provides for the matter to be referred to some third party for decision. Ultimately, of course, disputes may need to be resolved in the courts. In this case the specific provisions of the major bargain assume considerable importance as the courts are likely to regard them as an accurate description of the parties' intentions.

An important category of provisions in major bargains in construction is that dealing with the consequences of variability and interference. There are commonly provisions which seek to compensate teams delayed by others and penalize those causing the delay. The effects of bad weather, or more usually of exceptionally bad weather, of unexpectedly poor ground conditions, of strikes, wars, fires, floods, earthquakes and similar interference from the environment are normally dealt with by providing for payments and schedules to be adjusted. The more such provisions are included, the more likely it is that the basis of the original major bargain will be changed but also the more likely it is that a bargain will be agreed in the first place. Taking the effects of weather in the UK as an example, the most widely used building contracts provide for general contractors to accept the direct financial risks and the client to accept the direct schedule risks of exceptionally bad weather. This provision tends to ensure that building projects in the UK are completed late irrespective of the weather actually experienced. The fact that a fairly easy excuse is allowed by the major bargain for late completion tends to reduce the incentive to finish on time. On the other hand, the fact that the provision exists is likely, on balance, to encourage contractors to accept terms which might otherwise seem just too onerous. The fact that the contractor carries the direct financial risk is presumably based on the idea that he is best placed to minimize the costs of bad weather. This aspect of the contract provisions is likely to lead to contractors seeking better terms initially than would be the case if the client accepted the risk. However, once work is underway, bad weather does not change the basis of that original financial bargain.

The example of bad weather in UK building contracts well illustrates the relationship between the major bargain and subsequent transactions. As far as costs are concerned the major bargain removes the need for further decisions, but as far as schedules are concerned, it tends to ensure that bad weather will be the subject of frequent and potentially protracted negotiations. On balance there seem to be advantages in dealing with matters in the major bargain insofar as they can be fully and clearly defined. Conversely, it seems better to leave matters to subsidiary transactions where an attempt to deal with them in the major bargain would lead to ambiguity. This is because either party faced with problems will be tempted to exploit the ambiguity in an attempt to alter or even abandon the major bargain.

Subsidiary transactions

The complete set of major bargains in individual construction projects are intended to provide roles which among them have the capacity to do all the required work. Within that overall structure subsidiary transactions provide the decisions needed for day-to-day implementation. Subsidiary transactions rely primarily on the authority and responsibilities established in the major bargains. That is they rely on teams accepting instructions from their superiors. The relationship is usually seen as being essentially one way or at least substantially one-sided. Thus, failure to obey a legitimate instruction is widely regarded as sufficient grounds for dismissal. The one-sided nature of the relationship is commonly reinforced by requiring that work should be properly carried out before the workers are paid. The timing of the two sides of employment contracts tends to increase both the employer's plain and bargaining power. This is so since once work is satisfactorily complete the employer may have nothing further to gain from the transaction whilst the employee may need the money due to him to buy the necessities of life. That is the employer's effective preference will shorten since presumably he will prefer to pay as little as possible particularly as he already has what he wants from the transaction.

At the same time the employee's preference may lengthen as his need for money may persuade him to accept less than he is due in return for prompt payment. Indeed it is not uncommon for commercial contracts to include provision for a discount in return for payment within a stated period of time. The difference in timing of two halves of construction transactions reinforces the implied possibility that payment may be withheld which appears to be the essential source of authority. It adds further pressure to persuade subordinates to obey legitimate instructions in order to avoid providing an excuse for the employer to reduce, delay or entirely withhold payment.

Construction contracts and conditions of engagement do not always provide for payment to follow the successful completion of the work. It is not uncommon for construction contracts, especially in difficult and uncertain environments, to provide for an initial mobilization payment. This is a sum of money paid to a contractor before he has done any work. Such provisions tend to reverse the normal authority: responsibility relationship. Mobilization payments provide the most obvious example but there are others. Most large construction contracts provide for payment at regular intervals during the progress of the work or for payment as defined stages of the work are completed. Contractors may seek to structure prices in bills of quantities or agreed stage payments so that from the early stages of projects the employer is, in effect, paying in advance of the work being carried out.

Figure 7.5 illustrates a pattern of payments and costs which produce this result. From time period 1 the employer has paid more than the value of the work completed. This reduces his authority. He is more likely to find that the contractor questions instructions than in projects where payment follows the satisfactory completion of work. This arrangement of payments has further disadvantages for the employer. From time period 7 onwards the contractor will be working for no profit since the mean payment and cost curves are parallel. At this time he has little financial incentive to complete the work and may well seek to cause disputes by challenging instructions in the hope of re-negotiating the major bargain on terms which will allow him to work profitably. Professional fee scales often have similar characteristics so that clients are caused to pay too much for the work done during the early stages of projects. When this happens, consultants may be

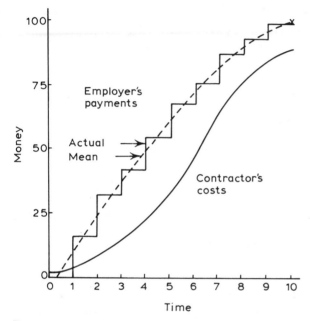

Figure 7.5 Payment sructure producing positive cash flow for contractor

financially better off when projects are abandoned than when they are completed successfully. Such front-end loading of payments creates a temptation to skimp the supervision of construction stages since the fee remaining may well not cover the costs of full and proper inspection and control.

We can see from these examples that the balance of power in subsidiary transactions may well vary as projects progress. In practice, the balance depends on the precise terms of the major bargain but also on events during the course of the project. These include events within projects and in their environments. One team working slowly or a design detail which has to be modified may change the balance of power in all the transactions involving teams affected by the problem. Similarly the weather or the level of demand for construction resources may alter the effective preferences of clients and of teams within construction projects. This, in turn, will influence the willingness of these teams to obey instructions. So subsidiary transactions are not simply a matter of exercising legitimate authority, that is of issuing orders within the scope of those envisaged in the major bargain.

Legitimacy depends at root on employees accepting instructions. It is, of course, a matter of fact whether any specific instruction falls within the categories envisaged by the relevant major bargain. Taking the case of an instruction which falls outside the categories originally envisaged, if it is obeyed and continues to be obeyed when repeated, then in effect, the major bargain has been implicitly re-negotiated. This is true whether an employee resents the fact that he is doing things which his employer has no right to ask him to do or whether he initially objects and has to be persuaded or forced to obey. What was previously illegitimate, has for all practical purposes, become legitimate. In much the same way, when an employee refuses to obey an instruction which falls within the categories envisaged in the major bargain and the refusal is accepted, the major bargain has, in effect, been changed. The range of legitimate instructions has been narrowed. The third case to consider is where an instruction is refused and the employer will not accept the refusal. In effect the major bargain has broken down. Either the team's contract is terminated or the major bargain is negotiated on the basis of new terms. In all three cases legitimacy depends solely on the acceptance of instructions. This is perhaps made clearer by considering the most formal way of establishing the status of a disputed instruction. This is to refer it to some higher authority which both parties accept. This may mean referring the matter to an independent adjudicator, submitting to arbitration or resort to the courts. A decision by higher authority that the disputed instruction is legitimate and should be obeyed may well make it legitimate in law. As far as the management of construction projects is concerned, it is effectively legitimate only if the instruction is in fact subsequently obeyed. It is the acceptance of the higher authority's decision which makes instructions effectively legitimate rather than the decision itself. A continued refusal to obey may cause further resort to the courts and may result in great inconvenience, costs and hardship to the employee. The employer may obtain compensation but if the refusal continues the major bargain has failed and the employer for all practical purposes has no legitimate authority.

The practical consequences for project managements is that they must so arrange the terms of major bargains and so behave in subsidiary transactions that they obtain consent to their exercise of authority from the teams who occupy project roles. It is generally not sufficient to arrange a neat set of major bargains which provide for all the required work to be carried out. Even assuming an unusual project in which no unanticipated problems arise it is still likely that teams will need to be motivated to complete the work efficiently and to proper standards. The general principles described earlier in this chapter provide the basis for handling subsidiary transactions. In particular it is helpful to recognize that a failure to reach agreement is most likely to result from effective preferences not overlapping. Therefore, conflict resolution in most cases requires that one or other or both effective preferences must, by some means or other, be extended. It is also helpful to remember that there are many factors which influence effective preferences beyond simply providing more money. Workers need to be motivated and so their superiors must ensure that they understand their work and know that it is valued. Recognizing these realities leads on to the final factor to be considered in dealing with problems in subsidiary transactions. This is that it is helpful to use the preferred method of reaching agreements. That is by using communication rather than transaction or organization.

Major bargains in practice

The main practical issue raised by the principles described in this chapter is the need to decide how far the required end product should be defined in major bargains. *Table 7.1* describes the relationships between levels of definition and the general type of work required in particular projects. Once the appropriate level of definition has been identified there is much to be said for adopting a consistent approach throughout a project. As was described in Chapter 5, the key characteristics of projects tend to cluster into internally consistent groups. Therefore, introducing standard or traditional work into an essentially innovative project creates coordination requirements which are likely to differ from those at work in the rest of the project. It may, nevertheless, be sensible to accept and deal with more varied coordination requirements in order to make use of an existing answer or established professional knowledge rather than to allow the project organization to search for a new answer merely for the sake of consistency. Thus, in practice, projects may well comprise a mixture of programmed, professional and problem-solving work. In determining the overall character of projects problem solving dominates professional work and both dominate programmed work. That is, dominate in the sense of determining the coordination devices needed and establishing the overall style and character of the project organization. This is not to suggest that one innovative detail in an otherwise standard project is sufficient to alter the whole project organization. However, it is entirely probable that as little as 10% of a total design comprising innovative answers will entirely invalidate a programmed organization. Therefore, consistency is important in ensuring that organizations are able to work efficiently.

The choice of the correct level of definition of the end product is, if anything, even more important. This is relatively easy to achieve in cases where full and detailed descriptions of the required end products, the means of producing them and the tests they must satisfy, can all be included in the major bargains. In these circumstances the role occupant is responsible for carrying out the defined actions to produce the defined end product which must satisfy the defined tests. The essential character of this approach is consistent with a bargain based on a firm lump sum payment in return for the work being completed within an agreed schedule. Ideally there should be no provision for the project management to order variations nor should the team carrying out the work be provided with allowable excuses for failing properly to complete the work on time. In other words the role occupants accept the risks of uncertainty.

On the other hand, their responsibility is limited to providing the defined work. It is the project management's responsibility to ensure that it accords with the overall project objectives. Work which can be handled by paying for defined outputs is likely to comprise standard components which are not closely interrelated with other elements. Prefabricated portal frames, cladding systems which simply bolt on to supports, free-standing air-conditioning units which plug into a power supply and standard external fencing, are examples of work which can usually be made the subject of the first type of major bargain.

The other end of the range of possibilities is an instruction to the role occupant to do their best in cooperation with other teams involved with the project to produce a satisfactory outcome. In this approach management is buying skills, knowledge and experience usually because they are not able to define the required end product. They have to trust the experts. The role occupants are responsible for producing answers which accord with the project objectives. The relevant objectives may well need to be identified as the work is carried out by proposing alternative answers, reviewing them and then trying again to find better answers. The work is essentially innovative and often only the role occupants themselves are in a position to know whether they have performed well.

The essential character of this approach is consistent with a bargain based on payment by time. That is, the role occupant is paid an agreed rate per hour, day, week or other unit for the time they actually spend doing the work. In its pure form this approach allows management to alter its requirements as often as it wishes. Since management is paying for the input costs rather than on the basis of the output it bears the full costs of such variations. Also it takes the risk of costs arising from the effects of uncertainty. The role occupant's responsibility is limited to exercising the care and competence which can reasonably be expected of a person undertaking the particular type of work. Work which can best be handled by paying for defined inputs is likely to be innovative or uncertain. Original design and much civil engineering especially that which is influenced by deep ground conditions provide obvious examples of the types of work likely to be made the subject of the second type of major bargain.

The pure output and the pure input types of major bargain sit at opposite ends of a range of options. However, they are in a sense, the only options available. The basis of bargains can be either the output or the input. There is nothing else which could form the basis of construction transactions. Therefore, the range of options which lies between the two pure types comprises a mixture of output- and input-based major bargains. A useful way of considering these is to concentrate on the methods used to calculate payments. Considerable ingenuity has been devoted to devising methods of calculating the payments due to role occupants to cope with various mixtures of output and input bases used in practice.

An approach widely used in the UK and also in countries which have adopted the British approach to procuring construction work, uses bills of quantities. These documents divide lump sum payments relating to outputs into many separate elements each of which is priced separately. This enables project managements to use bill rates to value variations without destroying the essential major bargain. The arrangement is satisfactory so long as the variations are relatively minor and issued before the role occupant has incurred costs which are wasted by the change. In practice the convenience of being able to order variations which can be evaluated by means of a straight-forward administrative process has led to abuse. Gurth Higgin[2] found that in many projects bills of quantities had become a hypothetical construct which in detail did not describe the work the role occupant would subsequently be required to carry out. Variations had, in many cases in the UK building industry, undermined the essential major bargain. Most standard forms of contract which envisage the use of bills of quantities now make elaborate provisions for this eventuality. In essence they revert to paying the role occupant the cost of his inputs. This leads to conflicting objectives since role occupants' financial interests are likely to be best served by being paid on an input basis for all the items where their costs exceed the bill rates. Conversely, project management will wish to regard bill rates as establishing the limits of payments. The more variations are issued or the more elements the role occupant can claim have been varied, the easier it is likely to be for them to be selective in choosing which elements they should be paid for on an output and which on an input basis. There is also scope for misallocating inputs so that resources actually devoted to an element paid for on an output basis are counted in with one dealt with on an input basis to the role occupant's advantage. In all events mixing output and input bases appears to have a strong tendency to give rise to many subsidiary transactions which are not concerned with the direct business of completing the project but are concerned rather with re-negotiating the major bargain, or at least substantial parts of it. The cause is not the use of bills of quantities which provide a useful means of describing the required work, but their misuse mainly through over-use of variations.

An output-based approach closely related to bills of quantities is to use a schedule of rates. This is a list of descriptions of items of work which are priced with unit rates by the role occupant. Then, as work is identified, the quantities actually required are measured and priced using the unit rates to calculate the payments due to the role occupant. There is no initial lump sum basis for contracts which are based on schedules of rates, simply an agreement to use the rates to calculate payments. This apart, the approach works in much the same way as a bills of quantities based one. The pressures on the two parties are similar. Bills of quantities and schedules of rates are appropriate when the work is well-understood by both parties and the amount required is likely to vary only within fairly narrow margins. When the nature of the work is altered during the course of its execution the major bargain is likely to be lost in a mass of subsidiary transactions.

An ingenious output-related approach is one often used to calculate professional fees. This is to base the payment on an agreed percentage of the price of the direct construction work. There is an obvious incentive for the role occupant to maximize the price of the construction work and to minimize his own input. As with other output-based approaches, changes cause problems. When they lead to an increased construction price the fixed percentage addition may provide an equitable reward for the role occupant. However, if the change involves extensive additional work and results in a reduced construction price, the outcome is clearly not equitable. Equally the arrangement can be inequitable to the client when these circumstances are reversed. Most professional fee scales based on percentage additions contain provisions which attempt to deal with such matters. However, the extremely weak relationship between input costs and rewards has led increasing numbers of experienced clients to move towards either input-based methods of calculating professional fees or firm lump sums.

There are a number of input-based options in common use in construction in addition to the rate per unit of time described in the pure case. Most of these are related to the actual direct costs of carrying out the work. A common approach is to add a percentage allowance for overheads and profits. The obvious problem with such an approach for project management is to control costs, since the higher the costs the greater role occupants' profits and the more their overhead costs are covered. Other options seek to overcome this problem. One is to agree a fixed fee to cover all except defined direct cost. Another is to agree a maximum target cost and then for the role occupant and client to share any difference between that figure and the actual costs. The difference may be shared equally or in any different proportions which the parties agree. The greater the proportion borne by the role occupant the greater their incentive to control costs. This approach acquires some of the characteristics of output-based ones. In particular, departures from the assumptions incorporated in the target cost may, depending on the terms of the major bargain, have similar consequences to variations. Particularly where the role occupant bears a high proportion of any differences between target and actual costs there are considerable temptations for them to seek to establish that project management has undermined the original basis of the transaction.

Any of the methods of calculating payments described thus far may be either fixed or adjusted to allow for the effects of inflation. The particular method adopted when payments include price fluctuation allowances may create further incentives to modify major bargains. In particular, when prices are rising the role occupant has an incentive to arrange matters so that costs are incurred or at least are accounted for late in the project. In this way the allowance for inflation is maximized.

The different pressures to depart from major bargains generated by the various approaches to calculating payments arise most forcibly when output and input bases are mixed and when the method used departs from the pure cases. It is therefore helpful for project managers to bear in mind the essential characteristics of each of the two main types when they are negotiating major bargains.

Output-based approaches depend on project managements providing clear definitions of the required end products in return for firm lump sum payments. In their pure form they depend on the major bargain not being varied. The role occupant determines the inputs needed and takes all the risks of the consequences of uncertainty. Coordination requirements are minimized by the pure output approach. The role definitions provide coordination since the outputs should fit together without leaving gaps or creating overlaps in the end product.

Input-based approaches depend on project managements defining the required resources in return for payments based on the amounts of these resources used. The end product is defined by the role occupants in agreement with project management as the work proceeds. The client takes the risks of the consequences of uncertainty since he pays for all resources used whatever the cause. The coordination requirements generated by this approach are likely to be considerable. This is mainly because the coordination devices used have to be selected and established, at least in part, as the work proceeds and in parallel to agreements on the end product. They therefore need to be flexible and will tend to be labour intensive rather than being able to rely on standard procedures, formal management hierarchies, establishing realistic goals or the use of sophisticated information systems.

There is a balance to be struck by project managements in the light of their particular project objectives between the costs of pre-defining the end product and the costs of coordinating teams operating with input-based agreements. Total costs are likely to be minimized by using contracts or conditions of engagement which approximate to the pure cases rather than mixing, or allowing circumstances to mix, output and input bases in the same one major bargain[3].

Summary

Transactions are concerned with the transfer of valued things between controlled systems. Agreements depend on the parties having different effective preferences. The plain power possessed by an individual in negotiation is directly proportional both to his own effective preference and to that of the other party. His bargaining power is inversely proportional to his own effective preference but directly proportional to that of the other party. Negotiations are all the actions which seek to find the bases for agreements. In negotiations, each party seeks to discover the limit of the other's effective preference without revealing his own. Also, each party seeks to persuade the other to lengthen his effective preference.

Agreement based on communication is generally preferred. Its outcome is unanimous acceptance of the terms of a transaction. The next preferred approach is agreement based on transaction. Its outcome is acceptance of a bargain in which all make concessions. Finally, agreement may be imposed on one party by superior authority or power.

Negotiations may involve goods and bads. Goods are valued things while bads are things which at least one party is likely to wish to avoid. In negotiations bads may be threatened or actually applied.

Competition tends to lengthen the effective preferences of those competing and shorten that of the party with whom they are negotiating. A cartel between the competing parties tends to reverse these effects. Generosity tends to lengthen effective preferences while hostility shortens them.

Negotiations are essentially a search for a transaction in which all parties judge that their future benefits exceed their future costs.

Transactions can usefully be divided into two levels. The first is major bargains which are concerned with decisions about roles and teams. It provides the structure of project organizations. The lower level comprises subsidiary transactions which are concerned with day-to-day interactions between teams. The balance between major bargains and subsidiary transactions depends on the nature of individual projects and varies as projects progress through the design and construction stages.

Major bargains establish authority and responsibilities. They specify the type and form of legitimate instructions, sanctions which may be imposed for non-performance, the basis of payments, methods of resolving disputes and provisions for dealing with the consequences of variability and interference.

Subsidiary transactions rely on teams accepting legitimate instructions as specified in the relevant major bargains. In practice, effective legitimacy is determined by teams either accepting or challenging instructions. The practical consequence is that project managers need to so arrange the terms of major bargains, and so behave in subsidiary transactions, that they obtain consent to the exercise of authority from the teams who occupy project roles.

Major bargains are either output- or input-based although, in practice, transactions may have a mixed base. Output-based major bargains tend to minimize coordination requirements and the need for subsidiary transactions. An input basis tends to produce large coordination requirements. However, mixed arrangements within one major bargain tend to maximize subsidiary transactions many of which are not concerned with meeting project objectives but with re-negotiating the major bargain.

References

1. KUHN, A. and BEAM, R. D., *The Logic of Organization,* Jossey-Bass (1982)
2. HIGGIN, G. W. and JESSOP, W. N., *Communications in the Building Industry,* for the National Joint Consultative Committee of Architects, Quantity Surveyors and Builders, Tavistock Publications (1965)
3. A good review of negotiating from the viewpoint of an experienced practitioner described in terms which do not conflict to any significant extent with the fundamental principles described in this chapter is provided in: SCOTT, W. P., *The Skills of Negotiating,* Gower (1983)

Chapter 8

Client's role

The client's role is crucial to the success of construction projects. The requirements for its proper execution can be stated under the five headings of providing the primary objectives for the project, defining the main outlines of the organization, selecting role occupants for the main roles, establishing the project culture and exercising authority over the organization. The tasks implied by the five headings are essential in all construction projects. When the client does not carry them out, another team within the project organization will do so but not necessarily, or indeed not even probably, in a way which meets the client's needs. Therefore, the five headings provide a framework within which we can identify the essential minimum set of tasks necessary for clients to create the circumstances for successful construction projects. It may well be that many clients need to employ additional help and advice in order to carry out these necessary tasks. Also, they may well wish to appoint a project manager to act as their agent. These decisions will depend largely on clients' previous experience of construction and the time and resources they can make available for the project. In the ensuing discussion the term 'client' is taken to encompass all and any of the arrangements which may be adopted to assist clients in undertaking their essential role.

Objectives

Clients' first necessary task is to provide the primary objectives for projects, that is their large overall objectives whether these are to make a profit, to house homeless families in decent conditions, to create a status symbol, to help win an election, to glorify God, or whatever else it is that at root persuaded a particular client to undertake a construction project. No-one except the client can provide these primary objectives. It may be sufficient to state the large overall objectives but it is usually risky for the client to leave things at that. It is nearly always safer to approve a model of the end product and the necessary organization, and for the project objectives to be to translate the models into reality. It is safer because clients are likely to be better judges of the kind of constructions and the kind of organizations which will meet their larger overall objectives than anyone else. They are likely to be a better judge of the performance they require, of the costs they can afford and of the timings which fit in with their overall objectives.

Thus the developer client on Red McGregor's present project was able to agree the change from building factory units to building the Roman Leisure Centre because either of these constructions met his larger overall objective of making a profit from the site.

No-one except the client could have made that decision.

A client's statement or agreed model of the required end product is usually described as the brief. This is a key document in ensuring a successful project. Robert Townsend[1], that very effective manager, provides clear advice on handling briefs under a heading of 'moving the head office'. His view is that one man should be put in charge of the whole operation. His terms of reference should be to provide offices which are all the same size, small and furnished with the same basic furniture. On no account should the one man consult or listen to any of the people who will occupy the new offices. Once consultation is allowed the end product, in Townsend's view, will take twice as long and cost three times as much and all the key prople in the firm will be completely preoccupied with status symbols and have no time for their work. His criteria for success are that the building should be ready on time, work reasonably well and that the cries of outraged vanity and offended taste should die out within thirty days.

A different view is taken by Goodacre *et al* in the Department of Construction Management at the University of Reading[2]. Drawing on much published material and studies of current architectural design practice, they concluded that briefs should be produced jointly by clients and their design teams over a period of time in which the client's needs and priorities are probed in depth and alternative ways of meeting them are explored in a search for the one offering the best overall value. They also take the view that clients who decide for themselves what kind of building they need are often wrong and that working closely with an experienced architect is likely to identify significantly better answers. They quote examples from their studies of a family who's brief was 'we wish to make our kitchen bigger' and a soft drinks manufacturer's which was 'we wish to build a new bottling plant'.

In the first case, in-depth probing identified the primary objective as 'we want to stop the children getting under the wife's feet while she is cooking' and the better answer was to leave the kitchen undisturbed and build an adjacent playroom. In the second case the primary objective was to take advantage of a predicted upturn in the sale of fizzy drinks. In the event, further data analysis revealed that the upturn was erroneous, and rather than expand their fizzy drink capacity the firm should have been diversifying out of the market. Goodacre and his team recognize that when briefing is seen as a dynamic process it is likely to expose different, and often conflicting, views on the proper objectives within client organizations. They take the view that this is healthy and the architect should confront the conflicts, seek to have them resolved and ensure that firm decisions are made. Their studies include cases within the UK National Health Service Hospital Boards where unresolved differences in objectives between administrators, doctors and nurses were hidden in vague briefs. The conflicts emerged as criticisms of the architect's design at a later stage. This approach allowed the Board to ignore its latent internal conflicts and to blame design problems on a lack of competence on the part of their architect. Clearly, unless the Board in question were led to provide a clear brief, the project would be faced with client changes throughout its life as one faction, then another, temporarily achieved a dominant position. Goodacre and his team see such cases as supporting their view that briefing must be approached in a problem-solving manner as a dynamic process rather than expecting clients to produce a clear and thorough statement of their objectives at the start of the projects. This seems broadly to be the view adopted by most architects, not that they know better than their clients what they ought to want, but that they, as professional architects, are skilled and experienced in relating problems and needs to a built solution and that many clients are not good at doing this.

We turn now to a third way of establishing clients' objectives. Greycoat Estates, one of the most successful UK development companies, takes a different approach from that recommended by either Townsend or Goodacre. Greycoats produce high-quality, well-designed office buildings in central London which are built significantly quicker and cheaper than other comparable ones. They regard the provision of a detailed, clearly-defined brief as an important feature of their approach. The following description is drawn largely from an unpublished case study carried out by the Department of Construction Management, University of Reading.

Greycoat's briefing document lays down the minimum standards which they will accept and invites the design team to use it as a basis for discussion and improvement. It is comprehensive and covers far more items than a conventional brief. The first page states the essential philosophy:

'This is a guide to the standards of the Greycoat Group. This document will form part of each professional's contract and if no comments are received it will be taken as read. It is intended as a discussion document but outlines minimum standards. It is intended to offer total architectural, engineering and energy conservation freedom of design but at the same time a cost-efficient approach is expected from the development team. Parts of the document are incompatible in certain circumstances and require input from the team. Input on all points is always welcomed and encouraged.

'All new projects give scope to advance through attention to architectural detail and methods as opposed to extra expenditure.

'Architectural quality on a Greycoat project requires high cost-efficiency (we do not require hidden high-quality concrete, etc.).'

In other words, they recognize that there is a need for dialogue between designer and client, but that this must be based on developing and improving from the level of knowledge already achieved. Their briefing document is adapted and adjusted for each project from a single file held on a wordprocessor. The process of assembling a brief for a particular project is undertaken by the Greycoat's in-house management team which is multi-disciplinary in background and able to draw on architectural and construction expertise balanced against very strong commercial criteria. The resulting project briefing document does not inhibit design freedom. There are no predetermined overall layout features except for a standard office block width and a suggested toilet layout. The brief clearly states the client's space requirements, particularly in areas which reduce lettable space. For example: plant areas and lifts are included within a 10% allowance for corridors and storage. Plant areas are further limited to 7% of total gross floor area. From these assumptions the building can be sized for the lettable area ratio of 1 person per 140 ft^2. The document contains reports and background information from Greycoat's own research. From observing the differences in the approach adopted by other countries particular elements have been highlighted for study. They are the structure, the cladding and services.

Greycoat have adopted a US-style structural steel frame with profiled steel welded deck and lightweight concrete topping with an objective of achieving an erection time of at least one floor a week. In order to achieve this specification it has taken 2½ years of intensive work between Greycoat, their structural engineers, the Fire Officers and the City of London's District Surveyors to surmount obstacles created by a traditionally conservative interpretation of the Building Regulations. Interestingly this work has been successful in that a US-style frame can be built in the UK, which suggests that it is an unwillingness to make the effort to challenge the existing situation, and not technical problems, which often inhibits change in the UK.

Greycoat have evaluated stone and curtain walling external cladding systems. The problem with stone in the past has been a requirement to use thicknesses in excess of 40 mm and to provide a mechanical key on to the building. US practice shows that thicknesses of 32 mm can be satisfactorily used. Greycoat have, therefore, devised an approach, again after exhaustive discussions with the District Surveyor, which enables a 30 mm granite panel to be cast on to a precast unit which is attached to the building in the normal way. This method gives a significant saving in the cost of stone, enabling off-site manufacture and fast on-site production. Curtain-wall cladding has been investigated by visiting the best European and UK design manufacturers and producers to learn about their processes. The brief contains a report and recommendations which draw the attention of designers to the lessons which have been learnt and are to be incorporated in the project, a sample quotation from which is:

'We in the UK can significantly improve the method by which we buy curtain walling without introducing any special new procedures. On large or complicated projects, specialist window sub-contractors could be asked to supplement the design team in pre-tender design development in return for a fee (as we already do with services sub-contractors).

'Make greater use of the dry powder coating process, which has cost, maintenance as well as architectural attractions.

'Invite tenders for glass supply direct from glass manufacturers and novate to window contractors, who shall quote for fixing only of glass (including supply of accurate cutting schedules).'

Greycoat have examined air-conditioning systems, plant, ductwork, lifts and lighting and converted the results of their study into a set of recommendations and instructions which mimic US practice modified to take account of a UK context with the object of achieving speed and economy. One further example illustrates the intentions contained in a whole list of 'dos and don'ts'. Ductwork has been examined both in the USA and in the UK and consequently their UK specification now uses thinner-gauge metals as existing specifications in general use appear to be based on 1950s hospital building specifications and provide for very heavy construction. 'The designer should question the use of threaded rods with angle-iron supports for ductwork support and question the need to insulate ductwork, particularly in plenum spaces. The air-conditioning plant should be purchased direct from the manufacturers (particularly equipment originating in the USA) to avoid the UK pricing factor when purchased through UK agents.' Generally the instructions to the consultants seek to cause them to challenge all current UK practice and some very direct guidelines are given to enable them to do this.

Throughout Greycoat's briefing document, conventional UK design practices are questioned. Examples have been given above, based on research into the practices adopted by other countries, but the document abounds in examples which have been tried and tested in the UK. Every part of a design is questioned to ensure that it achieves maximum value for money by removing redundancy, excess equipment and over-design. Greycoat's experience is recorded and therefore the designer does not have to rely entirely upon his own experience which may be limited in some areas.

The status of the answers proposed in the brief is reinforced by requiring designers to justify in detail any proposals for improvement to Greycoat's established answers. At each stage of design development, when making proposals which depart from the briefing document, the design team has to prepare an evaluation of the implications on:

Cost,
Value,
Speed of overall programme,
Speed of design,
Speed of construction,
Ease of construction and pre-manufacture,
Ability to 'fast track',
Energy use,
Maintenance,
Flexibility and efficiency of office use from tenant viewpoint,
Cost of tenant installation.

This is a set of requirements which exceeds the normal design evaluation and requires a very wide knowledge base. It is intended to ensure that design is purposeful, well thought out and generally in accordance with the methods Greycoat know work well.

Choice of construction

Townsend, Goodacre and Greycoat provide three different approaches to producing clients' briefs. Each view deserves to be respected and, taken together, they serve to illustrate the problems facing clients who have little experience of construction. Clearly they cannot follow all the advice provided by these three sources because it conflicts.

The principles described in the preceding chapters provide a framework which helps to resolve the differing viewpoints. Townsend's approach leads logically to standard answers, to seeing constructions as commodities which ought to be bought efficiently in much the same way as one buys cars, plant, equipment, raw materials or any other resource needed for a commercial enterprise. As a successful entrepreneur, Townsend knows that he must concentrate on running his own business. It is not his job to do the construction industry's work for it, nor does he want the confusion and conflict of a fragmented industry spilling over into his own organization. He therefore states what he wants in simple direct terms and expects the construction industry to provide it reasonably competently.

Goodacre's approach regards each project as a unique problem requiring its own individual answer. Seeing briefing as an interactive process involving clients and their design teams in detailed analyses of needs and priorities and wide-ranging searches for good answers, leads almost inevitably to innovative constructions. This may well not be Goodacre and his team's intention since they do recognize the possibility of a wide range of different answers including standard and traditional ones. It is difficult, however, for clients to withdraw once they have been drawn into a problem-solving organization. This is partly because innovative designers are commonly very good at selling their ideas and it is difficult for clients, especially inexperienced ones, to resist a beautiful drawing or an exciting model of an end product which will clearly speak to the world of their own culture and sophistication in commissioning a great work of art. So, although in theory Goodacre's approach may result in any type of end product, in practice once a client has set up a problem-solving organization he is most likely to be provided with an innovative answer.

Greycoat's approach can most accurately be seen as leading to a traditional answer provided by a professional organization. In order to recognize this it is also necessary to remember that their approach is being applied in the UK building industry where currently there is no well-developed traditional approach. The main reason for their extremely detailed brief is that they have had to invent their own traditional form of construction and having done so they need to describe it to the professionals they employ.

We now see that the three viewpoints broadly coincide with the three different approaches to construction identified in Chapter 5. There seems no avoiding the conclusion that clients must decide whether, like Townsend, they want a standard answer, like Greycoat's, they want a traditional answer (even if they have to establish their own form of traditional construction), or whether they want an innovative answer. Inexperienced clients are unlikely to be able to make this crucial decision without expert advice. Therefore, from this point onwards, we shall assume experienced clients or clients supported by competent advisors.

There seems to be merit in clients considering the possibility of a standard construction first. This is because if this approach can provide a satisfactory answer it is likely to be cheaper and quicker than the alternatives. So the first question clients should consider is whether an existing answer meets all their requirements. When the answer appears to be in the affirmative they should be able to visit a construction which is exactly like the one they wish to buy. Just as with a motorcar, there may well be a choice of optional features but once they are selected or rejected the client's brief is a simple statement of his choice of end product.

The next possibility to consider, if no standard answers appear to be appropriate, is traditional construction. This requires clients to consider whether an established method of construction provides an appropriate answer. An affirmative answer implies that existing constructions provide, in general, the level of quality and performance which the client wants. This includes the case which Greycoat's approach represents of selecting satisfactory details from a number of sources. Provided that the resulting method of construction is within the normal competence of experienced local design teams and construction teams it is likely that a professional organization will provide a satisfactory end product. Traditional construction probably places the greatest demands on the client at the initial briefing stage. As the Greycoat's example illustrates, clients need to make full and clear decisions about their requirements. When they fail to do so their projects can easily slide into a problem-solving style of approach and their needs will be met only at greater than necessary costs. In particular, they need to provide sufficient information to establish the size and complexity of the end product, the extent to which it provides repetition, the required speed of construction and the likely level of uncertainty to be faced. As we saw in Chapters 2 and 3, these factors are the key determinates of project management decisions. As we shall see when we consider the second of the client's necessary tasks, it is essential that the general order of magnitude of each of the key factors is established during the briefing stage. This does not mean that the brief is equivalent to a full design but it does require the main parameters of the end product to be clearly and firmly decided by the client.

When neither standard nor traditional constructions appear to offer satisfactory answers, and only in those cases, clients need to consider whether they should accept the costs and time involved in commissioning innovative construction. In these cases the brief should describe the problem to be tackled. Often the need for construction, from the client's viewpoint is just one part of a much larger process aimed at long-term objectives. Thus, a decision to market a new product is likely to be the result of much preparatory research and development work and to lead on to large-scale investment which involves a number of construction projects. Some of these may well be provided by standard or traditional constructions but for those which appear to need innovative constructions the client must decide how much of the background to include in the brief.

Newman[3], in a study of the relationships between clients and architects, found that experienced clients requiring buildings tend to see architects as technicians to be employed to formulate a design within their defined requirements. Such clients felt that architects were not competent to carry out the feasibility or analytical studies needed to understand complex manufacturing or marketing processes particularly where scientific, financial or organizational complexities of a high order are involved. On the other hand, Newman thought it paradoxical that architects interviewed in the same study expressed a desire to become involved early in their client's overall process of thinking in order that the design process could be illuminated by this information.

It may well be the case that the experienced clients interviewed by Newman needed standard or traditional answers which would explain their statements. However, where innovation is needed, the architects' views are correct. They need to understand their clients' problems in order to propose relevant answers. The suggestion recorded by Newman that architects tend to have anti-scientific and anti-analytical attitudes which preclude them from understanding complex technical matters suggests the need for multi-discipline design teams rather than lending support to the idea that it is rational to keep designers in the dark. Nevertheless, clients need to decide how much background information to provide in their briefs. The only possible answer is enough to ensure that proposed design decisions are relevant. In which case briefing for innovative constructions is inevitably, as Goodacre suggests, an interactive process in which the client must be fully involved. The client's role is twofold. First, to provide access to the problem which the project is intended to solve and second, to review possible answers. This is essentially a learning process from which the exact nature of the project and, therefore, the brief gradually emerges. So we see that in each of the three approaches the client's first task is influenced by the general nature of the end product. A large part of the difficulties which clients experience with construction arises because the reverse is also true. The way in which clients' objectives are stated goes a long way towards determining the nature of the outcome. Therefore, the choice between standard, traditional and innovative, or between Townsend, Greycoat and Goodacre, is crucial.

Organization

Once the client has made his choice of objectives, the implications of that choice must be consistently followed through all the other necessary tasks. The second of these tasks is defining the main outlines of the project organization. That is, to establish the top part of the organization structure in terms of the roles and responsibilities which shall exist and laying down a constitution which specifies the conditions of engagement or forms of contract to be used in employing role occupants.

In the case of clients wanting standard constructions, the second necessary task is straightforward. They need to ensure that the form of contract used by the firm selling the product which they have selected is fair and reasonable. The starting point for the client should be that performance, quality, price and delivery date are guaranteed – there are no excuses for failing to meet these performance standards – and that the client will be fully compensated if the firm does fail to perform. In many countries in the wake of recent consumer protection legislation, the common law provides an entirely adequate basis for buying standard constructions provided the initial agreement includes a clear description of the end product. Many of the conditions of contract used by firms in this sector of the construction industry attempt to limit or reduce the common law rights of their clients. Therefore, an exchange of letters setting out the terms of agreement and referring to an existing construction or to a comprehensive specification, and scheme drawings in order to define the performance and quality standards, may well be all that is required and is often better than signing a contract provided by the seller.

Traditional construction requires clients to think carefully about their project organizations. Essentially their task at this stage is to allocate clear responsibility for design and for management within a professional organization. The way in which these responsibilities are allocated to roles depends on the relative weight particular clients attach to their various objectives, on the key characteristics of the required end product and on the nature of particular project environments. The organization set up on the basis of these decisions must first behave in a problem-solving mode. It must decide the spaces to be provided, the relationships between them and the overall layout of the end product, as well as its shape, style and general appearance and its relationship to the site. These questions may well require considerable research, development and ingenuity to find a really satisfactory scheme design. Therefore, the roles which the client must identify may include a wide range of skills and knowledge.

However, by definition, traditional construction leads to a largely predetermined set of roles and relationships in the construction stage. The early organizational decisions must bear this need in mind. This usually means emphasizing the management requirement of producing answers within agreed budgets and schedules. On all except the smallest and simplest of projects it is likely to be an advantage for the client to create separate management roles. This will help ensure that the requirements of traditional construction are respected by the design team. The reason for requiring the restraint provided by separate management roles is that designers, especially when faced with difficult scheme design problems, are likely to want to continue their problem-solving mode of working into the detail design stages. This would turn the professional organization into a problem-solving one producing innovative construction with the likelihood of considerable cost and schedule penalties for the client.

Clients, in making their initial organizational decisions, when they want a traditional construction end product, express their own objectives by means of the responsibilities and authority they give to individual roles. Thus, the British Property Federation[4] whose members are mainly commercial development companies, recommends the creation of a management role with authority over a design leader role. This reverses the orthodox position of architects and engineers in which they act as project organization leaders responsible for both design and management. Clearly the British Property Federation has taken the view that the orthodox arrangements as supported and recommended by the professional institutions is unlikely to meet the objectives of commercial developers. The balance between design and management is important in establishing clients' objectives. Equally an emphasis on early completion can be established by creating a separate role with responsibility for schedule and time control; an emphasis on good internal design or high-quality landscaping by creating an interior design role or a landscape design role; or an emphasis on fire safety by creating a fire protection design role. Thus, clients can, and indeed must, incorporate their objectives into the very structure of project organizations. They must also take account of the key characteristics of the required end product since these have a direct effect on the initial choice of roles. We shall examine each of these characteristics in turn to describe the effect.

Size clearly affects the extent to which major responsibilities are divided into separate roles. Small projects will inevitably give rise to few roles. Large projects will be divided into many roles. These will necessarily include some which are primarily concerned with coordination. For example, in large projects it is likely to be worthwhile investing effort in producing formal project procedures, setting performance, cost and time goals, using computerized information systems and creating lateral coordination roles. There is also a tendency for teams on large projects to be larger than on small ones. This is obviously because there is sufficient work of any given type to keep many members of each profession, trade or specialism occupied. However, larger teams also reduce the number of roles required and so in effect transfer coordination requirements from the project as a whole into individual teams. This in turn often means that team responsibilities on large projects are more demanding than on smaller ones. Obviously, size has a direct and often subtle effect on the project organization.

Complexity also has a direct effect on the number of roles. The more different kinds of work required and the more closely interwoven they are, the greater the required number of roles and the more demanding the coordination requirements. These effects are likely to have their greatest effect in the construction stages. However, they affect clients' initial organizational decisions since provision needs to be made for managing a complex construction process from the earliest stages. This could, for example, mean creating a construction management role to ensure that design decisions take proper account of the selected method of construction. There is also likely to be an earlier direct effect since complex projects often give rise to difficult design work and cause problems in coordinating the work of different design teams. Therefore, special attention may well need to be given to a design leader role both in deciding the skills, knowledge and experience to be emphasized in subsequently selecting a role occupant and in providing effective design coordination devices.

Repetition creates opportunities for clients to aim for high levels of productivity and fast construction. High productivity, in-so-far as it is influenced by repetition, depends on the same teams repeating similar activities in a consistent sequence. On the other hand, fast construction can be achieved by employing several teams of each type to work in parallel. Thus, in making initial organizational decisions on repetitive projects, clients must, to some extent, trade off efficiency against speed or vice versa. When fast construction in its own right is one of the required key characteristics of projects, then clients, in addition to seeking to create repetition rather than complexity, should seek to reduce uncertainty. This may require providing for slack resources in larger than strictly necessary teams in the hope of ensuring that schedules are achieved. It may also require roles with responsibility for insulating projects from interference from their environments. Obvious examples are including experts in the project organization to deal with authorities whose approval of the project must be obtained, creating roles with responsibility for ensuring the supply of resources required for construction, or taking special precautions to overcome the effects of weather. Similar strategies are likely to be required in projects facing high uncertainty. Although in such cases it will usually be sensible to accept and to plan for slow construction and perhaps also to reduce the effects of variability and interference by sub-dividing projects into self-contained smaller projects.

The effects of project environments work their way into the key characteristics by increasing the level of uncertainty. The main strategies which clients faced with a difficult environment need to consider have already been mentioned above. However, the remaining possibility to consider is solely a response to environmental factors. This is the decision of where the boundary of the project should be set. By choosing to manufacture components on site ahead of construction for example, clients can seek to remove the risk of delay caused by late delivery. Similarly, providing a hostel or even a hotel, for the workforce may help to ensure the necessary supply of labour. In these and other similar ways the construction stage may be insulated from the effects of the environment. It is not so straightforward to incorporate environmental factors which are otherwise likely to adversely affect the design stage. There are, however, some steps which can be taken. One possibility is to include roles with public relations responsibilities in controversial projects. This may help to reduce objections and so make it easier to obtain essential approvals. Another possibility sometimes used by experienced clients is to include a research institute in their project organization to deal with possible technical objections to their proposals rather than waiting for local authorities to appoint their own experts to consider unusual features in the design.

Thus, we see that traditional construction requires clients to balance their various objectives, the general character of the desired end product and the nature of the particular project environment. In doing so they need to so arrange checks and balances between design and management responsibilities that the set of roles they select behaves as a professional organization and does not turn itself into a problem-solving one. Organizations, to produce innovative answers, should be designed for that purpose by their clients, not emerge by default. We now turn our attention to how this should be achieved.

Innovative constructions are in some ways less demanding than traditional ones in terms of the decisions to be made by clients in setting up the main outlines of their project organizations. Since, by definition, it is not clear at the onset what form of construction will be produced, the first task is to develop a better understanding of the client's problem. It is, therefore, only the client who can determine the relative weight to be given to design issues and management issues. In most cases both are likely to be important and therefore, the creation of a matrix organization which can give balanced consideration to design and to management may well be the right strategy. Where it is clear that one or the other of these major responsibilities is more important in the context of a particular project, this should be reflected in the allocation of authority. Thus, a client wanting a beautiful building irrespective of costs or time will create a design role with great authority over the project. In these circumstances management is likely to be restricted to an advisory role with little or no authority. It must be said that very few clients really are unconcerned about costs or time. Even when initially they adopt such an attitude there is nearly always a change of heart by the client as costs mount up while little tangible progress is being made. Consequently it is nearly always safest in projects which require innovative construction to base the initial project organization on a matrix structure which balances design and management responsibilities.

Role occupants

Having identified the main roles and their responsibilities, a client's next necessary task is to select role occupants for each, that is to appoint his first-line agents who in addition to their particular and defined responsibilities are always responsible for representing the client's interests in dealings with lower levels in the organization, with suppliers and with relevant actors in the project environment. It is important to define the requirements of roles, especially main roles, before selecting teams to occupy them. The opposite sequence is likely to result in the selection of impressive but unsuitable role occupants, that is unsuitable in that their talents do not match the skills, knowledge and experience required for the particular project. To avoid this problem clients should prepare a careful, formal role description which specifies the required attributes.

The aim in selecting first-line agents is to appoint teams with the required skills, knowledge and experience who are enthusiastic about their client's objectives. Experience of the particular type of project, the method of construction if this is already known, the local construction industry and the project environment are nearly always very important requirements. Role occupants need to be technically competent in the tasks required by their responsibilities. This is so that they can divide up the necessary work into sensible roles and give instructions about their performance. It is also necessary in order to judge teams ability to perform so that they can assign roles to effective role occupants. First-line agents in particular also need the interpersonal skills which motivate workers. That is to make team members feel good about their involvement with the project or, in the language of Chapter 7, to cause them to extend their effective preference. First-line agents are likely to have major responsibilities for coordinating the work of separate teams and so need to understand and be competent in the use of the relevant coordination devices. Finally, they need the strength of character to replace teams unable or unwilling to perform properly and to judge when this is necessary. These are the essential technical requirements for first-line agents. In addition the client should select teams to fill these important roles with whom he can communicate confidently. That is they should share a common understanding of the important concepts to be used in the project.

There are a number of ways of helping to ensure that good role occupants are selected. Perhaps best is the use of competitive interviews based on potential candidates' proposed approach to the defined role. In selecting designers this could usefully include a limited design competition in order to demonstrate the approach and attitudes each competitor is likely to contribute to the project. In selecting managers the candidates could be invited to evaluate the brief in terms of overall costs and times in order to demonstrate their potential contribution. A particularly powerful approach is to allow each competitor to criticize and question the proposals put forward by the others. This enables the client to observe potential role occupants working in a dynamic situation and there is a real possibility that the interchanges will help to clarify important features of the project. It is important to remember that it is not the design or the budget and schedule which are being selected, but the role occupant. Although having emphasized the primary objective of the competitive element it must also be admitted that it is an advantage for the client to have first-line agents selected on the basis of proposals which can be used in the project. Subsequent work is likely to proceed smoothly in such cases since the first-line agents are likely to have a greater commitment to their own ideas than to any imposed on them. Having gathered objective evidence on the capabilities of potential role occupants, clients must decide which to appoint. It is valuable to record the basis of the choice since the process of producing an agreed formal justification often helps to avoid judgements based on weak evidence or prejudice.

Project culture

Having selected his first line agents the next necessary task for clients is to establish the project culture. All organizations develop their own beliefs, values, languages and behaviours. Working together and communicating about their work causes the members to tend to see the world in much the same way and to adopt similar attitudes towards what they perceive. The greater the matching of beliefs and values, the more likely members are to communicate. This is because we all prefer to communicate with those of a like mind since the acceptance and approval of our view of the world provides pleasure. The more the members of an organization communicate, the greater the similarity of their internal patterns of knowledge and values. Over time a distinctive culture develops which determines the attitudes and beliefs about the role behaviours which are expected and acceptable within the organization. This process of culture formation takes place within construction project organizations. However, generally teams are involved with any one project for too short a time for any well-defined culture to emerge. This is not true of large projects especially when they are in remote geographical locations and, therefore, their members are largely or even totally dependent on the project organization for social intercourse. However, generally projects are too short term for a distinctive culture to emerge naturally. Therefore, clients need to create a project culture by their behaviour, the beliefs and values it demonstrates and by recruiting, at least to senior positions, teams who will reinforce the chosen culture.

It is useful to remember that culture is communicated. Therefore, regular briefings for all the project teams given by their immediate team leaders is crucial to building up shared beliefs and values and thus, to developing a commitment to project objectives. Teams are motivated by ends which they believe are good. Therefore, it is as important to explain why something is to be done as it is to state what is to be done. The regular team briefings should include information about progress in which the main priorities are emphasized, whether these are quality, productivity, safety or some other matter. The briefings should describe changes in policy which may affect the team, changes in people within the team or elsewhere in the project of interest to the team and highlight points which need to be given special attention in the immediate future. Provided that the briefings are positive and encouraging they can become an important two-way communication channel. Since teams are made aware of the overall objectives of their projects in this way they can channel their efforts, ideas and initiatives towards relevant and useful ideas. The Industrial Society in the UK has, over the years, provided much valuable advice on effective team briefing. The approach it recommends[5] can usefully be applied at all levels in construction projects from clients down so that there develops a close match between the values of all those who make up the project organization and the overall objectives. In this way clients create a project culture which is supportive. If they do not take the trouble to do this the culture which emerges may be supportive but it is just as likely to be antagonistic towards the client's beliefs and values. That is unlikely to result in a successful project.

Client's authority

Having provided the primary objectives, defined the main outlines of the organization, selected the first-line agents and established the project culture, a client's remaining necessary task is to exercise authority over the organization. This means continuing to carry out the four necessary tasks already described in the face of changing circumstances and providing appropriate rewards and punishments. That is control consists essentially of ensuring that objectives are clear, that the whole project is divided into rationally related roles, that the teams who are to perform these tasks are informed of what they are to do and motivated to do it and that teams unable or unwilling to perform are replaced. Significant changes in project environments or poor performance within their projects require clients usually aided by their top management, to search for and if they can be found, to implement modified decisions which promise to provide better results.

An important source of control information for clients comes from walking around the workplaces of the teams involved with their projects and talking to team members. They should ask specific questions to ensure that their own objectives and decisions are known and understood. Good examples include asking what are your achievements against targets, who told you what your targets are, do you know how your team is doing, was last week better or worse, do you know who your boss is and how could the job be done better? It is useful to ask team leaders about absenteeism, whether it is causing difficulties and if so, what they are doing about it. This is important since the level of absenteeism provides a reliable guide to motivation and morale. Clients should check for tidiness and proper welfare provisions, inspect the toilets, look at noticeboards, check targets and schedules and ensure that proper quality and safety standards are being applied. Above all they should listen to anything which project members wish to say to them and give praise and encouragement whenever possible. When they find faults they should reprimand the leader, not the individual.

The information gained from walking the job helps clients to interpret the formal reports from managers and data from information systems. It will help them make decisions which are capable of being implemented successfully. Poor performance often results directly from decisions made remote from the scene of the action. There is no substitute for first-hand direct experience of the conditions and circumstances of workers and without this it is easy to choose answers which are unreasonably difficult, dangerous, wasteful or simply impossible to put into practice.

It may be felt that the five necessary tasks represent unreasonable demands on clients' time and resources. In fact, all are essential for successful construction projects and if clients are unable, for whatever reason, to undertake them they should appoint a project manager to do so on their behalf.

Complex clients

The discussion to this point has been written as though it is assumed that clients generally are consistent and clear individuals. Construction projects would be greatly simplified if clients did indeed display these admirable characteristics. Clients in the real world tend to be organizationally complex in terms of who wants the building, who will use it, who must approve it, who provides the finance and other relevant responsibilities and powers. An example which illustrates this is provided by the situation surrounding projects to provide new schools in the public sector in the UK.

In Britain, public sector schools are owned by local authorities. Matters relating directly to ownership, including for example the purchase of the land and the formation of contracts concerning the design and construction, are normally dealt with by the County Secretary. The construction of schools is financed by loans from central government which must be repaid out of the authorities' normal resources, part of which come from central government grants, part from borrowed money, part from the local rate-payers and part from a number of other local sources. The County Education Officer is responsible for defining what is to be built through a multitude of specialist advisors within his own department. However, other departments often contribute to the total brief. It is not uncommon for the County Surveyor to lay down standards of construction for entrance roads and car parks. The County Architect may similarly require particular methods of construction and particular components to be used. The County Treasurer will establish the system of financial control needed to ensure that the necessary funds are available as they are needed. The County Quantity Surveyor will establish a detailed financial policy aimed at ensuring that the authority's expenditure on construction is achieved efficiently. The timing of the project will normally be determined by the County Education Officer but other officers may lay down additional time constraints. The planned quality of the project will effectively be established by the standards being achieved and accepted in the authorities other new school projects. The users of the school could be held to include the County Education Officer and his specialist advisors, the teachers who almost certainly will not be appointed until the building is virtually complete, the pupils, most of whom will not be born at the time the initial decisions concerning the new school are taken, their parents, the board of governors and the local community surrounding the school. All the local authority officers' decisions in this list are subject to the approval of the councillors who have the authority to alter any of them at any point in the client, design, management and construction process. This right is not frequently exercised but its existence does normally ensure full member involvement in policy decisions. There is one further important client participant. This is central government. The Department of Education and Science provides general rules which control all new school building and, in addition, overall levels of expenditure are established centrally. The application of this national policy framework to specific projects and, therefore, the definition of what is to be built can be the subject of protracted discussions and negotiations between the two levels of government.

All the people mentioned may, in one sense or another, be regarded as the client for a new school construction project. It should perhaps be emphasized that the example is not selected to illustrate a situation of extreme or unnecessary fragmentation. Indeed, the construction of schools in the UK is internationally regarded as a significant success story. Neither does the fact that a public client has been described alter the degree of fragmentation which may be encountered in practice. Rather it is a characteristic of decision making in large organizations, especially in those which have a major impact on their local environment.

The conventional wisdom in the construction industry is that clients should not allow their organizational complexity to flow over into their projects. The British Property Federation (BPF)[4] approach, for example, is that clients should nominate one individual who is authorized to commit the client contractually and take responsibility for all client decisions. This works well for experienced clients who know what they want. However, when the appointment of an individual merely hides unresolved conflicts within the client organization, the project is likely to experience major problems at later and more expensive stages as the disagreements surface and lead to design changes and delays. Therefore, clients should establish a client organization with as much care and thought as has been suggested they devote to the project organization. Their aim should be to provide a clear statement to the project organization of who, within the client organization, has authority in particular areas and who is responsible for specific decisions. This may require a client team or indeed several coordinated teams rather than one individual. As projects proceed and as firm decisions are made, it may well be possible to simplify the client organization. This is likely to benefit projects provided that it does not hide problems which will subsequently be allowed to surface.

The client organization should be arranged so that all the objectives are revealed. It is unlikely that the direct objectives of providing specific amounts of space to achieve stated performances at certain costs within given times will be ignored. However, clients often have other objectives which may have social, cultural, political or religious dimensions. They may be to provide status and prestige for the client, they may be to provide a service for a particular community, they may well be commercial, economic or technical, they may simply be to provide entertainment, pleasure and fun or to enhance the environment in some way. Most construction projects, like many other human activities, are undertaken with several of these categories of objective in the client's mind. They are not always explicitly expressed or indeed consciously recognized but they do exert a real and direct influence on the client's decisions in respect of his project.

An example may help to emphasize this important point. It is based on a synthesis of several actual projects. A man commissioned an architect to design a factory to house a new manufacturing plant. The man intended the new factory to be the culmination of his life's work. He would set up the factory, get it running properly and then retire. He saw the factory as giving expression to his undoubted local power and influence and solid business acumen. He had not revealed these long-term plans to anyone, least of all to the architect, in case news of his retirement disrupted his smoothly-running organization. The architect, over-impressed with the man's hard commercial approach, designed a simple, technically competent and efficient corrugated, fibre-cement-clad shed to house the new plant. The client was impressed by beautifully presented drawings of the design and enraged when he saw the shed being built. This kind of story is all too common in construction. The results are wasted time and resources, and either projects end up as an unsatisfactory and awkward compromise between the designers original concept and the changed brief, or else clients conclude that the construction industry is incompetent.

It is useful at this point to describe another project which again illustrates the importance of taking all the major objectives into account. It also throws some light on the relationships between clients and the construction industry. This time the example is taken directly from practice as reported to the author. All the names have been omitted to avoid embarrassment.

A talented and sensitive architect was commissioned by the Social Services Department of a local authority to design a health centre. The appointment was made on the recommendation of the doctors who would subsequently use the centre. Doctors in Britain have the right to choose whether to use local authority health centres or to provide their own accommodation. Those who the local authority hoped would use the proposed new building had visited and very much admired a health centre designed as part of a large city centre complex by the same architect. Everyone involved was confident that the project would be a great success. They were reinforced in this view when a pleasant wooded site in the middle of a delightful rural village was found for the new centre and the architect, in consultation with the doctors, produced a truly magnificent and imaginative design. It was widely admired and clearly would provide the basis for a fine health centre.

When the likely cost of the project was calculated the local authority quantity surveyors' report suggested that the proposals would exceed central government's normal cost limits for health centres by over 75%. The quantity surveyors also visited the architect's earlier city centre health centre and in a report to the authority, stated that the complex which housed it was a building of the highest quality, employing materials and standards of craftsmanship which had not previously been afforded in local authority health centres. It also appeared that the normal cost limit for the city health centre had been substantially supplemented by funds from other sources. The architect was applying the same high standards in his new design. In the main this accounted for the high cost.

There were no social or other grounds for taking scarce local authority funds from other badly needed projects to buy a fine piece of architecture for an already privileged village. The outcome was probably predictable and sad. After a series of long agonizing meetings and several half-hearted and patently unsuccessful attempts by the architect to produce a revised scheme within normal cost limits, the authority's Social Services Committee lost patience. The commission was taken away from the architect and his fee account was only partially paid, and that after prolonged and unpleasant argument. A prefabricated building based on an existing design was hurriedly put up to meet the original timetable for the doctors to move into the new health centre. It was well within normal cost limits. The doctors refused to move into the prefabricated building and have continued to practice from their existing surgery. The local authority are still trying to persuade them to accept the new health centre.

This clearly unsatisfactory outcome resulted in the main from a failure to make all the major objectives clear early in the project. This failure was largely caused by the Social Services Department, the doctors, central government and the Social Services Committee all undertaking elements of the client role in an uncoordinate manner. This is in fact, all too often a feature of construction projects especially where the client is a large organization. The legal ownership of the project, its financing, the technical definition of what is to be constructed, the imposition of controls over such matters as cost, time and quality and the actual occupancy and use of the finished product are frequently separated. It is only the client who can impose consistency, or at least create an organizational framework from which the consistency is likely to emerge. Consistency is essential for effective and efficient construction project management. Therefore, clients should expect to give as much attention to their own internal organization as they must to the project organization.

A useful discipline for clients in framing their objectives is to define the criteria by which the success of the project will be judged. Townsend's criteria[1] are simple and direct. He requires projects to be completed on time, work reasonably well and that the cries of outraged vanity and offended taste should die out within thirty days. Other clients are likely to set more demanding, or at least more complex, criteria. However, the process of establishing them provides a substantial contribution to successful projects.

Summary

The clients' role is crucial to the success of construction projects. It requires clients to provide the primary objectives for projects, define the main outlines of the organization, select occupants for the main roles, establish the project culture and exercise authority over the organization.

A client needs to decide whether he wants standard, traditional or innovative construction. The nature of the brief and the client's role in providing it is largely determined by this choice. Standard construction requires a simple statement of the client's choice of end product. Traditional construction requires a full and clear statement of the client's requirements in sufficient detail to enable the key characteristics of the end product to be determined. Innovative construction requires a statement of the problem which is intended to be solved by undertaking the project. It also requires clients to be fully involved in selecting the main features of the proposed end product.

Clients need to establish the top part of the organization structures and lay down the constitutions for their projects. This is influenced by the basic choice of end product. Standard construction requires merely a simple contract with the firm selling the selected product. Traditional construction requires responsibility for design and management to be clearly allocated taking account of the relative weight attached to the various client objectives, the key characteristics of the required end product and the nature of the project environment. Innovative construction normally requires a matrix organization which balances design and management responsibilities.

Clients need to appoint first-line agents with relevant skills, knowledge and experience who are enthusiastic about the project objectives. Clients need to create a project culture by demonstrating, through their behaviour, the preferred beliefs and values and by recruiting teams who support these. Regular team briefings throughout projects help create and sustain the chosen culture.

Finally, clients need to exercise authority over their project organizations by making decisions in respect of objectives, organization, role occupants and culture in the light of changing circumstances and by providing rewards and punishments. Clients can obtain an important part of the information they need for control by walking around their projects and talking to team members.

Clients often consist of complex organizations. They should, therefore, provide their project organizations with a clear statement of the allocation of authority within their own organizations for making all the various categories of client decision.

References

1. TOWNSEND, R., *Up the Organization,* Coronet (1971)
2. GOODACRE, P., PAIN, J., MURRAY, J. and NOBLE, M., *Research in Building Design,* Department of Construction Management, University of Reading, Occasional Paper No. 7 (1982)
3. NEWMAN, R., JENKS, M. and BACON, V., *Brief Formulation and the Design of Buildings,* Department of Architecture, Oxford Polytechnic (1981)
4. *Manual of the BPF System: The British Property Federation System for Building Design and Construction,* The British Property Federation (1983)
5. GRUMMIT, J., *Team Briefing,* The Industrial Society (1983)

Chapter 9

The principles in practice

The principles described in this book are valuable in-so-far as they help practitioners in the construction industry to improve their performance. In this chapter we consider the practical implications for designers, managers and constructors in order first to illustrate the principles and secondly to highlight the main lessons for current practice.

The main decision makers in the construction industry are professionals and craftsmen. As we have seen, this means they have learnt an established range of answers through their education and training. They are also skilled in relating those answers to a range of problems. That is they are skilled in diagnosis. As we have also seen they form teams which undertake professional and craft work on a formal commercial basis. Where projects require well-established traditional construction, the teams of professionals and craftsmen perform effectively and efficiently. Their work fits together with little project specific coordination and produces good results. This is particularly so when projects are not large, not more than moderately complex, involve repetition, do not require fast construction, do not include unfamiliar design details or methods of construction and take place within reasonably certain environments.

Traditional construction produced by professional organizations is implicitly embedded in most of the industry's formal education, its literature and its institutions. It provides the concepts and language in which its practitioners discuss their work. Yet it is under tremendous pressure. The pressures arise from two sources. One is from the nature of projects, many of which require standard or innovative constructions rather than traditional answers. The other pressure arises from the rate of change in the technology available to the industry both in respect of the materials, components and constructions which form the end products of the industry and in respect of the organizational implications of information technology. These two kinds of pressure give rise to many signs of stress. These include poor quality end products, low efficiency, over-complicated organizations and perhaps, most significantly, clients demanding better performance. These signs are, however, symptoms and the pressures causing them are that professional and craft education and training are inappropriate for many projects especially when combined with the demands and opportunities of rapidly changing technology. We can examine the pressures and their effects by reference to practice.

Standard constructions

Projects which require standard constructions exert pressures on the professionals involved in a very direct way. Leopold and Bishop[1] in a study of the design of houses in the private and public sectors in the UK found that architects had a limited role in speculative house-building firms. In the preliminary design stage their role is to produce, at extremely short notice, a layout for each potential site which incorporates a given number of specified standard house types chosen in order to maximize sales potential. In the detail design stages the architect's role is largely dictated by site management and the sales force. Management or marketing may suggest an alternative material with better performance or appearance or which will save money. Often the change is suggested merely to overcome component supply problems or to take advantage of the opportunity of obtaining a low price. In other words, commercial criteria dominate architectural issues.

On occasions, management may require the correction of a faulty detail discovered in constructing an earlier generation of the same type of house, or to introduce a new feature on the basis of feedback from the sales force. Even in these cases the initiative lies with the commercial managers and is not rooted in aesthetic considerations. Leopold and Bishop conclude that in these circumstances the architect's traditional design responsibility largely disappears. They contrast this with the fully professional role of architects working in public sector housing projects. In this case architects are able to consider the optimal development of sites from traditional architectural premises. They analyze from basic principles and use unique combinations of features to produce workable and attractive environments. Compared with those in the speculative house-building firms, the public sector architects are less constrained by time, by the costs of time, or by the type and number of dwellings to be built. In the detail design stage too, the public sector architects retain a fully professional role often being allowed a free reign to review principles and details as and when they see fit. These distinctions continue through into the construction stages. The architects in speculative house-building firms typically never visit sites, while those in the public sector are responsible for supervising construction on behalf of the client and playing the full traditional role of the architect. Clearly, the largely commercial pressures of a programmed organization have stripped away all except absolutely essential tasks from the architect's role in speculative house-building firms. What is left is essentially a sub-professional or technician role dictated by the requirements of marketing and management.

This is the case in respect of individual projects. However, speculative house-building firms require a more substantial input from architects when they decide to develop new house types. At this time the design role is fully professional. However, the development of new designs is infrequent. Leopold and Bishop found that in many cases responsibility for the professional work involved was given to a separate design group or to consultants. No doubt this organizational separation, as well as enabling firms to employ experienced and individual designers, served to insulate projects from the corrupting influence of professional attitudes. Thus, the architects employed to provide a service to individual projects are restricted to a very limited design role and in many cases, are not allowed the compensation of developing new house types.

Programmed organizations provide similarly limited and constrained roles for all the professionals and craftsmen involved. In-so-far as standard construction satisfies the requirements of a growing range of project types, it exerts increasing pressure on the established norms of the construction industry. In response the industry's professionals tend to attack standard constructions in any way possible. Examples of this include regulations which are loaded against standard answers by giving local officials considerable detailed discretion over such matters as planning requirements and fire safety requirements; publicity from professional institutions aimed at dissuading clients from adopting standard answers; articles and books in which efficiency and cost effectiveness are denigrated in favour of craftsmanship and aesthetic quality. Despite all this, a large part of the pressure on professionals arising from standard construction comes about because they appear to be losing the argument. Clients see that standard answers often provide technically competent, pleasant and very cheap constructions which satisfy their requirements.

The better approach for the industry's professionals would be to recognize that standard constructions provide good answers for many clients and whilst the roles required do not match the normal professional divisions, they are entirely worthwhile. Generally, the roles required are broader in covering a wide range of skills and knowledge but this is balanced since they apply to only one particular set of standard constructions. Thus, Leopold and Bishop found that in firms undertaking speculative house building it was common for one individual to take on the joint roles of marketing, project management and architectural design. Such individuals would benefit from education and training which covers this group of subjects together with the industrial design principles and production technology which underlie standard construction. This would prepare them for challenging roles in programmed organizations in which they are likely to have considerable authority in projects which provide an important part of the construction industry's output.

Innovative constructions

Projects which require innovative constructions exert a different set of pressures on construction professionals. In a sense these pressures are self-imposed. Many professionals are reluctant to use traditional construction and take a delight in searching for better answers through innovation. However, in doing this, they appear in many cases to want to preserve the roles and relationships appropriate in professional organizations. Thus, architects in problem-solving organizations will try to adopt the role of the client's primary agent which has emerged in small, straightforward building projects using traditional construction. In the same way quantity surveyors and general contractors will seek to use tendering and contractual arrangements devised in the context of well-established traditional construction. The common results are delays, claims by the contractor and a poor quality end product for the client. It is useful, therefore, to consider the kind of roles which are in fact required in problem-solving organizations.

Gilbert and Horner[2] provide from first-hand experience a detailed description of the planning, design and construction of the Thames Barrier. The following commentary draws freely on their account. By any standards the Thames Barrier project required innovative construction and therefore a problem-solving organization. The problem to be tackled was that central London faces a growing risk of a major flood disaster. The solution finally settled on was to build a structure capable of closing off the Thames Estuary. The barrier is designed to prevent the sea surging inland to flood an area of land housing over one million people and containing the most important administrative centre in the UK. The underground railway system in central London was particularly at risk and, if flooded, would take at least a year to return to full operation. In addition, basements, ground floors and many streets in central London could be under water within an hour of a high surge tide reaching London Bridge. The total damage was estimated in 1966 at £2000 million which is equivalent to at least £15 000 million at 1985 prices. Clearly these levels of damage would constitute a major disaster. The risk of it occurring is increasing due to a combination of natural causes which produce steadily more frequent and higher flood tides in central London. The floods of 1953 breached the flood defences all down the east coast of England. Over 300 people and much livestock were drowned. In central London the tide lapped the top of the parapet walls along the river. These events and the knowledge that the risks were increasing persuaded Government that the capital city must be protected.

The decision to build a barrier was preceded by a long and thorough analysis of the problem. At this stage the organization was more a problem-analyzing than a problem-solving one. It was necessary to quantify the threat facing central London and to identify the constraints on the various possible answers. For this purpose a large amorphous organization gradually emerged. A major weakness in the early stages was that responsibility for providing protection against the flood threat was not clearly the responsibility of any one body. That is there was no single client to provide objectives and to create and lead the necessary organization. It was not until the setting up of the Greater London Council (GLC) in 1965 that a body existed willing to play the client role. By this time much data had been collected but no clear way forward had emerged.

The GLC set about investigating the most important issues by establishing seven working parties to study questions of navigation, pollution and siltation, groundwater, amenity, oceanography and meteorology, civil engineering and costs of delay to shipping. This last in recognition of one of the major constraints facing any flood protection structure. Namely that London in the 1960s was still a major sea port and consequently the Thames had to remain navigable to ocean-going ships.

Day-to-day direction and coordination of the working parties was carried out by a project management team. Detailed control of this team was provided by a steering committee of senior officers drawn from the GLC, three different central government departments, two local river authorities, three separate bodies representing the interests of shipping and the Hydraulics Research Station. Overall direction was provided by a policy committee of politicians and chief officers drawn from the same bodies. Inevitably if such a large organization is to be successful, clear leadership must be provided. The chairman of the steering committee and the leader of the project management team emerge from Gilbert and Horner's account as key actors in this respect.

The working parties drew on the best scientific and technical knowledge available. The studies needed to range very widely as the working party titles suggest. The one responsible for oceanography and meteorological issues serves to illustrate important principles. It included experts who had made detailed studies of the incidence and probability of high waters along the east coast and who had undertaken research on the adverse change of high waters relative to land levels. They needed to draw on meteorological theories on changing patterns of depressions over the Atlantic. In other words all the available records and ideas had to be drawn together to assess the probabilities of surge tides of various heights. This was complicated by the particular shape and pattern of the Thames Estuary.

To help in the work two models were constructed. One was a physical model of the whole Estuary from Teddington to Southend with a 1:600 horizontal scale and 1:60 vertical scale. The model filled the floor of a 380 ft long shed at Didcot which was reasonably close to the Hydraulics Research Station. The second was a mathematical model of a tidal estuary produced by the Liverpool Tidal Institute. The two models were bound to give different results but some very significant information emerged when the research engineers responsible for each were required to present and defend their results in front of each other.

Out of all this work there gradually emerged a detailed understanding of the flood threat to central London. The other working parties were similarly engaged in assembling, sifting and analyzing the available data so that the relative importance of the major factors was understood. An interesting early problem was to establish the basis on which decisions should be made. Economists believed that a cost-benefit analysis approach should be adopted in which the estimated damage was balanced against the probability of the damage occurring and the costs of preventing it. The alternative view which was essentially that of the engineers involved was that since a major threat existed, something should be done about it. This was resolved by appointing a high-ranking scientist, a man of Nobel Prize calibre with a powerful intellect and no preconceptions, to report on the problem. The man chosen was Professor Bondi, FRS, FRAS, an astronomer, who was then Professor of Mathematics at Kings College. His conclusion was that a major surge flood in London would be a disaster of a singular and immense kind. It would be a knock-out blow to the nerve centre of the country. Therefore, even though the probability of a high surge tide is not great, the extremely severe effects on the life of the country make it appropriate to take preventative measures.

The question then was what measures were best. A good deal of work had already been done on this question. As early as the mid 1950s two firms of consulting engineers were appointed to examine the options. They considered a lifting bridge, a swing barrier and a retractable barrier and estimated the costs of the various possibilities at £13 to £17.5 million at 1958 prices. After several years' delay and indecision the two firms of engineers were each commissioned to prepare outline schemes and estimates of their preferred answer. Rendel, Palmer and Tritton produced a scheme for a low-level retractable barrier at an estimated cost in 1965 of £24.55 million whilst Sir Bruce White, Wolfe Barry and Partners produced a scheme for a high-level retractable barrier at an estimated cost of £41.25 million. Each firm expressed reservations about the practicability and safety of the alternative scheme, although on further discussion and study, it appeared that in each case the objections could be overcome.

All this background work was taken into account by the GLC in deciding the best form of defence. They needed to look at all possibilities so that subsequent stages should not be delayed on the basis that a valid option had been overlooked. The GLC barrier team used brain-storming sessions to identify possible answers. The general public was invited to make suggestions. In all, 31 different structures were considered, with some of the schemes having two or three variations. The outcome was a decision in 1971 to build a barrier using rising sector gates at Woolwich. Rendel Palmer and Tritton were appointed as consulting engineers responsible for detail design, producing contract documents, letting contracts and supervising construction.

The decision to build a barrier gave rise to yet another stage of detailed, painstaking investigation. This included a detailed borehole investigation of the river bed at Woolwich. A comprehensive range of tests was carried out by a specialist firm on the boreholes and on the samples taken from them to determine the geological nature of the site. In addition, the design of the barrier involved research and development work. The gates illustrate this. They formed a box girder which had to be revolved in a tidal river. The loads imposed by water pressure varied with the position of the gate and the state of the tide. The design was based on a complex finite element analysis by computer. However, the calculations were checked by means of two physical models.

The first, constructed by a specialist research model building firm, was an Araldite model of 1:25 scale which was used to check the computer modelling used for the design of the gates. This identified the need for changes in the original analysis. Secondly a larger steel model of 1:6 scale was produced by a university engineering department. In this second model all the components in the actual structure were reproduced. It was used to determine the ultimate load carrying capacity of the structure. The tests identified weaknesses in the design which were eliminated.

A similarly careful approach was adopted to the design of all parts. This included the architectural treatment of the nine piers which carry the gates. The architect to the GLC considered a wide variety of architectural designs before selecting curved housings clad in stainless steel on a timber structure. The Timber Research and Development Association designed the structure and wind tunnel tests of the housings were carried out by yet another university department. Each part of the barrier brought together in this way a varied group of experts to propose, select and develop the best possible answers. In this context 'best' was taken to mean the best compromise between construction costs, speed of construction, reliability, running and maintenance costs and acceptance by powerful interested parties including particularly those concerned with navigation in the Thames.

As the final design was almost complete a construction plan was prepared. To enable work to start early and to avoid any one contract being of more than moderate size or duration it was decided to split the work into 21 work packages. Even so the civil engineering work in the piers and cills was an extremely large contract with a contract period of at least 4½ years. It must be said that the late decision on the work packages conflicts with the principles described in this book for problem-solving organizations. An earlier recognition of the need for a very large work package for the piers and cill might well have caused the design to be rethought to enable the work to be further sub-divided. In all events the civil engineering construction was beset with problems.

Tenders were invited from five firms or consortia in July 1973. Two withdrew and three tenders were received in November 1973. All were heavily qualified in respect of costs of labour, materials and possible delays. During the ensuing negotiations a further firm withdrew. In July 1974 a contract based on modified standard civil engineering conditions of contract was entered into with the Costain Civil Engineering, Tarmac

Construction, and Hollandsche Beton Maatschappij BV consortium. An important provision was that contract rates should be reviewed after two years in the light of experience to date.

Work started on-site in January 1975. The conditions of employment adopted by the consortium did not fit into the normal pattern of work in Woolwich and the early days were beset with labour problems. A particular problem was the decision to work two twelve-hour shifts in an area where the men were used to working a 40-hour week. There were also, inevitably, technical problems particularly with finding a satisfactory means of excavating flinty chalk sub-soil below water. The end result was that at the review of contract rates in mid-1976, the work was six months behind schedule. After prolonged negotiations it was agreed that the contractor should be paid his full costs to date whilst the rates were increased by 16% for future work, a lump sum was agreed to cover the costs of industrial disputes during the next two years and a new clause limiting the contractor's profit or loss was introduced into the contract.

Although the GLC was dissatisfied with progress and had the contractual right to terminate the contract, this was not really a viable course of action since a new contractor may well have performed no better. In other words, the GLC's effective preference had lengthened, thus increasing both the consortium's plain and bargaining power. The main benefit to the GLC from the review was the reorganization of the consortium's top management in the project. The new team realized the weakness of the twelve-hour shifts and changed to three eight-hour shifts. This immediately provoked a two-month strike due to the loss of overtime payments to the workforce. Eventually, however, agreement was reached and work restarted on a sounder organizational basis. In particular the new top management saw it as an essential part of their job to be on-site dealing with problems where and when they arose. However, the contractor never succeeded in making a profit so that the limitation-of-loss clause effectively turned the contract into a cost reimbursable one.

In January, 1978 a very high surge tide partially flooded the barrier piers and came within inches of flooding central London. The Government asked the GLC to expedite the construction even at the risk of higher costs. Therefore, the contract was re-negotiated to provide the consortium with a reasonable financial carrot to finish the work quickly. The revised agreement was based on an index-linked target cost of £165 million for expenditure after 1 January, 1979 with a provision that profits or losses of up to 5% were shared. There was also a sliding scale of bonuses for completion by the 1982–83 flood season. The workforce was paid a bonus of £500 to each man for each of seven stages in the work if they were completed without industrial disputes. Labour relations subsequently were markedly better. The work was completed on time and the maximum bonus was earned by the consortium. This outcome probably justifies the criticism voiced in 1978 that the re-negotiated agreement was too generous.

The overall result is a structure which represents fine engineering and good architecture. It provides protection from floods for central London for a long time into the future. It is difficult to criticize the design, but the management responsibilities appear not to have been given equal weight in the project. The failure to identify manageable work packages during the design stages must have contributed to the problems with the civil engineering construction work. The apparent failure to take account of the uncertainty surrounding large, innovative construction projects in difficult environments in preparing estimates undoubtedly contribute to large cost and schedule over-runs. Without a clear management framework based on realistic estimates, it is impossible to set effective objectives for teams. In these circumstances cost reimbursement became the only alternative to abandoning the project. These effects were undoubtedly accentuated by the initial use of the traditional form of contract embodying the orthodox professional relationships between engineer and contractor. The final cost of £440 million illustrates these weaknesses when it is compared with the highest of the 1968 estimates adjusted for inflation to the mid-point of construction in 1979. This produces an updated total cost of about £100 million, or less than one quarter of the actual outcome.

The effects illustrated by the Thames Barrier occur on many large construction projects[3]. They arise from attempting to apply arrangements developed in professional organizations to projects which require problem-solving organizations. The challenge for professionals as they undertake innovative construction is to work in multi-discipline teams within matrix structures which balance design and management. The roles will be more specialized and draw on a greater depth of knowledge, skills and experience than their traditional professional work. Much of the time they will be essentially learning by exploring new ideas rather than applying learned answers. This is challenging and risky since there is always the possibility of failing to find a good answer. Added to this is the fact that working in teams where everyone's ideas may be challenged and must be defended is too demanding for many professionals. It is not surprising, therefore, that some of those involved with projects which require innovative answers feel themselves under pressure.

The way forward is for all the construction professions to give attention to recognizing and developing those of its members who are innovative problem solvers. In particular, the innovators need to become familiar with research and development work, to be able to use its results and to understand and be competent in its methods. There are close links between research, innovative design and basic human thought processes as described in Chapter 6.

Whilst some minds have a limited ability to make new connections between concepts, within all the construction professions there are many individuals who can imagine new answers and have the tenacity to turn them into reality. They need to be identified and provided with specialized education and training to develop these talents. Then, in setting up problem-solving organizations, special attention should be given to ensuring that such individuals are recruited to form the multi-discipline teams needed. Attention should also be given to setting up the teams in such a way that personal growth and development is encouraged. This means posing large open-ended problems and giving teams doing the basic work real responsibility and matching authority in respect of proposed answers. In this way the industry will gradually help its innovators to grow and so, together, will become better at tackling the most difficult of construction projects.

So we see that standard and innovative constructions both provide pressures, albeit of very different kinds, on construction professionals. They are also under pressure from rapidly changing technology.

New technology

Over the past two or three decades there has been an enormous increase in the kind of materials, particularly composite materials, commonly used in construction. During the same period the range and sophistication of prefabricated components has increased dramatically. There is now a substantial international market in windows, door sets, kitchen fittings, fitted furniture, partition and cladding systems, electrical, heating and ventilating equipment and many other elements. This hardly existed even twenty years ago. To further complicate matters there has also been a tremendous growth in methods of construction and the plant and equipment available to support them.

The important effect is that in many parts of the world there is no clearly established simple form of traditional construction. The consistent pattern of craft following craft has been joined and largely replaced by a burgeoning multitude of specialists. This is confusing for the craftsmen who find that the context of their work varies significantly from project to project. They must learn new construction details, fix to unfamiliar materials and use methods they do not fully understand. Specialist firms who can afford to invest in training for their construction teams and guarantee their end products have grown up to cope with this complexity and uncertainty. This appears to be an irreversible trend and indeed, at least one UK brick manufacturer is considering the practicability of certifying bricklayers as competent to use their products in the hope of providing an assurance of good-quality brickwork. Clearly if this is necessary, traditional craft training simply is not coping with modern construction. Since professional organizations rely on established traditional construction, construction professionals are finding that they must also adapt. The signs of these effects can be seen, for example, in the sustained interest in project information systems for construction projects over the past twenty years[4].

Construction professionals are about to face an even greater pressure from new technology. As computers begin to reproduce more and more of the processes of human brains, large parts of the routine aspects of professional work will be automated. That which remains for the humans is likely to be substantially altered. Computer-based expert systems can now be used to capture bodies of knowledge and make it available to users in response to free-ranging questions. The systems are able to determine when they have insufficient knowledge to answer a particular question and to cause the computer to pose questions of its own in order to discover the required information. The resulting new knowledge is then stored and is available to deal with similar questions in the future. The systems can also be programmed so that they draw new inferences from the knowledge available to them in response to users' questions. The most celebrated examples of expert systems are those used to aid medical diagnosis[5]. They are entirely relevant to considering likely future developments in construction professional practice since as we have seen earlier diagnosis is the most characteristic professional activity. It is unlikely that construction poses more difficult professional problems than medicine. This is confirmed by the emergence of a number of systems which capture specific bodies of construction knowledge. Examples in construction include expert systems which aid the selection of cranes and lifting equipment for particular projects, the calculation of general contractors site organizations and the supporting accommodation and other facilities they will require for particular building projects, and the design of scaffolding systems for various construction situations[6].

The effect of expert systems on professional work, based on the currently available evidence, is likely initially to be an improvement in the reliability of decision making. In the long run it seems inevitable that much routine professional work will be automated. Traditional construction will become very largely a process of selecting from a range of established specialist options. Having made the selection, computers will provide substantial assistance to the professionals in checking such matters as performance levels, compatibility between elements and compliance with regulations. They will then call up the required materials and components, produce instructions for construction teams and provide expert advice on selecting and managing the necessary organization. Clients will be able to use such systems with the minimum of professional assistance. In this way professional organizations will tend to become more like programmed ones. Individual projects will require less professional work than is the case today but there will be greater investment in developing and maintaining the systems on which professional organizations of the future will rely. However, that is for the future and in the meantime, information technology will change the methods used by professionals even within their present organizational structures. There are a number of examples of computer systems which illustrate this. In general they make it possible for construction professionals to provide better answers by using more efficient, more sophisticated techniques.

Construction Project Simulator

A good example of such a system which relates very closely to the principles described in this book is the Construction Project Simulator produced by Bennett and Ormerod[7]. It is worth considering in some detail, since it illustrates the kind of effects computers are likely to have on the work of construction professionals. In addition it demonstrates the strength of the model of projects which is described in Chapters 1, 2 and 3 and which underlies the subsequent chapters. The following description is based very directly on Bennett and Ormerod's report to the Science and Engineering Research Council who provided funds for the work. It starts with a general justification for the basic concepts which the simulator uses.

In the construction industry it is generally accepted that the provision of a firm commitment to a tender price and duration, for any project, is a 'best guess' as it seeks to predict the future. This is further complicated as each project is unique, takes places at a different location each time with its own problems and involves setting up a temporary production 'factory'. Also, construction is prone to many unpredictable effects such as: the influence of the weather, variable rates of productivity, supply problems of materials and components, labour shortages and strikes, the attendance of sub-contractors, and is critically affected by the flow of design information. Everyone can no doubt add one or two factors of their own to this incomplete list.

These factors are the source of what is generally referred to as uncertainty. The underlying hypothesis of the simulator is that uncertainty is considered to be made up of two major components: inteference and variability. Interferences are those external factors affecting the project which cause a stop to work on a particular task. These result from such things as: lack of design information, inclement weather, delivery problems, sub-contract non-attendance, plant breakdowns and the many other influences of project environments which cause delay. Variability refers only to variations in the rate of productivity with which work is executed. This can be explained as being caused by the variation within human performance, since in each group of people of a given discipline or trade there is a wide range of capabilities which tends to produce uneven performance from gang to gang and week to week. *Figure 9.1* illustrates a typical pattern of productivity rates for bricklayers. It is based on data collected by the Building Research Establishment and described by McLeish[8].

In the face of these many factors which generate uncertainty, historically management has sought to simplify the problem by dealing with 'average' cases and applying contingency factors for cost and duration based on a subjective 'feel' for the project. Much of management's effort is then devoted to controlling these factors or reducing their impact on a project. Certainly in the past any attempt to take account of each of the components in such a complex problem has been doomed to failure. All solutions to date have been deterministic in assuming a single fixed value and many people feel that even the best techniques, such as network analysis, are too inflexible and complicated to help effectively in the planning and control of construction projects. Indeed most projects are planned as simple bar charts.

The technique used to deal with uncertainty is 'simulation', also known as 'the Monte Carlo method' from the gambling aspect of the process, or 'stochastic simulation', which means having a random element.

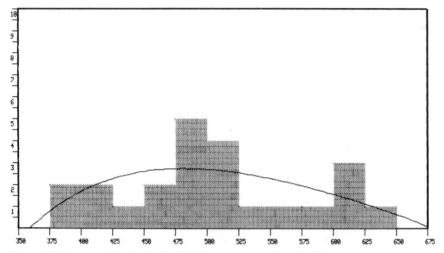

Figure 9.1 Frequency distribution for bricklaying output on housing sites

A building project represented by a deterministic plan is envisaged to be made up of operations of a set duration and cost, which has a single solution and is the only way the project is built. Using simulation the duration and cost of each operation is considered to be variable and represented by a population of possible values, not just one fixed value. During simulation the value of an operation is influenced by the effects of uncertainty by being chosen at random from a range of possibilities. The total project duration and cost are calculated from these randomly chosen values. This represents only one possible way in which the project may proceed. The whole process of choosing durations and costs under uncertain conditions is repeated and the result calculated to produce a different answer. Each calculation is known as an 'iteration' and, in the Construction Project Simulator, the simulation is complete when 100 different answers as to how the project might proceed are obtained. This gives an objective assessment of the range and pattern of possible solutions to a project under realistically uncertain conditions.

In the 1970s, the first attempts were made to employ this technique by applying expensive computing power to obtain a solution. Now, through the advent of the new generation of powerful 16-bit microcomputers, and the promise of 32-bit machines, this technique is a viable option within the budget of all but the smallest practice or company. The hardware used for the Construction Project Simulator comprises a 16-bit Sirius microcomputer, with a large amount of free memory (512 k) employing twin floppy disc drives with 1200 k of storage space. This drives a graphics quality dot matrix printer. The total hardware cost in 1982 was £4000.

The software philosophy has been to make operation simple and 'user friendly', through the extensive use of computer graphics and by minimizing the use of the keyboard. These techniques allow construction programmes to be entered directly into the computer in the form of a bar chart, the associated costs in tabular form, and production and weather data to be input as histograms of the form illustrated in *Figure 9.1*.

The basic program of the simulator is a versatile, interactive bar chart routine; where a series of bars are graphically entered against a user selected time scale (days, weeks or months) and the logical connections between the bars drawn in. Holiday periods can be entered and bar durations and logical links can be changed and the results automatically presented. The operation of the program is a very simple process and is achieved using only 10 keys on the keyboard. The resulting bar chart is illustrated in *Figure 9.2*.

A basic tenet of the simulator approach to planning is a hierarchy of bar charts. This is based on the way successful managers plan and in addition it serves to order and structure the data entry. The use of a hierarchy of bar charts reflects current practice because planners do not conceive a plan in its entirety, but develop a number of hierarchical stages with gradually increasing degrees of detail, structured around the way a building evolves on site and thus matches the management task posed by a project. The whole structure of the simulator has been modelled around this approach to allow ease of use and present a choice of levels of answers to increasingly complex questions, as schemes and strategies for a project develop.

Where projects are large, separate constructions, the first hierarchy level could represent distinct sub-projects; however, as most projects consist of one construction a sub-division into major work packages; is generally considered as the first hierarchy level. This first level usually consists of 10 to 15 major work packages – referred to as Primary Work Packages (PWP). The user has complete freedom to select the work packages; however, the list used in *Figure 9.2* has proved suitable for many building projects.

The simulator allows the user to take each PWP (e.g. external envelope) and to define in more detail the constituent Secondary Work Packages (SWP). The level of detail which is considered appropriate for an activity at this level is, in practice, governed by the three criteria of technology, territory and time. That is, the need for separate knowledge, skills and experience, work in distinct physical locations and work separated in time by the logic of the construction method. This results in a detailed bar chart at a level equivalent to a good contract construction programme. Once a PWP is chosen for examination, the program automatically presents a screen with the correct calendar with a time scale of the user's choice. The bar chart can then be entered by the user exactly as for the first hierarchy level. *Figure 9.3* illustrates the resulting secondary hierarchy level.

The duration of a bar at either level entered through the bar chart program is set by the user first defining the time unit of the bar chart and then a cursor on the screen moves in one time unit steps to set the start and end of a work package. When entering the duration, the time allowed is that required to complete the operation with the appropriate resources without making any allowance for uncertainty. That is, the user should not include any allowances for contingencies.

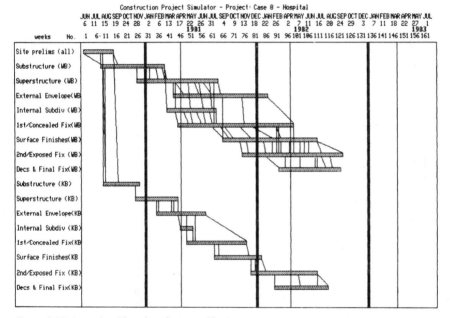

Figure 9.2 Primary level bar chart for new office block

Once a bar chart has been input the costs associated with each activity can be entered. This automatically presents the activity descriptions in a tabular format, leaving only the actual values to be entered by the user. Each activity cost has two components, a fixed materials cost and a variable labour cost. Again no contingencies for uncertainty are included as the purpose of simulation is to calculate the risks associated with a range of predictions of costs and time. The costs entered against each work package should be those for directly incorporating the materials into the project. Costs for establishing and managing the construction site can be entered as a separate cost category called 'preliminaries'. To enable this to be done the simulator automatically presents the primary bar chart, with the majority of the link graphics omitted for clarity and each required preliminary category can be set up by attaching its start and end to any link. Each preliminary category has a fixed cost and weekly (or monthly) cost, from which its total value is computed during simulation. The user has complete freedom to select up to 25 categories; however, the following

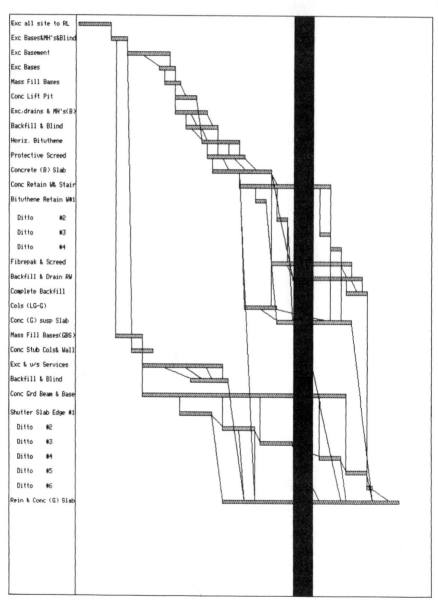

Figure 9.3 Secondary level bar chart for primary level 'substructure' bar of *Figure 9.2*

list has been identified as having the most cost significance: staff, plant, scaffold, accommodation, temporary power, cleaning and others. As with the direct construction costs no contingency amounts should be included. *Figure 9.4* illustrates the resulting representation of preliminaries.

The effect of the weather can be simulated by entering weather records, obtained from the Meteorological Office, for the project location. The activities on the primary bar chart can be designated weather sensitive or not and the effect of weather delays modelled by randomly choosing the actual weather delay, on each iteration, from the weather distribution. *Figure 9.5* illustrates a typical weather input from which successive iterations select a value to represent the time lost.

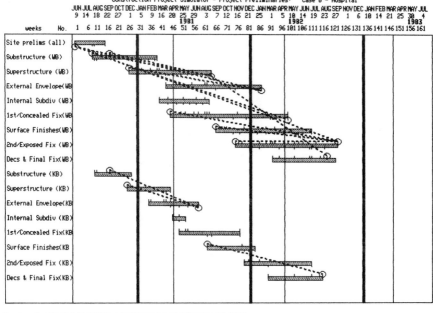

Figure 9.4 The 'preliminary' category costs and their interactions

Once all the data entry of bar charts, costs, preliminaries and weather has been completed the automatic simulation of the project can be undertaken. On each iteration, for every activity, a random number is generated and applied to the duration and cost distributions, to choose the actual values to be used. Another random number is chosen to determine whether or not each activity is interrupted and if it is, the length of interruption is chosen randomly. The resulting value sets the actual duration of each activity on this iteration. The bar chart is re-scheduled in accordance with the logical links, a final overall duration recorded and the costs are summed. This process is repeated 100 times to build up a frequency histogram of the possible duration and cost of the project. This simulation process occurs for each expanded PWP and then for the whole project plan, using the results from the more detailed level simulations which are transferred into the higher level simulation. The effects of weather are simulated at the primary level together with the costs of the preliminary categories, which then form part of the final cost and duration results of the simulation.

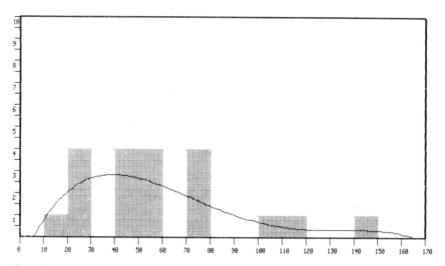

Figure 9.5 Number of working hours lost in Januarys from 1963 to 1982, for west London

As indicated before, each iteration result represents only one possible way in which the project may turn out. The purpose of repeating the process a number of times with different random choices of interferences and variability is to obtain a range of slightly different answers to indicate the worst and best case and the pattern of possible results. These results are presented as a graph with a frequency distribution and a cumulative plot. A separate graph is available for the cost and duration result which are illustrated in *Figures 9.6* and *9.7*. At first sight, having a range of possible answers may appear confusing. However, the picture they provide corresponds to real life where it is intuitively felt that more than one outcome is possible and that some answers have a better chance of success than others. Thus, the simulator provides an objective assessment of the worst and best cases, an indication of the most likely and for any particular cost or duration, an indication of the chance of success.

The simulator could be used at an early project stage, when several design and organizational solutions are available for appraisal; simulation

Project name: Case 8 - Hospital

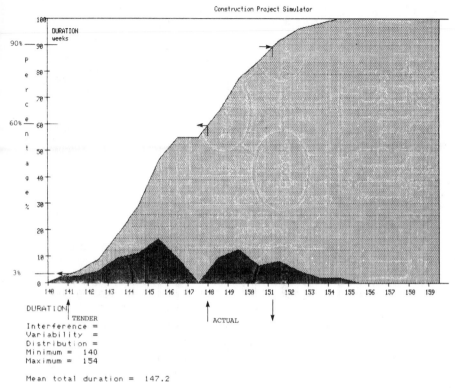

Mean total duration =   147.2

Figure 9.6 Distribution and cumulative curve for project completion versus the percentage chance of success

could be quickly executed at the PWP level to produce an objective comparison between schemes. Once a few schemes have emerged as front runners, they can be analyzed in more detail by applying different values of uncertainty, to allow sensitivity testing and, objectively, to assess the robustness of the schemes being considered. The client at this early stage would be aware of his likely exposure to risk and the size and configuration of his contingency allowances for cost and duration could be assessed on a rational basis. Once a single scheme has been selected and as design details are produced, a more detailed study can be undertaken by expanding the simulation to include SWP. This will allow a comparison with the earlier assessments and allow design and construction solutions to specific problems to be tested in terms of their likely effects on costs and time, so providing an aid in judging the buildability and other construction implications of individual answers.

The simulator can also be used to aid control of the project during construction by providing as input the percentage of work completed and then resimulating the remainder of the project. The results can be compared to the original and to previous month's figures and risk levels, to

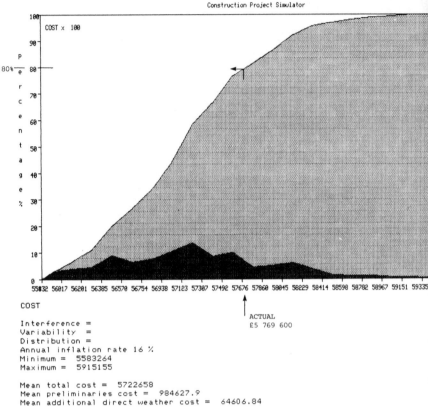

Figure 9.7 Distribution and cumulative curve for project cost versus the percentage chance of success

judge the likely outcome. The effect of design changes or client variations can be tested and their effect and influence on the whole project assessed. At all stages the simulator will help identify the areas of the project most at risk or which are causing most problems, so helping management to decide where to concentrate their effort.

The availability of cheap computing power has made the application of computer intensive methods feasible using techniques which are not an extension of manual methods. This brings fresh insights to the task of design, by revealing the probable implications of decisions prior to actual construction, and to the managers of the industry, by directing their attention to controlling variability in performance and external interference and by demonstrating that work packages should not be considered as independent but should be regarded as part of a dynamic system with a range of possible outcomes.

These are perhaps large claims but they are supported by experience of using the simulator on live projects. As Bennett and Ormerod report, the results produced on four substantial live projects were based on much less data than is required by present manual methods but they provided better predictions of the actual costs and times. It therefore seems certain that models similar to the Construction Project Simulator and its further development will provide a better basis for construction management decisions than manual deterministic ones. Computers will have similar effects on much of the work of construction professionals in changing the nature of their methods. They will not, however, in any sense, eliminate the need for professional work in the various forms described in this chapter. Nevertheless, pressure to change is deeply disturbing for many currently in the construction industry.

The future

We have now considered the major pressures currently faced by construction professionals. It remains for us to identify the net effect by considering the nature of professional organizations in the future. The right place to start is with the teams who will undertake the actual construction. It seems clear that construction will be carried out by specialist firms. Many will emerge from manufacturers faced with the need to ensure that sophisticated components are used properly and installed correctly. Firms manufacturing such components may employ construction teams trained in the proper construction techniques. Alternatively, they may adopt some form of franchizing in order to reduce their financial commitments while still providing clients with the assurance of properly installed components.

Other specialist firms will be based on the use of plant or equipment. They will provide a design service to ensure that projects take proper advantage of expensive capital items. Then they will hire out the appropriate plant or equipment complete with teams of operators supported by a head office team of trouble-shooters to deal with any unusual problems which arise during construction. Other firms will specialize in producing particular elements of constructions. As is common with mechanical and electrical services now, they will provide a complete design, construction and commissioning service. It seems likely, possibly under pressure from consumer protection legislation, that they will guarantee the performance of the end product. Finally, as with the traditional crafts, other firms will specialist on the basis of skills and knowledge, in using particular materials. As with the brick manufacturer who already sees the need to find some means of assuring clients that they will receive competent brickwork, it seems likely that successful firms of this type will need to guarantee their end product in order to compete with component manufacturers. There will, in other words, be a rich variety of competent firms responsible for detail design, negotiating and forming contracts, constructing and commissioning guaranteed elements of construction projects.

Professional work, given a basis of such firms, comprises selecting elements which will combine together to meet clients' objectives. As we saw in Chapter 8 in the case of Greycoats, some experienced clients already recognize that this is necessary and have developed their own form of traditional construction. In the example quoted, this is supported by construction firms who provide and in many cases, guarantee the set of elements Greycoats have selected. Other clients will need professional help in selecting elements and organizing the firms who provide them. The professional design firms who contribute to this service will need to understand the performance of elements in combination. That is they must understand complete constructions so that they can meet particular client objectives. They will be less concerned with detail design than is normal at present but will give much more attention to junctions between elements and to calculating and evaluating the total performance of the end product. The professional management firms who contribute to modern traditional construction will understand how teams interact and how their work may be coordinated. They will, in other words, understand the contents of this book.

Much of the emerging pattern of professional organizations is anticipated in the system for building design and construction proposed by the British Property Federation. This club of expert clients commissioned a study which examined the best construction professional practices worldwide and recommended a particular approach to their members[9]. The resulting analysis of the roles which must be undertaken in order to produce good buildings is very competent. It closely matches the description given above. It correctly places great emphasis on the client's role. It then proposes a management role which is given the title of Client's Representative and a design role with the title of Design Leader. The BPF manual provides detailed descriptions of the responsibilities of these two first line agents. These make the management role pre-eminent which reflects the primarily commercial interests of the BPF members. Other clients may choose to reverse the BPF allocation of authority or to create parallel and equal responsibilities for design and management depending on the balance of their own objectives. The manual also gives clear recognition to the role of construction teams in providing detail design. However, in order to accommodate the current UK orthodox approach, the system assumes a general contractor role so that detail design responsibilities run parallel to management and construction responsibilities which will almost inevitably result in duplication, confusion and divided responsibilities. This contrasts with Greycoats' approach in which specialist construction firms provide their detail design contribution for a fee before the client is committed to the resulting construction work. That apart, the BPF system goes a long way towards anticipating the form of professional organizations of the future.

It is worth considering the place of general contractors in the future construction industry since the pressures which are shaping their role typify those which other construction professionals must face. Much of the pattern can already be seen in developments over the past decade and even more clearly in the past four or five years. Some firms will remain as general contractors specializing in particular types of project. It is already common for large general contractors to sub-divide their organization on the basis of type of work. Obvious examples include refurbishment work, small alteration work and maintenance. In many cases it may be hard to draw a distinction between general contractors and specialist firms. Other general contractors will gradually turn into design and build firms selling standard constructions. This is already common in respect of housing and small factory or warehouse units. Others will relinquish their construction role and concentrate on management, so becoming consultants. Again there are clear signs that this is already happening. It seems unlikely in the long run, despite the BPF systems approach, that general contractors will be used for large or even medium-sized traditional constructions. The inherent advantages of flexibility and efficiency in using separate specialist firms coordinated by consultants motivated by clients' objectives is likely to be decisive.

In a very similar way consultants will tend to specialize. Recent decisions in the UK by professional institutions which now allow their members to advertise will reinforce this tendency. Firms will need to advertise particular services in order to have a clear and convincing marketing message. This will need to be backed up by a record of successful experience in the particular field advertised as clients take advantage of further changes in professional institution rules which enable their members to compete for commissions.

Thus, we see that under pressures generated by the current recession in the world's economy the principles of construction project management described in this book are being ever more clearly expressed in practice. When these developments are reinforced, as they will be, by the developments in artificial intelligence now emerging from the research laboratories of the computer industry, the principles of construction project management will be fully applied in practice.

We shall end as we began, with Pete James. Looking a little way into his future we see him at home sat at his computer terminal. He is working on a bid for an extension to the hugely successful Roman Leisure Centre. His terminal is connected to the project memory which is a computer database containing models of the proposed end product and project organization.

Pete's terminal was provided by Ibstock Building Products, a major brick manufacturer. They also provided a database which provides full technical details of all their products and a wide range of approved standard construction details. To enable Pete to use this information, Ibstock also provided programs which allow him to call up high-quality pictures of the details, to combine them, to examine junctions between different details and to relate them to specific scheme designs. This is what Pete is doing at the moment. *The scheme design which he has called up includes awkward junctions between the brickwork and the steel stancheons. By looking at the project schedule Pete sees that the brickwork and steelwork are to be constructed simultaneously. This could create problems so Pete calls up a more detailed level of the project schedule to learn the exact sequence of steelwork and brickwork. The secondary level schedule tells him that the stancheons will be in place before he builds the brickwork around them but that the roof steel will still be under construction.*

The Ibstock standard details provide three possible answers to the particular detail. Pete uses further facilities in the programs to calculate the materials required, the likely labour content and the overall cost and time implications. Only one of the details really fits into the planned project schedule and it requires very accurate bricklaying.

Pete now has three teams of bricklayers. The new project needs Doug Henderson's team to ensure the required accuracy. Pete calls up his own management file to see if Doug is available when the Leisure Centre work is needed. He sees that the new work will fit in very well with Doug's commitments. Pete makes a tentative entry on his management file so that if Doug calls in to see what is planned for the next few weeks, the record will be right up-to-date.

Pete continues to select details ensuring that they match the scheme design and will work well together from the point of view of construction. When he has finished making his decisions, the program calculates all the material and labour requirements and the overall costs and times. On this project the brickwork team will be required to provide their own scaffolding. Pete has a long-term agreement with a scaffolding contractor which is provided as part of the franchise arrangement with Ibstock. He has already called up the costs and times of the scaffolding which allow for the window team to use it for access to their work places. When he adds in the times required by the scaffolders Pete finds that the time allowed in the overall project schedule has only a 15% chance of being achieved. He likes to work at 60 to 70% confidence levels and so he looks back at his management file to see if he can borrow an extra bricklayer from one of the other teams. This will be difficult so Pete decides, as he often does, that he will work as one of Doug's team. He feeds the revised team size into the data for the project and waits while the effects are calculated. The new costs and times are lower and both now have an 80% chance of success. Pete adds his name to Doug's team in the management file, adds his profit margin to the estimates and sends his bid to the project memory. The bid is held with other competitive bids in a secure file which Pete is unable to access. It consists of records of the details Pete proposes to use, his price and schedule for the work.

Pete is much richer than when we first met him. He still enjoys laying bricks and takes every opportunity to join one of his teams His is now much more in control of what he builds and takes a real pride in his reputation for high-quality brickwork produced on time. He knows he can afford to charge more than most of his competitors because of his deserved reputation. The decision to enter into a franchise agreement with Ibstock had been the most difficult of his life but he had never regretted it. He could see that the construction industry, by taking advantage of information technology, had improved its performance and as a result had never enjoyed such a high demand for all its products. Pete the bricklayer was proud to be part of an efficient modern industry.

Summary

Pressures from clients whose objectives can best be met by standard or innovative constructions rather than traditional answers combined with rapid changes in technology are reshaping the orthodox professional roles in construction projects.

Programmed organizations using standard answers give rise to roles on individual projects which, when compared with the orthodox role of any one profession, are sub-professional. However, individual roles in programmed organizations tend to cover the work of several professional disciplines and so are demanding and worthwhile. Additionally within firms providing such project organizations the development of new standards gives rise to orthodox professional roles. Therefore, the industry's professionals could, with advantage, find challenging and satisfying employment in programmed organizations.

Problem-solving organizations give rise to roles which require their occupants to go beyond established professional methods and techniques. They require individuals to work in multi-discipline teams within matrix organizations which balance design and management. They require individuals to question each other's proposals and to defend their own ideas in order to develop more robust answers. Such organizations are challenging and suit only those professionals who can imagine new answers and have the tenacity to turn them into reality. The industry needs to give attention to developing its innovators in order that the most difficult construction projects may be undertaken effectively.

Professional organizations under pressure from rapidly changing technology will require professional roles which are different from the present orthodoxy. Construction and detail design will be carried out largely by specialists. Professional roles will consist of selecting combinations of the answers provided by the specialists in order to meet clients' design and management objectives. Computers will play a large part in helping the professionals to evaluate proposed answers.

The patterns of roles which can be seen to be emerging in contemporary practice tend to confirm the principles of construction project management described in this book. Imminent developments in artificial intelligence will reinforce them.

References

1. LEOPOLD, E. and BISHOP, D., 'Design philosophy and practice in speculative housebuilding', *Construction Management and Economics,* **1,** No. 2 (1983)
2. GILBERT, S. and HORNER, R., *The Thames Barrier,* Thomas Telford (1984)
3. KHARBANDA, O. P. and STALLWORTHY, E. A., *How to Learn from Project Disasters,* Gower (1983)
4. In the UK there has been sustained interest in project information on the part of Government and professional institutions for at least 20 years. Important publications include:

   Building Research Station, *A Study of Coding and Data Coordination for the Construction Industry,* HMSO (1969)
   Department of the Environment, *Structuring Project Information,* HMSO (1972)
   Project Information Group, *Project Information,* Department of the Environment (1978)
   Coordinating Committee for Project Information, *A Common Work Section Arrangement for Specifications and Quantities,* CCPI (1984)
5. WARNER, H. R., *Computer-Assisted Medical Decision Making,* Academic Press (1979)
6. Ongoing work by C. Gray in the Department of Construction Management, University of Reading, supported by the Science and Engineering Research Council
7. BENNETT, J. and ORMEROD, R., *Construction Project Simulator, Final Report of SERC Research Grant,* Department of Construction Management, University of Reading, Occasional Paper No. 12 (1984)
8. McCLEISH, D. C. A., *House Building Productivity: A Study of Labour Requirements on Scottish House Building Sites Using Activity Sampling Methods,* PhD thesis, University of Aston (1978)
9. *Manual of the BPF System: The British Property Federation System for Building Design and Construction,* The British Property Federation (1983)

Glossary

The terms in this glossary are those defined in the book. The definitions often limit the meaning of words in general use in order to establish their meaning in the context of construction project management.

Acting system:	a system in which two or more elements interact
Action:	the exertion of energy or influence. (Note – the actions of central concern in construction project management are communication, transaction and primary work.)
Authority:	the ability to grant or withhold rewards or punishments in return for the performance or non-performance of instructions
Bargaining power:	the ability to get a particular good by giving relatively little in return
Benefits:	the goods or satisfaction received or receivable from a transaction
Bit:	the amount of information needed to select unequivocally between two mutually exclusive and equally probable items
Boundary (of a system):	the limits of a system which is identified by listing all the elements of the system, any elements not so listed form part of the system's environment
Brief:	a statement of project objectives
Budget:	an estimate of future expenditure and/or income used in the planning and control of the financial aspects of projects
Client:	the person or organization whose motives concerning a project constitute its objectives

Coded information:	information that has been separated into distinguishable patterns
Coding:	the initial transfer of signs which mean a communication from the source to a medium
Communication:	the transfer of information between controlled systems. (Note – a communication is a message transferred from a source to a receiver.)
Competition:	a situation in which two or more parties compete to complete the same transaction
Complexity (of a project):	the complication inherent in a project which is conveniently measured in terms of the number of roles requiring different kinds of knowledge, skills and/or experience
Contract:	a formal agreement to complete a transaction
Control sub-system:	that part of a controlled system which processes information to provide instructions for the operating sub-system. (Note – in construction projects the client and teams occupying roles responsible for design and management constitute the control sub-system.)
Controlled systems:	a system whose elements and their interactions maintain at least one variable within some specified range or return it to that range if the variable goes outside it. (Note – projects, clients, project managers and role occupants are examples of controlled systems.)
Construction:	production of the physical product or its elements. (Note – constructions are the products of the construction industry.)
Coordination:	conscious direction of the behaviour of more than one team towards their objectives
Costs:	the goods or satisfaction given up as a consequence of obtaining other satisfaction
Culture:	knowledge which is communicated and learnt and is common to a collection of persons

Decision:	response selection under conditions of complexity; a commitment to action (which includes the limiting case of a decision to take no action)
Decoding:	recognition of the meaning of the signs in a communication
Design:	selection of the elements of the physical product and their relationship to each other and to their physical environment. (Note – a design is a specific selection.)
Detection:	the transfer of the signs in a communication from the medium to the receiver
Effective preference:	the terms preferred by a party to negotiations which, if agreed as the basis of transaction, they are able to put into effect
Elements:	the basic parts of systems which may be any identifiable entity – concrete or abstract, object or event, individual or collective. (Note – in practice the term tends to be used to describe the basic parts of physical products.)
Environment:	anything outside the boundaries of the system. (Note – in practice only things capable of affecting the system need be regarded as making up environments.)
Feedback:	information about the effect of the system's actions on the environment
General information:	information about construction which is not specific to individual projects and is published generally
Goals:	the desired state of role variables concerning the role products and/or process
Hierarchy:	*see* Management hierarchy
Information:	concepts which enable inferences to be made about things other than the concept itself
Information system:	a system whose elements consist of signs. (Note – in practice the term also encompasses the medium which carries the signs.)
Innovative construction:	construction which uses new decisions and therefore tends to create interdependent work

Interference:	undesirable effects in projects caused by their environments
Knowledge:	coded information in a human brain
Lateral coordination role:	role requiring the occupant to provide coordination between other roles at the same level in a management hierarchy
Major bargain:	an agreement that there shall be a relationship of a particular kind
Management:	being responsible for the actions of others. (Note – the management within a project is the client and any of their agents or subordinates responsible for the actions of other project participants.)
Management hierarchy:	an arrangement of levels of management roles in which each higher role has authority over designated roles in the immediately lower level which, in turn, are responsible to the role in the higher level
Management information:	information specific to a firm or other separate legal entity
Matrix structure:	an arrangement of management roles based on more than one (usually two) divisions of responsibilities in which each higher role has shared authority over designated roles in the immediately lower level which, in turn, are responsible to more than one role in the higher level
Matter – energy:	matter, energy or both
Medium:	the matter – energy on which a communication is coded by the source and from which it is detected by the receiver
Message:	information transmitted by signs in a communication
Negotiations:	the communications by which two or more parties determine whether, and on what terms, they will conclude a transaction
Noise (in communication):	any matter – energy of the same general sort as that used in a communication medium and which tends to obscure the message
Objectives:	the desired state of project variables concerning the product and/or the process

Operating sub-system:	that part of a controlled system which processes matter – energy in directly undertaking the primary work of the system. (Note – in construction projects, teams occupying roles responsible for construction constitute the operating sub-system.)
Organization:	interaction between controlled systems to facilitate action. (Note – a project organization is the teams who occupy the roles which make up the project and the devices used to coordinate their actions.)
Perception:	the process by which uncoded sensory inputs from some pattern in the environment selectively activate a concept stored in a human mind and leads to the conclusion that an instance of the meaning of that concept currently exists in the environment
Power:	the ability to bring about desired external states
Primary work:	work which contributes directly to a project's objectives
Problem:	any situation requiring a decision
Problem-solving organizations:	organizations set up to produce innovative constructions
Procedures:	formal rules which regulate behaviour. (Note – procedures may be included in role descriptions, work descriptions or general rules.)
Process:	the behaviour of the people and organizations within a project, and in particular the interactions between them and the resulting modifications of their behaviour
Product:	the results of the project whether intended or not
Productivity:	a measure of the effective work produced by teams
Professional organizations:	organizations set up to produce traditional constructions
Professional person:	one who has learnt established decisions and the types of problems which they solve and is practised in implementing those decisions; expert in a well-defined field

Professional work:	applying learnt, established decisions and practised skills to complex problems
Professionalization:	selecting teams with knowledge and experience relevant to their role in a project
Programmed organizations:	organizations set up to produce standard constructions
Project:	the consciously coordinated actions of two or more persons or teams aimed at discreet objectives
Project information:	information specific to a project which passes between teams within the project and between these teams and others in the project environment
Project manager:	a person or organization within a project responsible for the overall process and its product
Receiver:	the controlled system to which a communication is transmitted
Redundancy (in communication):	additional information included in a message to provide a means for the receiver to check that it has been communicated accurately
Repetition (of projects):	the extent to which work is repeated in a project which is conveniently measured in construction management in terms of the number of times sequences of similar roles are repeated
Responsibility:	the obligation to perform as instructed in return for rewards
Risk:	the chance of bad consequences
Role:	instructions to a project participant specifying the actions including interactions with the occupants of other project and non-project roles he is required to take and/or the desired product of his actions
Schedule:	an estimate of the timing of work in the future used in the planning and control of the progress of projects
Sign:	a word, number or symbol transmitted in a communication which stands for a concept which is its meaning
Size (of a project):	the magnitude of a project which is conveniently measured in construction management in terms of the number of roles

Slack resources:	additional resources provided in order to reduce the level of performance required from a team
Source:	the controlled system which originates a communication
Speed (of a project):	the rate of progress of a project which is conveniently measured in construction management in terms of the number of roles completed per unit of time
Standard construction:	construction which uses predetermined decisions
Strategic phase:	the early problem-solving stages of projects in which objectives, product and organization are established
Structure:	the pattern of an organization described in terms of its sub-systems and their roles. (Note – structure is also used to describe an arrangement of information when it matches the pattern of an organization.)
Structural configurations:	types of project organization
Sub-project:	a division of a project with minimum interaction with the rest of the project, thus providing the basis for self-contained role
Subsidiary transaction:	a transaction over some detail of a continuing relationship on the assumption that the major bargain will continue
Symbol:	any pattern produced by a controlled system in a medium external to itself which corresponds to an internal concept which is its meaning
System:	any group of elements which relate to each other in a sufficiently regular way to justify attention
Tactical phase:	the stages of projects in which the primary emphasis is on executing roles defined within a framework established in the strategic phase
Task force:	a team comprising persons drawn from interacting teams brought together to find an answer to a joint problem
Team:	a formal group consisting of few enough persons that each can take explicit cognizance of each of the others, together with the tools, equipment and other

	resources needed for them to undertake roles jointly
Traditional construction:	construction which uses established decisions and, therefore, tends to allow independent work
Transaction:	interaction between controlled systems relating to the transfer of valued things between them. (Note – a transaction is an agreement to exchange valued things.)
Uncertainty (of a project):	the combined effects of variability and interference
Value:	the position of anything in a preference order
Variable:	any part of a system which can take at least two distinguishably different states
Variability:	the range of performance achieved by teams isolated from other teams and interference
Variations:	formal changes to objectives
Work package:	a sub-division of projects defined by teams in the acting system and by roles in the information system

Index

220   Index